"IN GOD WE TRUST"

One man's search for eternal life

GLEN AARON

Editor: Sanja Bulatović

Cover designer: Luka Dubretić

Book Layout & ebook Conversion by manuscript2ebook.com

To those who fearlessly search for truth,
Regardless of where the path may lead.

CONTENTS

PART II: MY COMPLETED STUDY OF ABRAHAMIC RELIGIONS

PART III: SCIENCE AND ATHEISM

PART IV: THE FIRST AMENDMENT AND SEPARATION OF CHURCH AND STATE

INTRODUCTION

MY NAME IS Glen Aaron. I was born in the early 40s to ordinary people in West Texas who grew up in the Depression, experienced World War II, along with everyone else in the nation, and joined in the postwar economic growth as it evolved. My mother worked as a secretary. My dad worked in the oil industry. They were good people.

As 1951 approached, and I headed for junior high school, my hometown of Midland, Texas had a population of about 15,000 people and was hitting an affluent economic stride. It was and still is an oil town. To those of us who lived there, it was like any other U.S. town of similar population. Of course, in some ways, it was like other American small cities. In other ways it wasn't, but we thought that where we lived was just like everywhere else in America. Our town was all white, except for a small black community across the tracks that we never saw. There was no poverty as far as we could see, but if we ran into it, we were sure that it existed because people were too lazy and refused to get a job.

Everyone belonged to a mainstream Christian church,
Southern Baptist and Church of Christ leading the Protestant way,
while there was also an active Catholic community. The Pentecostal
explosion had not yet occurred. If you wanted to succeed in
business or participate in politics, a prerequisite was a good,
solid family base in one of the leading churches. Everyone was a
conservative Democrat, but distrusted Democratic leadership and
was convinced that labor unions had not only better stay out of
this part of the country, West Texas, but that these labor organizers
were communist sympathizers. In the 60s, everyone switched to
become a Republican, because of the hippies and the liberals and
the communists.

Interestingly, several leading citizens of our town raised money
for Fidel Castro during the 50s in his revolution against the Batista
regime and supported him in nefarious ways, the hope being that if
Castro took over Cuba, perhaps some of our exploration companies
could acquire oil concessions to drill around Cuba. In those days
in West Texas, people were still drilling wildcat exploration wells,
and discovering new large oil fields. The exploration companies
were major corporations like Shell, Humble, Standard Oil of Texas,
with operational headquarters placed in Midland, my hometown.
If you didn't work for a "major," you either worked for a small
independent or some other type of oil service company.

The conservative structure of society was supported by Texas
Tech University, 100 miles to the north at Lubbock, Texas. Between
Lubbock and Midland was a vast plain of sandy, but irrigated
cotton farms pumping out of the non-rechargeable Ogallala water

formation. No one believed or thought that oil or water would ever run out. Money and profit came from pumping it out, using it up and selling as much product at the best price as you could, as fast as you could. Environmental protection was surely communist-inspired or might have something to do with that liberal Supreme Court. Billboards on the highway stated, "Impeach Earl Warren."

Sixty years later, as I begin to tell the story, not much has changed, except for the number of people, about 400,000 in the surrounding area of Midland, and the ethnic mix of the population, a majority being brown. It is still an oil town, and white elitism is still present, but everyone is now a Tea Party type Republican, regardless of ethnicity, and still believes that the budget problem is caused by the black woman at the checkout line, with her Lone Star Welfare Card talking on her iPhone. The word that the middle class has shrunk is just liberal propaganda. It is common knowledge that policy implemented by the federal government is not only erroneous, but it is also an encroachment upon individual freedom, and more importantly, corporate freedom. Religiosity has also changed – the Pentecostal revolution brought about a considerable conversion and establishment of independent Christian evangelistic mega-churches. Even the mainstream Protestant and Catholic churches became more evangelistic and wrapped in proselytism by following some of the Pentecostal techniques.

Midland, Texas is a clean, safe, good place to live, as long as you conform to Christian and political conservatism. That doesn't mean that anything bad is going to happen to you if you don't. It is just like any other small town in that if you don't conform to the majority mindset, meme, and platitude expressions, people just prefer not to be around you or do business with you. I suppose I was a "sleeper" in the community because my mind has always asked questions about the truthfulness of our group thought. I would often search independently for answers and come up with information that did not support the opinions around me. For the most part, I dodged the bullet of social rejection by not contesting the popular mantras of the community. I kept my counter opinions to myself. When you are in business and raising a family, you just tend to go with the flow, not rattle any views, and get on with life.

As a boy, no love was ever greater or purer than my love for my dog, Schatzie, and her love for me. At the age of nine, we were a common sight in the neighborhood, as Schatzie ran along beside my bike in the exploration of our next imaginative mission. On the handlebar, I had a little squeeze horn. If Schatzie decided to pause to investigate, all I had to do at any time was to squeeze the horn, and she would come running. Every day, we explored the community and neighboring countryside together, after school on school days, all day in the summer. She and I couldn't wait for the morning to begin the process again, side by side. Schatzie was my perfect friend and my confidant. We kept our secrets.

This story is my meager attempt to rectify that complicity of accepting what you are being told versus the search for truth, albeit in the twilight years of retirement. It all began early on in my life when a car hit and killed Schatzie. I started to ask questions I had never thought of before. These questions became a search for answers that followed me throughout my life. Some people are satisfied, or at least less disturbed, by being told the truth by an "expert." I have always wanted to know the source information the "expert" used to evaluate the fact. Having been raised by a devoted Southern Baptist mother, I naturally thought that the church had the answers to my earnest religious questions, or that the mayor or someone like him had the right bent on political issues. Until I left home for college, I was at the church every Sunday morning and night. On Monday nights, the youth group Royal Ambassadors met, and although my mother went to prayer meeting every Wednesday night without fail, I usually stayed home and studied. This and school and a part-time job of sacking groceries at Piggly Wiggly made my life through pubescent years. There was no reason to question anything, at least not until the loss of my best friend.

Little did I know at the time, but the tragedy of my best friend's death created the beginning of a very long travel, that would take me not only on a search for answers to end-of-life questions, but ultimately to a vision of how religious thought and mandated responses are under control of a sinister marriage between Christian religion and government influence in this country, which also goes for all religions in every country. This is the story of my quest for comfort which the religious belief could give me in the question of life after Schatzie's death, followed by a brief look at how religion has depended on government throughout history for its growth and how government has depended on religion for its stability.

This is my quest.

PART I

MY EARLY
COMPARATIVE STUDY OF THE
ABRAHAMIC RELIGIONS

Chapter 1

My dog Schatzie; The Acceptance Period; The Gandhi Period.

I WAS ELEVEN years old when a car hit my dog Schatzie. I was devastated. Something hurt, really hurt, deep inside me that I had never experienced before. I couldn't explain it, but I couldn't accept that Schatzie and I would never be together again. She and I had been joined at the hip for several years. Such a tragedy brings every young person to their first thought about what it feels like to hurt and die, whether you have to hurt when you die, and then what happens to you when you die. Do you go somewhere?

There are probably sagacious parents that take the child in hand and quietly explain the meaning of life and death, but I have only read of such people, never actually known one. My father was the male authority role in our family. He was the strong, silent type. Since he handled anything that would portend to violence, or threaten the peace of the family, I immediately went to him to seek out answers to my questions about my best friend, Schatzie. He was the type of man who was stoically prepared to face another adult in a short conversation about a death event, but as he looked down into the watering searching eyes of his only son, he had no idea what to say. He didn't want to be brutal in a cynical response. He knew my heart was in pain, but he didn't know whether there was an animal heaven or if we Christians (he being relatively new in that he had not been in a church until he married my mother at age 24) were even supposed to think of a dog going to heaven. Was that kind of thinking heretical? He didn't know and couldn't connect the dots.

My only other source for answers, since I had no siblings, was my mother. To the issue of whether Schatzie hurt, my mother was straightforward. Schatzie was hit by a big car, poor thing. She had to be in pain, but probably at some point, the hurt went away, and she just died. Where did she go after she died? Well, the Bible doesn't say anything about animals going to heaven, so it may be that she didn't. On the other hand, the Bible doesn't just come out and say that your favorite pet doesn't go to heaven, so perhaps Schatzie did. Mother's advice was just to think about it and decide for myself and have faith. She also suggested that I be sure to say my prayers. She assured me that it would help.

I suppose that was about the best that one could do for an eleven-year-old Southern Baptist boy, who was posing his first questions on life, death, and the hereafter. Simplistic as they were, the same issues would resurface periodically throughout life, always without a definite answer. As I look back on it now, some sixty-plus years later, I see that the search was always there, at times in the forefront, even as early as when Schatzie died, while at other times it was humming just below the surface. On the other hand, the quest for political truth didn't have that subliminal irritation that religious questioning did. You could debate policy, question what was happening, figure out what was causing it to happen and come to closure. Not so with end-of-life questions. As to religion and belief through those pubescent years and into college, I was a devout Baptist and accepted the stories of the Bible and the promise of the New Testament. I now call that period of my life, my "Acceptance Period."

I enjoyed viewing the political world and analyzing the implementation of governmental policy. In that realm, I felt I was on top of things, certainly more so than figuring out where Schatzie was after her death. I started representing my high school on the debate team in the interscholastic competition in the tenth grade and continued into my attendance at Baylor University. On the college debate team at Baylor, I competed against Southwestern colleges and Ivy League schools in national competition. My daily ritual from the tenth grade on was to check current events each morning and review the latest national discussions on governmental policy. That hasn't changed to this day.

At college, Baylor University, religion was not my major, although I did take a course in Hebrew history, one on the New Testament, and a philosophy course. My mind began to open to questions about any number of aspects regarding the Bible. I had always heard that while the Old Testament was historical, the New

Testament scripts were divinely inspired with the writings coming straight from God through the apostles. At the time of taking these religion courses at Baylor, I couldn't quite figure out how the Apostles wrote what they wrote, but there seemed to be a timing problem. I didn't attempt any detailed research, because of the time that was needed to meet other academic demands, not to mention extracurricular activities. In the back of my mind, however, questions remained, such as: who and when wrote the books of the New Testament? How could it be possible that a supernatural power impregnates a mortal married woman? If Mary, the mother of Jesus, was with Joseph, how could she be a virgin? Why was Christ a bachelor? Why was the resurrection and ascension of Jesus in a human form, a non-decaying body, though it had been tortured and died, and not as a purely spiritual soul?

Towards the end of my sophomore year, the Student Congress, of which I was vice president, announced that Prime Minister Nehru (Jawaharlal Nehru, 1889 – 1964) of India was coming to the United Nations headquarters in New York City. He had sent invitations to some colleges inviting them to delegate a student representative to speak with him. He wanted to know the views of American college students. Baylor was one of the invited colleges. The invitation stated that the Prime Minister would pose questions to the students and would request that the students do the same. I was nominated to attend as a representative of the Student Congress. At the time I didn't realize it, but this trip to the U.N. would create resurgence in my quest for after-life answers. However, before the trip, I felt a change stirring within myself.

At some point between my freshman and sophomore year, a charge of rebellion shot through my psyche, or perhaps it was more like a fast evolving metamorphosis of resistance. I suppose this happens with most kids at some point. The movie "Elmer Gantry" came out, and it was quite a hit among Baylor students. Burt Lancaster played the part of a hard-drinking, fast-talking, traveling salesman who hooked up with a traveling tent revivalist and her tent show as he decided to become an evangelist, himself. He preached and entertained the attendees, saving them from sin, talking the girls into bed, drinking whiskey, and leading sinners to salvation.

One Saturday night after a few beers, my suitemates and I reflected upon different revivalists and evangelists we had encountered in our lives growing up as Baptist boys. We each had reached that rebellious questioning stage during growing up. Suddenly, we hit upon the idea that it would be great fun to go over to the campus and set up a mock revival across from the row of girls' dormitories as they came in from their dates. Their curfew was 10 PM. Our revival would be a parody of the movie. I would be Elmer Gantry, as I would preach and mock play Gantry. Another suitemate would lead the singing with good Baptist songs like "Bringing in the Sheaves," which in our parody would be the coeds. My other suitemate would pass the hat for a collection and flirt with the girls.

It was a great hit! The coeds were having so much fun that many stayed out past their 10 PM curfew. As they sat on the grass of the quadrangle in front of their dorms listening to me preach, we passed a few bottles of beer and a pint of whiskey down the rows. Of course, my sermon was not "sex is bad," but that sex was enjoying and healthy. They should try it, and the fine gentlemen bringing them this entertainment might be good candidates.

The following midweek, the president of the college summoned my suitemates and me to his office at the administration building, Pat Neff Hall. As we sat soberly in front of the president's receptionist awaiting our meeting with the head of the University, I couldn't help but be struck by the beautiful view the president had of the quadrangle below, the place where we had held our "tent revival" the Saturday night before. The reverie was short-lived, however, as a big, bald man in a black suit and a bass voice opened the door to his office and told us to come in.

It was quite a scolding, not to mention a defense of our religion and the people in it. The president anticipated that the University would expel us. A decision would be reached later, but in the meantime, we were to continue attending classes. It may be possible to allow us to complete our semester courses so as not to lose our credits, but the president was not sure. He would consider it.

I was sweating bullets. I was the first one ever to attend college from my family. Hearing about this prank and my expulsion would devastate my parents. I never planned it this way, but the saving grace was the fact that one of my suitemates, the one who passed the hat and whiskey, was the governor's son, Price Daniel, Jr. His father was the governor of the State of Texas. In the final analysis, I suppose the administration considered it inappropriate to kick two of us out while allowing the governor's son to stay. As a result, none of us were expelled. I dodged the bullet and cleaned up my act.

It was shortly after that event that I was to go to New York to represent Baylor at the meeting with Prime Minister Nehru. Frankly, I knew almost nothing about Prime Minister Nehru, though I had at least conversational knowledge of Gandhi and the nonviolent Gandhian expulsion of British rule. In preparation for that trip and meeting, I did hit the books to learn more and came away with a new fascination of the man, Mahatma Gandhi. It struck me that such a humble man who purported the theology of liberation and peace might have answers to my Schatzie questions. It was 1962, and I couldn't wait to meet Prime Minister Nehru, but in retrospect, my greatest excitement was to return and study Gandhi.

There is such a vast sea filled with philosophic and theological thought when you begin to ask the simplest of questions. One learns in time and through much reading that the manner in which even brilliant philosophers and theologians cope with these problems is to develop experiential explanations of where and how their life is, and thus, how it must be in commonality. The opposite shore of that sea flows from a realistic vision of who God must be (Gandhi) to metaphysical and mythical belief in the meaning of life and the hereafter.

So, I returned from New York to Waco, Texas and to Baylor University with a new mission – to understand Gandhi's philosophy and get my questions answered. I now call this part of my search "The Gandhi Period." At first, I struggled a bit with the Sanskrit terminology that seemed unfamiliar, yet somewhat mystical. It took me into a period of confusion, because some parts of Gandhi's beliefs to me sounded similar to the teachings of penance in the Catholic religion.

It seemed a roundabout way to answer my questions, but I decided that perhaps this was the message I must first understand. There was no direct path to the answer. Gandhi seemed to maintain that the responses to my questions were the definition of truth and could only be known, understood, and observed by the daily practice of truth in thought, word, and action. To discover the answers required a path to knowing God and attaining "moksha," or spiritual liberation, while still encased in the body. God and spiritual liberation were integral to the Gandhian concept of Swaraj, or attainment centered equally on God and the human spirit.

In time, I realized that Gandhi's approach to reaching enlightened answers was an ascetic way of life in his beloved ashram, the iconic picture of spinning his cotton as representing the wheel of life with service to fellow humans, in particular service to the lowest of the lowest, the helpless. Emanating his concept of God, he practiced faith in action and saw God as both doer and non-doer, and the model for all who sought moksha.

Gandhi was terrific in his ability to extrapolate his concept of Swaraj onto the national psychic: that the best and simplest means of self-realization, or of being with God, was to serve God's creatures. He reasoned that God was incorporeal and not in need, whereas humans were corporeal and in need. Service, therefore, was a measure of faith; and India needed it. God had himself set the example of selfless service to his creatures, as though to say that there was no other way to serve Him. Indeed, no other way to find the answers. Only through service could the answer be found.

Over the year that I tipped my toe into Gandhian waters, I came to see that he believed that answers to such questions could only be found through a lifetime of dedicated, ascetic service. There was no such thing as a point-blank question and a simple answer. The answers came as light through a glass darkly in the service of doing and non-doing.

I found that Gandhi did not feel threatened by the religion of the British. In the process of leading India to Swaraj, Gandhi evolved a unique system of conflict resolution. This system, based on Satyagraha with its components of Satya, Ahimsa, and Tapasya, clearly drew upon the Christian model of contrition, repentance, conversion, and reform. He remained Hindu, but extracted much of the value from Christian dogma and integrated it into his practices. One might say that his legacy to Christians, at least, was a challenge to do the same in the face of their materialistic addictions.

By the time I was a senior at Baylor, preparing for graduation and going on to law school at the University of Texas, I lost interest in Gandhi's teachings. While I recognized them in the foundation of service and admired him very much, I felt that it was nothing more than blind faith to think answers would come through persistent, daily, lifetime ascetic service. There was no question that much truth, meaning, and goodness did come from this philosophy, and Gandhi's life exemplified many revelations, but to me, he didn't start with the fundamental question – – was there a God? How do you know? How does death look? Where do we go or do we go anywhere when we die?

To me, Gandhi ignored such questions with the belief that in service to a preordained truth and humanity, all answers to questions either reveal themselves or lose significance to a level of not worth asking.

Chapter 2

To Question or Not to Question

IT HAS BEEN said that we begin dying the day we are born. In a sense, of course, that is true, but not in any meaningful sense, until one passes midlife and begins to see changes they knew they were coming, or when one realizes they have seen more sunsets than they will see in the future. Even then, one moderates their thoughts on death with views of being in the peak of life, perhaps with a view of having reached a pinnacle of children raised and some funds saved for that glorious anticipation of retirement.

But with the knowledge that death comes to all, the question begs to be asked. "Is there a hereafter?" Many spiritual leaders have said there is, but they based that knowledge on hearsay. Either by dream or epiphany, they were "told" that there is a hereafter. The question stabs every individual, young and old at one time or another. Perhaps because we don't have the answer, or don't like the one we have come up with, or don't trust the one we have heard, the questioning moves us throughout life and before death. The only relief for every sentient being is to suppress the question into some dogma so profoundly, that it becomes catatonically clinical and even then the questioning is just below the surface of consciousness.

I have observed that there is always the justification of belief, regardless of what that idea may be. There is also defensiveness and resentment if the surface of a belief is peeled off. In fact, there is anger as one tries to avoid the possibility that we have misguessed the answers to life's questions of purpose and mortality. Abrahamic religions have fought hard for centuries to suppress independent thought on what might be a non-dogma truth, while channeling motivated thinking into a religiously philosophized debate. Hindu religion developed a slick history of thousands of mythical gods to chase after the wishes and desires of mere humans, so as not to force a single dogmatic God. Buddha, on the other hand, at least in the early evolution of that religion, went within self in the search for answers.

I have also observed that the vast majority of people desire not to think too deeply about life and death questions, but prefer to check off to some pastoral verbalism or ritual and say to themselves, in effect, "Okay, it's done. I've thought about death. Now, I don't have to think about that for a while longer." It especially seems so as we serve in that age pattern of starting a family, gaining employment, developing wealth and then looking toward that golden perception of retirement. In other words, the period that covers the most of our lives.

One might say that there just isn't much time to question or to think about such things as death and immortality, or perpetual life. To dwell upon it much at all quickly becomes an irritant. Besides, whatever the answers are, unless you have forced yourself into thinking that there is a place within the entrance of Pearl Gates and golden streets or a place where many virgins meet each man, you know that you're probably not going to like the answer. Then, if you even allow yourself to reach the point of questioning, you will become retrospective about your life and say to yourself, "what was it all about?" Indeed, that is not a very comfortable feeling, and we all dislike discomfort. It is the dilemma for every human who may think of these questions, though it is evident that most do not allow themselves to do so, except in that subliminal state.

We, humans, look for absolute truth, absolute meaning, with no existential thought. It is the closed-end thinking part of our brain. All religions try to serve this fundamental aspect of our nature on various levels. You may think at this point that what I am writing is just another book attacking religion, which you will find that it is not. But it is writing about pushing forward into a less comfortable area of free and critical thinking. This is our life. This is our death, and we have a right to question it, examine it, and yes, ask questions and even contemplate answers, whether within or outside "the box" of mainstream thinking.

Of course, we each also have the self-determined right just to accept what is, without the interrogation of self-doubt. It appears by a surface glance that it would be the easiest path, the more comfortable one, but then there is that word "surface," again. If you haven't figured it out already, I must tell you. Your psyche will not allow you to get away with just surface thinking. Even an ostrich must at some point reach up for air, but then, of course, the ostrich with its head in the sand is a myth in itself.

Chapter 3

The Search for the Holy Grail and the Doubting Thomas Period

As A YOUNG person, excitingly anticipating life, one does not think about specific years falling into categories or "periods." Looking back now, I can see my childhood and entrance into college as my "Acceptance Period," where I accepted at its stated value what older, better educated or more experienced people told me. As I have mentioned, that was not without internal questioning, but it was without outward confrontation.

The trip from Baylor to New York City and the youth meeting with Prime Minister Nehru instigated the "Gandhian Period," though it only lasted a couple of years. But regardless of what label or categorization I might now place to describe a certain time, the overarching drive was questioning. The search for God? Why? How was it that "out there" was an all-knowing God, a God of truth, a superior force that directs what happens in this world with an underlying plan, even when the happening is disastrous to human beings or the earth itself?

Some people feel comfort in numbers gathering with raised hands in nearness to each other's protestation that there is a God because of the way they feel. Others gain confidence by being in the presence of a nominated holy icon. It affirms the feeling that God exists, that Jesus lived and died on a cross, and that there is a divine plan for saving sentient beings that rests in the hands of the deity. While the human genome may be closest to the chimpanzee, which also follows a familial social order, in mass, humans are group animals, more like a herd of wildebeest. Humans follow the group paradigm without question. Not only do they support the majority thought of where they are, but they are also excluded from the group if they do not follow the predominant paradigm.

The legend of "The Search for the Holy Grail" exemplifies the group (wildebeest), just-follow-along mindset. Why would anyone want "the Grail?" Because for the medieval mind, the legend, or myth if you will, was that the Grail contained the Blood of Christ. It had his "soul," possibly his divinity. Because it had been part of him, it must have a means of transmitting the direct knowledge of God, "spiritual essence." The Grail, itself, has been the item of creativity, pictured in different iconic ways, including a chalice or even a ciborium with a consecrated host inside. Frequently, it is described as "the platter in which Jesus Christ partook of the Paschal lamb with his disciples." Regardless of what the Grail was thought to be, Alfred Tennyson's (1809 – 1892) poems point them on the search and composer Richard Wagner's (1813 – 1883) creations are often portrayed in art as a chalice.

Although the Grail is biblically based only in the minds of those who created the story in truly Harry Potter and Gothic fashion, it does represent the deep wanting desire that God exists, that there can be an abiding daily, moment by moment, relationship by an eternal blessing of peace and immortality. That wish is so strong in the human psyche, that the group never asks the seminal question, "What proves that God exists, over and above our strong desire to have a God?"

Today, Stephen Prothero, a professor of religion, among other things, at Boston University[1], through lecture and writing has reached out to those limited numbers, like me, who want to revisit those early very personal questions such as, "How does death look like?", "What does this life mean?", "Was I meaningful?" Or, is that last question irrelevant? Prothero points out that eight rival religions run the world. Regardless of how many there were in the early years of humankind, how many there were throughout time or how many were snuffed out by other competing religions, that is what we have, today, eight.

These religions are significant for many reasons. They each have, at various times in their history, produced revelations in non-theological learning such as art, architecture, medicine, and many other disciplines. While searching for unity within their group, they are very human in their internal power struggles, their attempts to gain influence and to be the sole source of authority, and their willingness to enter into massive physical and philosophical battles to maintain superiority.

But as Prothero points out, two things quickly come to your attention when you look at the eight religions. One, they control the vast majority of thinking, behavior and everyday ritual of almost the entire human race. Two, because they are the daily spiritual source of humans, they dictate the nature and governmental organization of the statehood in which they exist. If there were no other reason to study the eight religions of the world, this would be more than enough to do so, but there is more. Each one of these faiths has spent thousands and thousands of years asking the same questions I naïvely ask about life and death. Each religion has spent untold wealth and energy and brought forth the very best minds, generation after generation, in search of – – the Grail. But in every quest in every religion there is the premeditated assumption that the Grail (God) exists and what follows in the search supposedly affirms that assumption. As the professor Prothero states in his book God Is Not One: The Eight Rival Religions that Run the World – and Why Their Differences Matter: "What the world's religions share is not so much a finish line as a starting point."[2] "The world's religious rivals do converge when it comes to ethics, but they diverge sharply on doctrine, ritual, mythology, experience, and law."[3] In this realization, it cannot possibly be said that God is one, and all religions climb a different side of the same mountain seeking the same ultimate point.

While the professor makes a good point that all religions are different, this realization does not help me in my original question of "Is there a God." I decided to look to the Western revolution that tried to break away from mandated or controlled thinking, the Age of Enlightenment, the age of reason. It was the cultural movement of intellectuals in the eighteenth century, whose goal was to escape conservative closed thinking, and to question, understand, and reform society and advance knowledge. Their charge was to promote science and intellectual interchange, oppose superstition, have a free exchange of ideas and experimentation, and above all, oppose intolerance and abuses by church and state that in Christendom began within the very century of Jesus' death.

Philosophers like Baruch Spinoza (1632 – 1677), John Locke (1632 – 1704), Pierre Bayle (1647 – 1706), physicist Isaac Newton (1643 – 1727), and philosopher Voltaire (1694 – 1778) sparked the early tentative steps toward free thinking in this era. If people had not invented the printing press in Europe in 1450, we would probably be oppressed by closed-mindedness to this day. The print allowed rapid dissemination of knowledge and a beginning for critical thinking, while at the same time producing and dispersing widely a compilation known as the Bible.

Of course, history is replete with the counterforce of pendulum swings from freethinking revelations to controlled dogma. By about 1800 what the Western world had known as the enlightenment era gave way to what came to be called "Romanticism's Enlightened Despotism," but that is another story.

How did those early enlightened philosophers and scientists come to think as they did? When did they first entertain my simple, straightforward questions in their lives? How did they wrestle with the matters through the decades of their lives? Did they have mentors? I know they had rich exchanges and debates on these issues. I wonder how each man considered the crucial question as he lay on his deathbed, knowing that for all the new enlightenment, this brief space of human-made time was over. Was there an epiphany or just the end?

As I left the "Acceptance Period" and the "Gandhi Period" for other pursuits like attending law school at the University of Texas, I set these questions aside and entered into what I now call my "Doubting Thomas Period." While the search for probability is fundamental, there is that period in each person's life where there is just no time to be irritated with such questions. In that period, one may be immersed in religious activity or non-attendance, but one feels the constant pressure of dealing with life and its rapidness.

Chapter 4

The Abrahamic Religions and the Re-Search Period

IN THE EARLY years of beginning law practice and starting a family, I had no time for contemplative thoughts on human existence. However, after seven years of trial practice, a gap occurred in my career and life that allowed for a return to contemplative thought, even research as it were. I came to call this my "Re-Search Period."

But my "Re-Search" had a new element that inspired me. Having been through law school and now seven years of trial practice, I was well aware that Americans live their daily lives on two tests of evidentiary proof. In criminal law, a conclusion of guilt must be proved by evidence beyond a reasonable doubt. We don't live by that standard in our personal lives. In all else, we measure our daily actions against what a sensible person would or would not do, believe or not believe. This comes to us from old

English common law as the foundation of our civil jurisprudence. It is the way we live and the standard that we must live up to, regardless of whether we are aware of it or not. It is called proof by a preponderance of evidence. We evaluate evidence as existing or not existing, as credible evidence or not based on what is more likely than not. That is the test. We do not live and make our decisions on a standard of absolute correctness, but what is more likely based on the evidence we subconsciously or consciously view.

If we can measure reasonableness of every person in this way, then why not test the existence of God with such reasonableness? In other words, by a preponderance of evidence, does God exist? Religion tends to gloat at the conclusion that science can prove neither that there is God nor that there is no God, but that begs the question because that is not the purpose of science. Science examines what is here that can be observed and tested. Just because there is no absolute evidence of existence, it does not mean that something must exist.

But if we, people, live our daily lives on the existence of what is reasonable and prudent in our actions, and if our everyday life involves religious acknowledgment and participation, then it is only logical to examine if we can prove the fundamentals of religion by a preponderance of evidence. "Preponderance of evidence," while mostly used in law, actually is the way we live our lives every day. We do not live on absolutes. We live and make our decisions on what is more likely than not to occur from a certain action that we may take or a decision we may initiate.

The cataclysmic nature of divorce coupled with a change in profession, mine being from trial law to oil exploration and energy finance can lead one to introspection – – to ask yet another question – – "what is it all about?" I had a period of some four or five months between jobs to enter such contemplation, and I thought it might be a good idea to turn to my religious roots to find some understanding. I knew from courses I had taken in college that there had been a 4000-year quest of Judaism, Christianity, and Islam (the Abrahamic religions) to answer my simple questions, but I had also heard that some of the mythical aspects of these faiths had existed long before the Abrahamic religions came into being.

I took this time to travel to several great libraries and began to dig into heaps of manuscripts, historical documents, and treatises. Since it was a period in which I couldn't sleep, anyway, I was able to cover a lot of ground, noting and outlining as I went. I don't know how large the Mediterranean Sea is, but if you imagined that it was filled with the history and philosophies of Abrahamic religions, you would quickly realize, as I did, that in a lifetime of swimming you would never swim through it, not to mention the significant Greek philosophers in their time.

I decided to simplify my goal to two prongs; first, where did each of these Abrahamic religions come from; second, could they give me a straight-forward response to my questions. Quite by happenstance, I began with a popular theory put forth by Father Wilhelm Schmidt in "The Origin of the idea of God"[4], published originally in 1912. His premise was that there had been monotheism before men and women started to worship many gods. Not able to explain physical events and being tribal, they acknowledged one Supreme Deity, someone, perhaps similar to themselves, but who created the world, controlled what happened in it, and governed human affairs from afar. This belief exists even today in many indigenous African tribes whose ancestors predate migration to the Mediterranean area. Archaeological findings throughout the nineteenth and twentieth century have reinforced this explanation of early belief in a deity. This single deity was not the God of Abraham but was a creation of several tribes, and looked differently from one tribe to another. It relied heavily on a yearning toward God in prayer and in sacrifice, as well as on a belief that he is watching over those who subjugate themselves and that he will punish wrongdoing, as various tribes have separately described it. At the same time, it was often an explanation for natural physical events.

Father Schmidt seemed to theorize that the early perception of this omnipotent being vanished in time, only to reappear later after having been replaced by lesser spirits and more accessible, tangible gods of the pagan pantheons. But then I read other treatises that surmised, no, the single Supreme Deity belief always circled and evolved through ordinary cultures, most often the common folk, which were the less powerful, particularly those communities who did not have access to the pantheons or were not part of a governing elite.

Wherever the human thought of a single God or multiple gods originated, I could see that the one thing they all had in common

was the idea of a mysterious force – – the concept that the unknown
of the universe was caused by an act of a mysterious god(s). People's
beliefs, more appropriately their base feelings, from the earliest
beginnings before Abraham through the ultimate evolution of
Abrahamic religions, centered on the daily thought that earthly
life was obviously fragile and no lowly human being could control
what happens. Danger, sickness, and death overshadowed life and
this constant awareness created fear. It was difficult to cope with
the fear of death, but if it could be explained or at least dealt with
through mystical explanations, there was an easing of the constant
stress, and it all began to build upon itself and take on its own
reality.

I wondered not only when the first thought of religion occurred,
but that of forming a government as well. Both religion and politics
joined for control of the people at some point. When was that? Of
course, it was different for different peoples at different times, but
when was the first? The amount of material written historically,
anthropologically, and philosophically, is so vast that no one person
could ever read it all. Each Abrahamic religion has for centuries had
thousands of scribes in wave after wave writing separately in each
of their disciplines. They have spent and continue to spend their
entire lives doing so, and indeed, the discoveries and the evolution
of thought in the varied paths followed is both enlightening as to
social paradigm, as well as admirable in its attempt.

When I went to New York City and the United Nations as a
college student to meet Prime Minister Nehru, I took a tour of the
New York City library. It was so impressive that I told myself that

someday I would return to do some research there and perhaps at some other great libraries in the city. I had no idea what I would research. It was just an odd fantasy, but now, in this gap in my stream of life between divorce and career change, there were several months that I could chase the dream, and I knew what I wanted to research. I wanted the answers to my end-of-life questions, first asked with the heartfelt loss when my dog died. I still wasn't satisfied with the idea of blind faith in some vague explanation, and divorce felt like death. It felt the same as when that car killed Schatzie, so now was a good time to see if one of these Abrahamic religions could give me a reasonable answer to what happens to us when we die.

It came to me one night late in the library, among scrolls and treatises, that for me it was an impossible task to cover only original sources. I would look at them when I could, but I must rely on scholars who had researched with critical discipline and written treatises that would lead the way. I realized that I would have to make a judgment call on my own as to which scholars follow a discipline for credibility, as opposed to those who might use motivated reasoning. In making that determination, I would have to go behind the text to who wrote it, what their credentials were, and what other scholars had to say about the writings.

While I had some basis to work from, having taken courses on religion in my college days at Baylor, there was much that I did not know about Judaism, Christianity, and Islam. To complicate matters, I had only a brief period to satisfy myself on the questions of what was dying like and what, if anything, happens after you die. Everyone I knew accepted what their religion or what their preacher, priest or imam said and went on about their business in the world. I couldn't do that. I had to see the answers to my questions in the foundational documents of each of these religions for myself. My burden, my quest, was relieved somewhat in that I wasn't doing this for anyone else or to try to convince anyone else of what I found. It was something that I had always wanted to do. It was to satisfy my curiosity without outside interference. This was the commencement of what I now call my "Re-Search Period."

Chapter 5

Early Hebrew, Jewish, and Arab History

I DECIDED TO work back in time of the founding of each of the Abrahamic religions, Islam first, then Christianity, and finally Judaism. My thought was that if I studied from the most recent to the earliest, I might avoid bias which was present in my fundamentalist upbringing. Nevertheless, I found that at the very beginning I must have at least cursory knowledge of early Hebrew history so that I could understand the political, religious, and philosophical atmosphere at the time of either the founding of Islam or Christianity. It took me several days, but I created the following synthesis or digest of that history, so that I could use it as an early reference, which I would develop later into more detail.

The archaeological record of today disputes the Old Testament teaching, mainly the Book of Joshua, that the Israelites conquered the lands of Canaan from the Canaanites to forge Israel. You remember

Joshua, "Joshua blow your horn and the walls of Jericho will come tumbling down." The Israelites were, in essence, indigenous Canaanites, and settled Israel peaceably, along with a mixture of diverse people who intermarried and evolved into what came to be called the Israelite people or later the Jewish diaspora. Similarly, even though the Old Testament and the Jewish Bible depicted the Israelites as monotheists, having one God from the beginning, this isn't true. They were multi-theists from the beginning, but at a point in history, a small and ultimately successful minority group of monotheistic revolutionaries took hold.

You had two kingdoms side-by-side in generally what is today Palestine, Israel, Jordan, Lebanon and part of Syria. To place it in date context, Israel and Judah were ruled by Iron Age Kings of the ancient Levant, which is that general geographic area just described. The Kingdom of Israel emerged as an important local power in the ninth century BCE before falling in war to the Neo-Assyrian Empire in 722 BCE. Israel's southern neighbor, the Kingdom of Judah, emerged in the eighth century, after Israel, and enjoyed a period of prosperity as a client-state and a trading partner of first Assyria and then Babylon. But in 586 BCE, it attempted to revolt against the Neo-Babylonian Empire and experienced destruction.

For Israel and Judah, these several centuries from the late seventh to the fifth BCE seemed to wash in war, power, and control from one side of the kingdoms to the other, back and forth. In the last decades of the seventh century, Assyria was overthrown by Babylon, but Egypt, fearing the sudden rise of Neo-Babylonian Empire seized control of Assyrian territory. Then, Babylon counter-attacked. In 599 BCE, the Pro-Egyptian party was in power, as Judah revolted against Babylon. Babylonian Nebuchadnezzar II laid siege to Jerusalem, and the city fell. In 597 BCE he pillaged both Jerusalem and its Temple and forcibly disbursed the Israelite people over a period of sixty years, not only to Babylon but throughout the Levant, which later led to the description of the people as the Jewish diaspora. This was the first destruction of Jerusalem. Centuries later, a half century after Jesus' death, the Romans would succeed in the second destruction of Jerusalem.

The destruction of the Jewish Temple and its centralized organization was devastating. The Babylonian captivity severely affected Judaism, which would provide an early source for the evolution of a new religion centuries later. It was during the captivity in Babylon that the current Hebrew script was adopted, replacing the traditional Israelite script. This within itself creates enormous difficulties in translations of what words say, or don't say, in attempting a correct view of the earlier history. But it was also during the Babylonian period that the Torah (the first five books of the Jewish Bible) emerged as the central role in Jewish life. However, evidence now shows that it was edited and redacted numerous times, though no one knows how many, from the period of the First Temple, often to bring together a more theocratic, nationalist view of the people for themselves. Before this exile, the people of Israel had been a mixture of numerous tribes, some large, some small. But in captivity, scribes and sages emerged as Jewish leaders, and later, the tribe of Levi (the priests) was the only one maintaining a central role. Thus, in Hebrew, they could write the Torah (Old Testament) in a historical manner of their own concept.

The South Arabians before Islam, however, were polytheists and revered a large number of deities, often emphasizing the sun, as masculine, and the moon, as feminine. It seemed to me that this was not unlike the general polytheism of the Israelites centuries before. The earliest known South Arabian Temple is the Mahram Bilqīs or Harem of the Queen of Sheba. South Arabians worshiped the Moon from 700 BC through 400 AD, when Judah and Christianity overtook much of the area and when Islam was ultimately created.

A second prominent Arab culture had sprung up and evolved from the Southern Sinai around 600 BC and in the land of the Edomites in Jordan from around 400 BC. Two tribes, the Edomites and the Nabateans both claimed a female descent from Ishmael, born of Abraham's marriage to Sarah, the descent being through Bashemath, one of the three wives of Esau and her sister Nebayoth. It also gave the Edomites descent from Isaac through Esau.

The Nabateans migrated from Arabia as shepherds and caravan traders and built a kingdom in the area of Syria. There seem to be numerous goddesses in Arab tradition and history. "El" and "al-Lah" simply means God, and "al-Lat" means goddess. It is said that Allat, identified with Aphrodite – Venus, became the goddess of the Nabateans, but they also had two principal gods in their pantheon, Dhu Shara and al-Uzza. Dhu Shara means Lord of Shera, a local mountain. Al-Uzza was a deity of springs and water.

But there were numerous Arab tribes, the Rechabites, the Kuryshites, and the Ansari, just as there were many tribes of Israel. All tribal, pre-Islamic worship seems to be of male and female deities, with great emphasis on astrology. The moon was considered the holiest of objects and was often the guiding light for rituals and festivals. They worshiped many deities, which is a practice proved by many archeological artifacts – inscriptions on walls, rocks and tablets. For example, every family in Mecca had at home an idol which they worshiped. The Arabs were passionate and fond of worshiping their idols, and they offered sacrifices through various rituals, but the idea of a one God theology had to come into contemplation as they viewed Judaism and Christianity.

We know that from 6,000 to 100,000 BCE was the period of the origins and early distribution of the human species originating in the continent of Africa. We know that from 100,000 to 11,000 BCE was the spread of modern humans in the Ice Age. After that, there were adaptations to a warmer world and the beginning of agriculture.

From there on, the history of the old world looks much like our modern world, only now, with a multi-billion fold increase in population. Disparate tribes formed into civilizations, each with a different religious creation. Within each civilization, there were power struggles between religious faiths, although all of them were there to give a supernatural explanation to questions not otherwise answerable at the time. Each was jealous of the other and strived for dominance by extinguishing the other. War, then as now, decided what religions would survive. It is clear that the seventh and sixth centuries BC were embryonic for religions, the most important centuries for establishment of religious ideas. Since the Hebrew kingdoms had first been conquered by Assyria and then by Babylon, Hebrews were beginning to be called "Jews" and deported to Mesopotamia. There, in the writing of the main books of the Old Testament, an influence of Mesopotamian mythology was clear. The Old Testament books appear to have been influenced by the Iranian prophet Zoroaster's espousal of monotheism and cosmic dualism, as well.

By 800 BCE, Assyria was dominant and went about colonizing the Phoenicians. By 500 BCE, early Mesopotamian empires expanded and contracted according to military capabilities of their rulers, whereas Persians had substantially conquered all of their neighbors.

Persia, under foreign rule since Alexander the Great, made a strong resurgence in the third century, when the native Sasanian Dynasty overthrew the Parthians in 224 – 226. The Sasanians were set on restoring Persia's ancient glory and became a formidable threat to the Roman Empire, which was already struggling with political instability.

The Sasanians attempted to conquer all the land to the edge of the Mediterranean Sea from the Romans, which would encompass Israel, Syria, Lebanon, Jordan, and Turkey, or at least much of that territory. The leader of the Sassanians by 227 AD was named Ardashir. He organized a powerful central government and took his army to invade Roman land in West Asia. Neither side won a clear victory. This result set a clear pattern for the next four hundred years; much fighting but no real change in borders, and a costly drain on each government's treasure. Does this sound familiar, as in today's world?

However, the Sasanians got very rich by running a lot of Silk Road trade between Central Asian kingdoms in China, Tibet, Egypt, the Byzantine Empire and East Africa. Through trade interaction, they were both influenced by such disciplines as the Roman law codes, the Ulpian Digest (about 211 AD), the Justinian's Digest of 534 AD, and the Talmud's commentaries on the Zoroastrian Avesta, written no later than the 300s AD. The greatest of these Sasanian digests was the Book of a Thousand Judgements, about 620 AD.

Zoroastrianism is one of the world's oldest monotheistic religions. A prophet named Zoroaster founded it in ancient Iran approximately 3500 years ago.

While I am not a professional scholar of religion, it appears to me that while Islam (created in the seventh century) is considered an Abrahamic religion, the writings and practices within Zoroastrianism must have had an influence:

- "Zoroastrians believe there is one God called Ahura Mazda (Wise Lord) and He created the world.

- Zoroastrians are not fire-worshippers, as some Westerners wrongly believe. Zoroastrians believe that the elements are pure and that fire represents God's light or wisdom.

- Ahura Mazda revealed the truth through the Prophet, Zoroaster.

- Zoroastrians traditionally pray several times a day.
- Zoroastrians worship communally in a Fire Temple or Agiary.
- The Zoroastrian book of Holy Scriptures is called The Avesta.
- The Avesta can be roughly split into two main sections:
  - The Avesta is the oldest and core part of the scriptures, which contains the Gathas. The Gathas are seventeen hymns thought to be composed by Zoroaster himself.
  - The Younger Avesta - commentaries to the older Avestan written in later years. It also contains myths, stories and details of ritual observances."[5]

During the 400s AD, Central Asian White Huns started attacking Iran from the North, while attacking the Roman Empire at the same time. To keep them out, Sasanians built a massive wall, like the earlier Great Wall of China. It was approximately 33 feet high and 16 ½ feet wide, covering the northern border of 124 miles in length. But the White Huns conquered Eastern Iran, anyway. It took the Sasanians until 550 AD to push them out again.

In the 530s, the Eastern Roman Empire reconquered much of the former Western Roman Empire. However, by the end of the 6th century, the Empire was again on the defensive against attacks from the Lombards, Slavs, Avar nomads and the Sasanians. After defeating the Sasanians in 622-27, the Emperor Heraclius reformed the Empire and made Greek its official language. Because of this, the Eastern Roman Empire is known as the Byzantine Empire from this time on.

While this chapter may be a heavy dose of pre-Islamic and pre-Christian religious history, this is not much more than an outline. I found it necessary to better understand what comes after. Weakened by centuries and centuries of war, both by tribal assault and by empires, the religious soil was ripe for a new seed to be planted. Islam!

Chapter 6

Islam

IN TRYING TO understand how Muhammad came to be, I began reading the writings of various imams and Islamic philosophers, filtering as best I could dogma or motivated thinking to produce creed from actual historical context. It was most difficult to do, but I suspected that there was a foretelling, perhaps in Arab folklore, of a man that would someday come, a prophet, like Muhammad. There were numerous interpretations by Christian theologians that the prophets of the Old Testament foretold of a man like Jesus one day coming to save the Jewish diaspora.

It didn't seem to me that the way humans worked, particularly tribal humans, that one day some deity or quasi-deity just popped into the community. A god becomes pre-destined through storytelling over long periods of time, and I wondered what the precursor was for Muhammad. Interestingly, most of what I found was Islamic writers relying on the Torah or Jewish Bible and dissecting what those prophets were pointing to as a person one day coming who was the representative of God. Some writers argued that the special person was Muhammad, not Jesus, while others claimed that the prophets foretold of more than one such person coming and both Jesus and Muhammad fit their descriptions. But what struck me most was that the Arabic culture and historical writings before Muhammad didn't seem to be there foretelling of the coming of a prophet like Muhammad. There was much literature, indeed, about other Arabic mythology and Persian spirituality, but not a tightly knit prophecy of a messenger of God coming. Most of the writings of Islamic theologians on the subject were retrospective, post-Muhammad, arguing that the Hebrew prophets of the Old Testament were speaking of Muhammad.

To me, something is missing here in Islamic history, and it is unfortunate. There is always a mythical beginning that leads up to a catalyst for people to believe in when it comes to religion. Where was that for Islam?

The whole idea of the coming of Christ came out of the Hebrew, and later Jewish prophets who had for centuries told that one day there would be a human incarnation of God. People who were commoners, separated from higher priestly participation or ritual, would speak of it, and over centuries there were various descriptions of the personality and the character of this person. Indeed, it was the evolution of a mindset, at times a pure superstition, at times a faith yearning, but off and on, the story would peak, fade, and sometime later peak again, often corresponding to the pressures of war and oppression. Ultimately, for some (actually only a small group) it would consolidate in the story of Christ.

It appeared to me that Muhammad had two things going for him; a messianic story to tell, a wealthy family to support it, and his father-in-law, Abu Bakr, a cunning manipulator, who knew what to do with it.

But I could find no real foretelling in the time leading up to Muhammad. I did find the writing of a Palestinian Christian historian by the name of Sozomenos, who drew from scrolls that some Arabs of Syria told stories where there had been rediscovered the authentic religion of Abraham, who is not Jewish, but the father of both Arabs and Jews. Apparently, the historical feeling among the group was that the Jews had stolen Abrahamic history and written in the religion to suit them. In their view, since Abraham lived before God had sent the Torah and Gospel, Abraham was neither Jew nor a Christian, as that religion later came to be. I saw various references to these stories that may have predated the advent of Muhammad, but most of what I saw was argumentative writings looking in retrospect. I suspected that somewhere, in some mosque or Islamic library, there is much to be found about prophetic stories of a new, real religion coming, one that would serve and unite the Arabic people within the historical basis of Abraham.

Muhammad ibn Ishaq (d. 767), Muhammad's first biographer, tells us that four of the Quraysh of Mecca (mercantile tribes that controlled Mecca) had decided to seek the hanifyyah, the true religion of Abraham. I couldn't figure out the timing, but it seemed that somewhere after that announcement, Muhammad received his prophetic call through a dream or vision. In reading this, I almost felt there was a competition as to who might be first with the new, yet original, religion. The mindset was in place. People could be ready for a revelation.

Three of the four banifs (pure monotheists) appeared to be well-known among the Arabs. Ubayd-Allah ibn Jahsh was Muhammad's cousin. Waraqa ibn Nawfal was an early spiritual advisor, and Zayd ibn Amr was the uncle of Umar ibn al-Khattab, who was one of all Muhammad's closest companions and the second Caliph (successor to Muhammad, as leader) of the Empire. This group provided a core power. My impression was that Muhammad was religious from early childhood, but was also sensitive to the mysterious, the spiritual, and the mythical. His belief in and dreams of angels as messengers from God produced revelations not only in which he could believe, but could catapult into both religious and political dialogue. The revelations could neither be refuted, nor could they be opposed to a counter-thought, because no one was there in these dreams but Muhammad and God's messengers, the Angels. It came in cataclysmic form, and since Muhammad had scribes, it could be written down and proselyted. Beyond that, it tended to satisfy the Arab desire for their own, original, religion of Abraham, just as Jesus had satisfied some Jews in their hope for the coming of a Messiah.

That is not to say that there wasn't a difference of opinion and resistance in Mecca. In fact, Muhammad and his followers moved from Mecca to Medina because of persecution, and there were wars over control and subject matter. But, Muhammad prevailed and ultimately his call to the Arab Ummah, the Arab community as a whole, and the development of the Ulama, Islamic scholars, was answered, organized and followed. The theology is to entirely submit to and surrender to the will of God, to testify that there is no God but God, and Muhammad is the messenger of God. The methodology to follow this will does not call upon reason but upon daily ritual practice, to pray five times a day, fast during the month of Ramadan, give purifying alms annually, and make a pilgrimage once in your lifetime.

Muhammad began his Abrahamic revision with the Kaaba, the history of the House of God first built by the prophet Adam, then rebuilt by Abraham and his son Ishmael. Idolatry, confusion and vague thinking had seeped into the history of the Arab world, and Muhammad took this seminal beginning as the place to purify the House of God from idol worship and to rededicate it to the worship of One God after years of Pagan practice in Arabia. His Sunnah, or way, constituted both his actions and sayings, which became the foundation of Islamic law and scribes wrote it all down for him. The dictates of the law were enforced militarily and through forceful submission.

Indeed, for Muhammad to have done all that he did and for the Arab world to accept his teachings and beliefs in his dreams is a fantastic occurrence. There is a rich and vast history, and beautiful art and architecture in the Islamic world. I came to admire it in this early study, not so much the religiosity but the art and architecture. I adore it now.

But I could also clearly see that it had been war and conquest that gave Muhammad the power and control over large numbers of people to impose a particular faith paradigm. I couldn't help but compare that in my mind with the similar historical evolution of Judaism and Christianity. War and religion are close cousins.

The hijra, Muhammad's migration to Medina in 622 to escape persecution for his teachings at Mecca, marks the beginning of the Muslim Era. Most pre-Islamic Arabs were polytheists, while Persians were monotheists, as described in the last chapter. In the Arabian Peninsula, there were Arabs, Jews, Christians, Zoroastrians and Banifs (Arab monotheists). You can see hints of all of these religions in the development of Muhammad's religious ideas. Muhammad did not think of himself as the founder of a new faith, as much as he saw himself as the restorer of the original religion of Abraham, which, to him, the Jews and Christians had misunderstood.

At Medina, Muhammad established a theocratic Muslim state in which he exercised both religious and political authority. The delicate hand of Abu Bakr, his father-in-law, could be seen in this process. Upon Muhammad's death, Abu Bakr was elected the first caliph (successor). The intent was for the institution of caliphate to continue to unite all Muslims into a single community.

The period from 1,000 BC to AD 650 saw the birth of all the major religions in the world that exists today. During this time, Hinduism, Buddhism, Zoroastrianism, Judaism, Christianity, and Islam spread. It is interesting to me that this period of a few centuries was the most creative the world has ever seen in the creation of the world's major religions. It also raises a question, did war create God?

Chapter 7

The Ummah and the Qur'an

IN MY STUDY of Islam, and as my first attempt in this sabbatical to find answers to my questions, I often moved from translations of the Hadith, the traditional account of things said or done by Muhammad or his companions and the Qur'an, itself. If Arabic Ummah were to have their Abrahamic history, it would nevertheless have to follow the documented Abrahamic history. That history had to be firmly based on the tension between the deity, the God of Abraham, and God's creation of humankind. The tension existed because of the aberrant will of God's people and a constant pulling back, or disciplining, by the deity to conform and constrain the people. Their deviant behavior was called sin and could be counted against each, individually, in a day of judgment. Various stories evolved through the centuries of iconic battles between good angels and evil forces and how the people, to survive, had to supplicate and make new sacrifices to the deity to receive repentance.

Indeed, Muhammad would have to honor this history in the finding of Ummah's religion under Abraham or at least follow the dictates of that recorded history. He did not disappoint. In fact, he revitalized every aspect of the Old Testament in the dominance of God and an individual's required supplication before him. Daily reading, prayer, and ritualistic practices were mandatory, and the deity chronicled each person's good and bad deeds, in order to make ultimate judgment. However, under Muhammad's teachings, I could not find the rich stories of the Ummah's history and their relationship with the deity, as you see in the Old Testament relating to the Hebrews.

As I turned to the Qur'an to seek its view of life after death, I had difficulty in making sense of it, as I did every time I read the Qur'an. Part of the problem was my orientation to the Western organization of writing. I didn't read right to left as in Arabic, and because the Qur'an was not written chronologically, to me, it didn't seem well organized. I came to realize that was my failing, because for someone growing up and educated in Arabic and reading the Qur'an it was all quite logical. The fact that I was relying on translations and documents by interpreters helped, but it was still a struggle.

Before getting to what the Qur'an could tell me about death and what happens after it, I came upon a Qur'anic criticism of previous recipients of divine revelation – the Jews and Christians. You find this in verse but more so in the Hadith. The Hadith is the supporting document for the Qur'an as the collection of different books, in which scribes recorded Muhammad's words, life facts, actions, and deeds, as well as those of his family and companions. It is a large study within itself. The Hadith casts a credibility attack against Jesus for not having written anything and having no scribes until half a century or more after his death. In an indirect and subtle criticism, the Qur'an and Hadith criticize both Judaism and Christianity for altering their scriptures after their prophets passed away. It was like, "see, we were more diligent, truer to the letter of the original Abrahamic religion. We were cautious with the proper collection and authentication of the Qur'an." I have read many times that Muslims firmly believe that God fulfilled his promise to protect the Qur'an from human corruption, and Muhammad was his faithful and dedicated messenger in bringing it to the people.

I worked back and forth in my attempt to gain what the Qur'an might tell me about death. The Qur'an is not chronological; Meccan passages and Medinan passages appear intermixed in many Surahs (chapters). Oddly, most of the Meccan Surahs appear at the back of the Book, and they are usually pretty short, yet Mecca is where it all began. It is said that eighty-five of the 114 Surahs were revealed during the Meccan phase. During this period, Muhammad focused most of his attention on calling people to Islam. He addressed more the humanity as a whole than the community of believers. But it was in this part that he spoke of the Day of Judgment and afterlife. Nevertheless, to get to it, I had to keep flipping from one place to another, from Qur'an to Hadith, with the help of scholars who had already traveled these academic roads.

The difference between the Surahs written in Mecca and those written in Medina is important to understand because of what was going on from a historical view. The Mecca Surahs are backward in chronology because even though they were first, they are in the rear of the Qur'an, while the later Medina Surahs are in the front. Why the reversal in the time chronology of Muhammad's life, I did not understand.

Historically, Muhammad was born in Mecca in 570; he was born to a minor faction, the Hashemites, of the ruling Quraysh tribe. According to Islamic tradition, in Mecca, in the nearby mountain cave of Hira on Jabal al-Nour, Muhammad began receiving revelations from God through Archangel Gabriel in 610 A.D. He began to preach his form of Abrahamic Monotheism against Meccan paganism and his view of corruption of God's message by Jews and Christians. It appears that he was about forty when Archangel Gabriel visited him in the cave.

After enduring persecution from the pagan tribes for thirteen years, Muhammad emigrated in 622 with his companions, the Muhajirun, to Medina. The conflict between the Quraysh and the Muslims continued. The two fought the Battle of Badr, where the Muslims defeated the Quraysh army outside of Medina, while a different battle, the Battle of Uhud ended indecisively. Nevertheless, Meccan efforts to annihilate Islam failed and proved both costly and unsuccessful. During the Battle of Trench in 627, the combined armies of Arabia were unable to defeat Muhammad's forces. It is clear that these battles, costing many lives, were fought to control the population and mandate their religion, whereas before success of Muhammad's army's there was what we might call freedom of religion.

In 628, Muhammad and his followers marched back to Mecca, attempting to enter the city for pilgrimage but were blocked by the Quraysh. Finally, in a joint oath, Muslims and Meccans entered into the Treaty of Hudaybiyyah, whereby the Quraysh promised to cease fighting Muslims and promised that Muslims would be allowed into the city the following year for pilgrimage. Two years later, the Quraysh violated the truce by slaughtering a group of Muslims and their allies. Muhammad, however, was now 10,000 strong and decided to march into Mecca.

The city of Mecca surrendered to Muhammad who declared peace and amnesty for the inhabitants. He then destroyed native pagan imagery and Islamized the region, proclaiming Mecca the holiest site of Islam. He unified the Arabian Peninsula, and Islam began a period of rapid expansion.

By all accounts, Muhammad was deeply reflective, even in childhood. He would spend days in complete seclusion while meditating and worshiping God. The writers and compilers of the Qur'an were very knowledgeable of both Judeo or Hebrew history, as well as Christianity. But just as the stories of Jesus' death and resurrection were a catalyst for Christianity, the story of Muhammad's experience in the cave was a catalyst for Islam. By his account, one day while he was meditating, a spirit spoke to him with the word, "Read!" Muhammad was startled by the voice and replied, "I do not know how to read." Suddenly, the spirit caught hold of Muhammad, squeezing him until he could bear it no more and once again urged him to read. Muhammad was shaken by the experience and repeated his claim, "I do not know how to read!"

Once again the spirit took hold of him, squeezing him tightly, and then finally letting him go. This time, the spirit, known as Angel Gabriel, revealed the first words of the Qur'an to Muhammad. "Read, in the Name of your Sustainer, who created man from a clot. Read! For your Sustainer is the most powerful One, who has taught man to use the pen – – taught man what he did not know." (96:1 – 5).

This experience marks the beginning of a divine revelation. It would become the centrality of Islam, the Prophecy of Muhammad, who continued to receive the Qur'an in stages through the Angel Gabriel as he would experience periodic revelations. This lasted over a span of 23 years from 610 through 632 of the Common Era. But apparently, Muhammad never learned to read and thus, unlike Jesus, he relied heavily on scribes to take down his revelations and record his history. Later, some scribes attempted to diminish the non-reading aspect of the story by replacing the word "read" in translation with the word "proclaim," but this was a weak excuse for the original text.

As an aside, I reflected back to my Baylor courses on whether Jesus could read. I knew that He studied in the temple, or was claimed to have done so, though there is no direct proof. But studying in his youthful days didn't necessarily mean reading. Not many in those days could read. Study or like references often referred to being taught, not necessarily reading. As far as I was aware, there is no evidence that Jesus could read. Isn't it interesting that the two men who founded religions that would ultimately control most of the world's population were illiterate, according to modern definition? Clearly, for Muhammad, the fact that he could not read and his admission of same weighed heavily on him. Thus, he had a strict dedication to the use of scribes for each current moment. Would that be good if Jesus had done the same?

Last day of apocalypse turned out to be the central doctrine in the Qur'an, where the world will be destroyed and Allah will raise all people, even the dead, and judge them. As for those who have already died, they will remain in their graves and do now, awaiting their resurrection. There is a premonition for some, however. Of those who are known to be bound for hell, they will suffer in their graves, while those bound for heaven will lie in peace until the time of resurrection.

Decayed bodies in graves are not a problem because Allah is all-powerful. As the Last Day resurrection takes place, He will recreate the decayed bodies (17:100 "could they not see that God who created the heavens and the earth is able to create the like of them?"). At this point, Allah will judge the people according to their deeds. They will either gain admission to Paradise, where they will enjoy physical and spiritual pleasures forever, or be condemned to hell to suffer mental and physical torment for eternity.

This paradise is a place of peace, pleasure and lofty mansions (39:20, 29:58 – 59), and there is delicious food and drink (52:22, 52:19, 38:51). There are virgin companions for men. Indeed, there is almost an obsession with the promise (56:17 – 19, 52:24 – 25, 76:19, 56:35 – 38, 37:48 – 49, 38:52 – 54, 44:51 – 56, and 52:20 – 21). There are seven heavens (17:46, 23:88, 41:11, 65:12), often described as luscious and beautiful gardens.

After Muhammad experienced his revelation for the first time, he returned to his wife Khadija, seriously unnerved by the experience. His wife comforted him and believed that he had just received a divine message. Khadija took Muhammad to her cousin, Waraqa ibn Nawfal for advice. Waraqa is said to have been a learned Christian monk, an Ebonite Christian priest, living in Mecca who had learned to read Hebrew. After hearing Muhammad's experience, Waraqa reassured him by saying:

"Surely, by Him in whose hand is Waraqa's soul, you are a prophet of his people. There has come unto you the greatest Angel who came unto Moses. Like the Hebrew prophets, you will be called a liar, ill-treated, and they will cast you out and make war upon you."

Sometime later, Waraqa converted to Islam and was a constant support to Muhammad. But the interesting backstory to Muhammad is that he was born in Mecca. Arabia was less developed than other regions in that part of the world. It was made up of nomadic tribes, which either worked the land or were in trade. Each tribe was made up of clans, or extended family groups. Much like the Navajos of North America, the blood ties of family, clan, and tribe were the primary manner in which people identified themselves. Muhammad Ibn Abdallah was born into the Hashim clan of the powerful Quraysh tribe, and his people were primarily traders.

He became an orphan at a young age. He was first taken by his grandfather and then his uncle, who raised him to manhood. Muhammad grew up illiterate like most people throughout the

Arabian Peninsula and the Levant. Interestingly, the wealthiest lady of mecca, Khadija, entrusted him with the task of leading her caravan into Syria. He was good at it; he was trustworthy and an excellent business person – the caravan yielded profits beyond Khadija's expectations. Soon, she decided to find a way of making him agree to marry her. Despite his poverty and being disadvantaged in social circles, he married into great wealth. Khadija was 40 when they married, while Muhammad was 25. Khadija's family would remain a ruling and integral force in the evolution of Islam.

Similar to the Torah and the New Testament, the Qur'an turned out to be obsessed with the brevity of life on earth, a person's actions, a nebulous definition of a soul, the end of times and judgment day. After the day of questioning, the soul reaches its final home, either in the delights of paradise or the torments of hellfire. The Qur'an attributes paradise to that soul which was near God on earth: "and those foremost (in faith and actions) will be foremost in the hereafter)" (56:10). While at the same time, those for whom the Qur'an attributes hellfire are the souls that overindulged in their worldly passions: "for, behold, in times gone by they were indulged in sinful luxury, and persisted in sinning." (56:45 – 46).

Muhammad explained to his companions that his divine revelations came to him in two primary ways through the Angel Gabriel. First, it came "like the ringing of a bell," until he grasped all that was revealed. Second, the revelation came through the Angel Gabriel taking the form of a man who would then impart divine inspiration to Muhammad.

In the Islamic tradition, there is a belief that the Angel Gabriel visited the Prophet Muhammad every Ramadan (the month of fasting in which the revelation of the Qur'an began) to review what had been revealed. In his revelations, the second most important doctrinal teaching came out of the Meccan phase of his life and regarded the preaching of the Day of Judgment and an Afterlife. It was a radical departure from the common practice in Mecca – Pagan beliefs that did not recognize accountability of moral actions for after death existence.

In the Qur'an, heaven is a garden; hell is a cauldron of fire. It calls the faithful to the garden and condemns those who did not serve well.

"O soul who is at rest, return to thy Lord, well – pleased with him, well – pleasing Him. So enter among My servants and enter My garden." (89:27 – 30).

If one goes to hell, the description gets very graphic. It has seven doors (39:71, 15:43) leading to a fiery crater of various levels, the lowest of which contains the tree Zaqqum and a cauldron of boiling pitch.

Although written differently, the imagery often reminded me of Revelations in the New Testament, and a mythical mindset seemed quite similar. Here was the perpetual desire to live forever overlaid with fear of judgment, the punishment of hell, and the visions of paradise, if all went well.

Chapter 8

The Qur'an and the
Promise of the Hereafter

I READ MANY disquisitions as to what Muhammad was and what he did. While he claims to be the interlocutor or a messenger of the Angel Gabriel and therefore his words are not to be contested or questioned, he states that he is neither the author nor the editor of the Scripture. In fact, the Qur'an refutes the notion that it was written by Muhammad by saying, "and you were not a reader of any Scripture before it, nor did you write it with your right hand. In that case, indeed, would the talkers of vanities have doubted?" (29:48). It marks an interesting pre-defense and avoidance of attack by dismissing the messenger, all the while retaining his authority and credibility. It is the age-old "Don't shoot the messenger, and you can't get to the source." It also begs the question, "was there really an Angel Gabriel, or is that just more Hebrew mythological development?" What is the evidence for this source? There is no evidence either from Muhammad or the Hebrew writings. You just have to accept that the story of the Angel Gabriel is true, lest you become a nonbeliever and subject to eternal Hell.

It is clear that the writer is trying to justify this writing as coming from God and is seeking credibility through levels of protection, first God the writer, then Gabriel the messenger, then Muhammad, the messenger. If we apply the standard of proof that we commonly and realistically live by, that being by a preponderance of evidence (more likely than not by reasonable deduction), the writer of the Qur'an fails. All three Abrahamic religions wrestle with this problem of words coming from God. They presuppose the existence of God.

There is definitely a lack of credibility, when this Surah claims that the words of the Qur'an are the exact words which Angel Gabriel gave to Muhammad without the presence of any other person, and then, orally Muhammad related them in order to be written down to some scribe or a group of scribes at a different location, and those words are exact and there can be no variance. I have often wondered how much time passed between Muhammad receiving these words in the cave to when he met with the scribes for transcription in that first encounter. Remember, he first went to his wife and told his revelation. She then took him to her cousin for another telling. Sometime after that, he told it to a scribe who wrote it down.

This is a strange defense. Which has higher veracity, words from an unproven supernatural who does not have the power to speak directly to the Ummah but must do so through an intermediary, or words of a mortal who claims to be a Prophet but can neither read nor write? The mindset seems to be that illiteracy offers credibility. If you can't read, who told you about the Old Testament, the New Testament and the mythical history of the Angel Gabriel? Even if you accept the premise of "messenger," to a reasonable person the question would arise, "why does this earth-shaking revelation have to be in secret? Would it not have been more credible for a witness or two to have been present either at the time God was speaking to Gabriel or Gabriel was speaking to Muhammad?" Why all the mysterious secrecy?

Nevertheless, Muslims believe, on fear of death, that the Qur'an is divinely created in form, content, message, and literal word, just as fundamental believers in the New Testament do regarding the books that make up that scripture. The Qur'an reflects the concept of revelation or divine inspiration known as "Wahy" in Arabic. It asserts in several passages that the inspiration Muhammad received came from the same source and experience as those messengers who came before, such as Prophets Noah, Abraham, Moses, and Jesus. And yet, in the quoted passage the Angel Gabriel is stating "… And you were not a reader of <u>any Scripture before it…</u>" (29:48), as a defense against copying what had been previously written. In this way, what becomes the Qur'an is interpreted to be its own original out of the mouth of God through these intermediaries. "So we have made the (Qur'an) easy in your own tongue, that with it you may give glad tidings to the righteous, and warnings to the people given to contention." (19:97) "We sent down the (Qur'an) in Truth, and in Truth has it descended; and we sent you but to give glad tidings and warn (sinners)." (17:105)

A reasonable mind would say that this sounds rather weak, for an all-powerful deity to justify the writings and anticipate criticisms before they are made. One also wonders why God apparently did not care or know about the other millions of people on earth in other geographic regions. Regarding the Surahs, since the "messenger" could not get to everyone in the world and obviously an appointed Arab in the middle of a great desert could not as well, were those not reached to burn in the cauldron of fire?

The Qur'an weighs heavy on the fear of dying, the fear of being judged by a supernatural power and not being accepted, and the fear of the unknown, i.e., what happens after one dies. It is an obsession and probably comes from Muhammad's life in the middle of wars where death was ever present.

"The Death from which you flee will truly overtake you: then you will be sent back to the Knower of things secret and open: He will tell you things you did." (62:8)

When it comes to being judged, there is plenty to fear not only if you are a nonbeliever, but if you were to treat the book, the Qur'an, wrongly:

"That this is indeed a Qur'an most honorable,

In a Book, well-guarded,

Which none shall touch but those who are clean:

A Revelation from the Lord of the Worlds.

Is it such a Message that you would hold in light esteem?

And have you made it your livelihood that you should declare it false?

Then why do you not (intervene) when (the soul of a dying man) reaches the throat

And you the while (sit) looking on,-

But we are nearer to him than you, and yet do not see-

Then why do you not, - if you are exempt from (future) account,-

Call back the soul, if you are true

Dust, then, if he be those nearest the Allah,

(There is for him) Rest and Satisfaction, and a Garden of Delights.

And if he be of the Companions of the Right Hand,

(for him is the salutation) "Peace be unto you; from the Companions of the Right Hand.

And if he be of those who treat (Truth) as Falsehood, who go wrong,

For him is entertainment in Boiling Water,

And burning in Hell-fire."

(56:77 – 94)

For the Qur'an, the soul has a journey in the physical body from pre-birth to the hereafter. Apparently, the soul is not something different from the physical body. We learn that a conversion takes place between every human soul and God before birth.

"And whenever your Lord bring forth their offspring from the loins of the children of Adam, He calls upon them to bear witness about themselves: 'Am I not your Lord?' – To which they answer, 'yes, indeed, we bear witness'" (7:172).

I wonder how Muhammad knows of Adam when he hasn't previously read the Scripture. Ah! I understand, now. Muhammad is illiterate, and he is merely passing the Judeo history on to his scribes at some date. He must have a photographic memory to be able to recite such history so accurately to his scribes. Nevertheless, the pre-world commitment occurs before every person is born. Naturally, the idea of free choice does not exist, except to the extent that you can reject Islam once you get into the world. Of course, that means you will boil in a cauldron of fire. But from this Islamic concept of pre-world non-choice, the Qur'an rejects the Christian concept of original sin whereby all humans are marked with sin upon birth because of Adam's first act of disobedience, that of eating from the forbidden tree.

The Qur'anic interpretation of that event is that God ultimately forgives and honors Adam. He becomes God's representative on earth and the first Prophet in a series of prophets that bring constant guidance to humanity:

"No soul shall bear the burden of another." (6:164)

Thus, according to the Qur'an, people don't carry Adam's sins and need to seek forgiveness from the beginning of life. Each person is singularly responsible for their good or evil deeds, and Allah will remember them all. In my observation, that means that there is no forgiveness in the Qur'an, only responsibility.

From this premise, the Qur'an describes five stages for the life of the soul, which began before birth and continues after death. After the pre-world commitment, babies are born with the original pledge to God in their subconsciousness. The Qur'an calls itself a "reminder" of that which the soul already knows at the subconscious level. The second stage, this birth and life on earth, with all its tribulations is a testing stage to check the individual's commitment to God.

"And most surely shall We try you by means of danger, and hunger, and loss of worldly goods, of lives and of (earned) fruits. But give glad tidings and to those who are patient in adversity." (2:155)

Following this second stage, life in its tribulations and its commitment or failure to commit, comes the third stage – the grave. The Qur'an describes the grave as a place of initial questioning where the soul faces the illusory nature of worldly goods. God makes good His promise to hold each person accountable for his or her deeds. But the grave is a place of waiting where righteous souls lie in peace and satisfaction and evil souls lie in discomfort and punishment. The grave is also a place for purification through punishment of souls who had much good in them, but committed evil deeds as well, so that on the Day of Judgment those souls will be forgiven and granted paradise.

So, it would appear that in the grave somehow there is prejudgment, but in my study, I wasn't sure by whom. The Qur'an often speaks in the plural, "We," with the capital letter. At other times, it speaks of Allah (God). I never understood whether the "We" was the Ummah, the Muslim community as a whole, the califs, Muhammad, Gabriel, all of the former Prophets, Allah, himself, or some kind of committee. Nevertheless, the message is clear: one must follow the dictates of the Qur'an literally. A failure to do so renders prejudgment in the grave which one should fear daily and then ultimate judgment on the Day of Judgment.

The Day of Judgment is graphic in the Qur'an, as it is in Revelations in the New Testament, describing the transitory stage from the grave to Judgment Day.

"And verily the Hour will come: there can be no doubt about it, or about (the fact) God will raise up all those who are in their graves." (22:7)

On this day, souls: "will come forth – their eyes bold from their graves, like locusts scattered abroad." (99:7-8)

For nonbelievers or sinners who are not forgiven:

"On the Day of Judgment We shall gather them together, prone on their faces, blind, dumb, and deaf: their abode will be Hell: every time it shows abatement, We shall increase for them the fierceness of the Fire."

For the believers who are accepted:

"Again, on the Day of Judgment, you will be raised up. And We have made, above you, seven tracts, and We are never unmindful of (Our) creation." (23:16-17)

This fifth stage is the final abode, the eternal bliss of heaven for the believer, or the eternal torment of fire – Hell. It is best summed up in the Qur'an's own words.

The description of the garden which the righteous are promised: "In it are rivers of water which time does not corrupt, rivers if milk wherein the taste never alters; rivers of wine delightful to those who drink it; and rivers of honey of all impurities cleansed, and the enjoyment of all the fruits and of the forgiveness from the Sustainer. (Can those in such Bliss) be compared to such as shall dwell forever in the Fire, and be given to drink boiling water, so that it cuts up their bowels (to pieces)?" 47:15

So, here is what we have. Islam is a religion based on hearsay and reinforced by fearful threats to anyone who does not believe and follow the scripts.

Traditionally, testimony that a witness gives, who relates not their own experience, but what others have said, which is therefore dependent on the credibility of someone other than the witness is hearsay and not admissible as evidence.

We have already questioned the accuracy of what could be told four times (God to Gabriel to Muhammad to scribes). Let's break down the stages of the soul.

Pre-birth Dedication: the unborn child is committed to this religion (Lord). How do we know this? We don't. There is no evidence that there is a place where the identity of a child can be had before conception and have a conversation with it. Saying that there is does not make it so.

The "Reminder": to accept that the eyes of a super-being are upon every individual, everywhere, and within their heads reminding them that he is watching them can be nothing more than self-imposed paranoiac superstition. Again, there is no independent evidence to support that belief and just saying it doesn't make it so.

Deed Counting: again, it is quite a reach to allege that there is a superhuman somewhere that counts and judges every action of every person on earth as that same supernatural tests each person with adversity. Has a role of deeds ever been produced? If not, how do we know it exists?

The Grave: accountability regarding good or bad deeds while decomposing in a grave is yet another fiction of imagination. What is in a grave is no longer sentient. We know from experience that it is just a corpse. There has never been any evidence that anything other than decomposition goes on in a grave.

Day of Judgment: mystics have been waiting for that day for a long time. Here again, such a day presupposes a powerful supernatural who has never been heard from throughout time, except as voices in the heads of a few people and somehow this deity keeps up with every action or non-action of every human throughout time, judges them, then transports each one to either heaven or hell.

None of this would be allowed as evidence in any court in the land, today because it is hearsay built upon hearsay. That is not evidence, and the protestations of the Qur'an are neither proof nor proven. Where is the proof that there is a God, any evidence that can be quantified? What human mind created the story of the Angel Gabriel and why is he given to know without error what God instructed him to say? In angel histology, angels often made mistakes.

Chapter 9

The New Testament

IN THIS INTERMITTENT sabbatical of mine, I turned from studying the Qur'an to a review of the New Testament. I felt that I knew the New Testament fairly well. As a child and through my teenage years, my mother had insisted that I attend Sunday morning Sunday school, followed by the main church session and then the evening services, not to mention a yearly evangelical revival. I had heard hundreds of sermons and interpretations of the Bible and had done a fair amount of reading on my own. At Baylor, I had taken a course in Hebrew History and one on the New Testament, though religion was not my primary study.

My teachings as a young man had provided a reasonably grounded Christian belief in the hereafter, based on blind faith, which was the accepted way of reasoning with questions of immortality. My understanding was that to have everlasting life,

life after death, one must first believe that Jesus Christ was the Son of God.

For me, there were always questions. My late parents, loyal Baptists, told the story that at about ten years old I asked them the question, "If God had a Son, Jesus, who was God's mother and father? Didn't He have to come from somewhere?" Of course, the core belief of Christianity is that there is a God, as in Islam, all-seeing, omnipotent. However, as far as I could tell, there was no story of who created God. What made Him, and why was He a Him?

Jesus became the ultimate sacrifice for the absolution of human sin, as he allowed himself to be crucified on the cross as the incarnate (personification) Son of the deity. For the longest time, I did not know the meaning of the word "incarnate," but it had the sound of authority. It turned out that God had a Son with a bodily form. Presumably, God did not, although there is that statement in Genesis that man was created in His image. To enjoy life after death, a person needs only to affirm that Jesus was the Son of God, who died for the forgiveness of that person's sins, predisposing that the person would sin. By believing in Him in this way, a person would have a life after death, eternal life.

As in all religions, the longer the history, the greater the expanse of machinations of ritual, the involvement of numerous icons, and the variances of religious philosophies and ideologies into sects, subparts, and denominations. Nevertheless, each religion promises satisfaction and certainty for that primal desire of immortality.

Now, in my "Re-Search Period," I wanted to see what scholars had to say about the writing of the New Testament. Since no original documents exist, I was interested in finding scholars who analyzed copied text, for the meaning of words and stories of that period. I did not know it at the beginning of this study, but through my search, I realized just how inconsistent the New Testament is. I came to understand what so many of the sermons I had heard as a young man were. They were a purposeful defense, an apology, an argument offering consistency, because a close view of the New Testament raised numerous questions of inconsistency. In the "preponderance of evidence," inconsistency is an element of invalidity.

My methodology and my new study were simplistic and not scholarly. After all, I was not preparing to write a thesis. At this period of my Re-Search, I never even contemplated writing this book. This work was to my satisfaction, and I decided that if I were to understand the New Testament's answers concerning death, I should start with the birth of Jesus. I created subject and verse reference outlines and columns and then worked back and forth, somewhat as I had done with the Qur'an. When I would get stumped, I would search what scholars had said about a given verse, looking for where it originated and how it was written. Interestingly, I found that numerous verses had been altered or written through the centuries after the death of Jesus, by scribes who felt that it was significant to do so. However, it is impossible to identify all alterations.

After my sabbatical and over the next forty years of my life, I would find authors and scholars who were knowledgeable, educated in the subject matter, but who would follow a similar methodology to mine of outlining. They would be both more complete and yet more succinct in accomplishing what I was trying to do in this early private sabbatical. Nevertheless, in these nights at libraries, and particularly the New York Public Library, which I chose for this personal study early on, I found the writings of numerous scholars who had compared the Abrahamic religions on various levels, as well as writings that compared verse by verse the documents of each religion pointing out their inconsistencies. What I considered to be a novel approach had been going on for centuries. Questions, doubts and attempted affirmations began in each religion early in its founding, and in each religious document one could find paranoia of not being believed followed by the threat, sometimes subtle, sometimes blunt as in the Qur'an, of what would occur if one disbelieved.

I chose the New York Public Library as a base for my search for two reasons. First, I had seen it while visiting as a United Nations representative to meet Prime Minister Nehru and had thought that someday I would like to return and spend some time there, as I mentioned earlier. Second, it was a long way from Texas, and going through a marital as well as a professional transition, I had the feeling of wanting to be far away.

It was a time before computers, or at least personal computers and digitized library catalogs. It took a few days of working card catalogs and getting used to different departments of subject matter, texts, and archives, but soon I was moving through the grand library with relative ease. The helpfulness of the staff made the process easier as well.

Each of the Abrahamic religions has its book, the Bible for Christians, the Qur'an for Muslims, and the Torah and Jewish Bible for Jews. The book, itself, is sanctified and protected and to denigrate it in any way, by accident or intentionally, can lead to outrage and retribution by the faithful. Asking questions is often viewed as denigration in itself.

For Christians, the compilation of the New Testament of the Bible ends the long search and hope for immortality, everlasting life. It tells of the coming of the Messiah, Jesus, long foretold in some Jewish traditions and purports to establish proof that by following specific rules of faith, one can enter a place called heaven, where friends and family who respected the same rules will also be.

The combining of the two books to make one Bible, the Old Testament coming out of the Jewish Torah and the New Testament compiled after the death of Jesus, is an interesting formatting. The New Testament with few exceptions does not cross-reference the Old Testament itself but leaves the freedom to practitioners and interpreters to do so. It provides flexibility to voluntarily combine passages or ignore parts of the Old Testament as either irrelevant or purely historical or allegorical.

Perhaps the sharpest criticism of the credibility of the New Testament is that it pretends to be timeless, eternal, and the unchanging truth. The diverse writings that were captured and selected to become the composition known as the New Testament were not given lineation until midway into the second century of the Common Era.

Jesus neither wrote nor had scribes writing down what he said. This seems quite odd, because there is an assumption by scholars that Matthew, John, and Peter could write, but they chronicled nothing in Jesus' time. Most certainly Jesus' good friend, Nicodemus, could write, but one could understand why he couldn't chronicle during Jesus' life. While being a Pharisee, the late enemies of Jesus as a group, he may well have also been an Essen, a member of a secret sect who healed others, used herbs and dedicated themselves to peace. It would have been dangerous for Nicodemus to write about Jesus.

Christians have almost no words that Jesus spoke in his native tongue of Aramaic, the ancient language of the Semitic family group (Assyrians, Babylonians, Chadians, Aramaeans, Hebrews, and Arabs), that language of multiple dialects. The few Aramaic words of Jesus that we do have are "Talitha Cumi" in Mark 5:41 and "Ephphatha" in the story of the deaf-mute in Mark 7:34. Then, there are his words attributed to his cry from the cross, "Eloi Eloi lama sabachtani" ("my God, my God, why have you forsaken me?"), which is a quotation from Psalm 22.

Through the early period of compilation and even up to the creation of the New Greek Testament centuries later, separate power struggles existed within the Roman Church and between the competing sects of followers of Jesus, as to which stories were true, which stories were false, how events occurred and what people said. It is difficult to imagine how exact memory can a scribe have, when writing of events told which happened a half to a full century before the actual writing. Just imagine for us in the twenty-first century if in the early twentieth century at the event of World War I there have been no historians, no scribes, and today we tried to re-create the story. A factual basis would be impossible to develop.

As a trial lawyer, if I had a case where my burden of proof was to establish the truth of the story, but my only evidence was a century of hand-me-down oral stories later written, redacted and rewritten, I would be much concerned. If the New Testament were part of the English jurisprudence test of proof by a preponderance of evidence, it would be difficult for me to see what reliable evidence there is to establish the credibility of the New Testament story. Nevertheless, I will continue to try in the following pages.

What little we do have of what Jesus said is as equally mystifying as what we don't have. Because of that, there is a distinct possibility of basic human mistakes. One mistake could be that scribes were putting into Jesus' mouth the words which he didn't say. Or, they were writing them differently than how he actually said them. The second type of mistake could be that the traditional oral storytelling embellished words or events, beyond the actual words or events. For one tacit admission in the New Testament, itself, there is that strange admission attributed to Luke at the beginning of the Gospel According To Luke. He seems to say that "many" before him had written accounts of the things Jesus said and did, and from reading them, he decided to produce his account, which apparently is in contrast to the others, but his account is "accurate" (Luke 1:1 – 4). Or rather, the writer of Luke would have one believe.

Linguists have struggled for centuries with the New Testament, and the result is often a garbled interpretation, because the linguist has to move from English to Greek (not current day Greek), the language in which the New Testament was written, but not the language of Jesus and his followers, so the Aramaic has to be first considered. To move into the world of Aramaic, the lingua franca of the Eastern Mediterranean since around 1000 BC, poses great difficulty. This Semitic language displaced Hebrew and became the language of the Jews and thus, Jesus. It was the liturgical language of the region, again, with difficult dialects and oral tradition for meaning.

I came across numerous examples of the problem. We all remember that odd metaphor about the eye of the needle and the impossibility of a camel going through it. It may not sound so strange today because we've heard it so many times, but for Jesus to have used it in the way reported, it would not have made sense any more than it does now.

"It is easier for a camel to go through the eye of the needle than for a rich man to enter the kingdom of heaven."

These mixed metaphors would not have made the point to the people of the region. But if you look at the Aramaic word of rope and compare it to the Aramaic word for camel, you find that they are almost identical. At least that is what I learned from the linguist I read who wrote on translation discrepancies. If this is correct, the metaphor would be more consistent, make more sense, and would have been contextual to those to whom Jesus was speaking. Thus,

"It is easier for a rope to go through the eye of a needle...."

One of the things always bothering me in the New Testament mythology is the virgin birth. During Christmas, it is talked about with hushed honor, unless you are a Catholic and then the Virgin Merry seems to be everywhere all year long. How Jesus came to be in the womb of Mary wasn't part of my questioning quest of what happens when we die, but I did run across a manuscript that pointed out a lapse of translation relating to the concept of "virgin." Apparently, neither the word "virgin" nor the concept of virginity appears in the Hebrew text of Isaiah that Matthew quoted as a basis for his account of Jesus' virgin birth. The understanding of "virgin" is present only in the Greek word "Parthenos," which was used to translate the Hebrew word "almah" into a Greek version of the Hebrew Scriptures. The Hebrew word for virgin is "betulah." "Almah" never means "virgin" in Hebrew.

This revelation gave me some relief, even though it apparently meant that the Virgin Mary tradition of Catholicism and New Testament Protestantism rested upon something as fragile as a mistranslation. History has shown some serious attempts to cover up this little glitch, as well as counter-explanations. But I felt relieved, because I had never really accepted the idea that some supernatural power came down out of somewhere, to a little place where Mary, a virgin, lived with Joseph, and then impregnated her with its sperm. In a good sci-fi novel, I could be capable of suspending my disbelief for the purpose of entertainment, but in a Biblical tale offered for the truth, it had been difficult to do. Most likely, mortal Joseph impregnated Mary as nature dictates.

As I researched the explanations of death in the Scriptures of the New Testament, I began to run across a plethora of inconsistencies which church teachers, ministers or orators, at least in my lifetime, had never mentioned. I randomly discovered myself some of them; different scholars found other inconsistencies and directed me to them. I knew that it was impossible to defend the New Testament as being the literal word of God, and yet I could not understand why where I lived in West Texas that was exactly what the people did. They are tribal when it comes to defending its literal meaning.

But even if translation and Machiavellian maneuvering of translations were not a problem with the New Testament, the failure of teachers to look at all verses was. For me, a close reading of the New Testament followed by the Old had to be disturbing for anyone of a humanist bent. Practitioners of Christian religion seldom, if ever, point out that while Jesus exhorted people to love their enemies and to pray for their persecutors (Matt 23:17), he called Gentiles "dogs" (Matt 15:26). He said he had come to set a man against his father and a daughter against her mother (Matt 12:46 – 50), which ignored the teaching of "honor your parents." Yet, this was the same deity that espoused the beautiful principles of the Sermon on the Mount, in direct conflict with the dysfunctional statements of hate.

These exhortations by Jesus do not speak to my questions about the end of life, but such talk does cause a pause for concern about the speaker. There are these New Testament ideas of destroying a herd of pigs and presumably a person's livelihood in order to exorcise a perceived demon (Mark 5:13), or of cursing a fig tree because it did not bear fruit out of season (Matt 21:18-19). Those ideas just don't rise to the intellectual level that one would hope for in seeking end-of-life answers. Then, the divine message says that if we fail in our understanding, we will be cast into the outer darkness, where there will be weeping and gnashing of teeth (Matt 25:30).

As I continued my study, these types of exorcisms initiated by fear of darkness harkened a parallel with the Qur'an for a later period and indeed the Old Testament for the earlier. In the New Testament, most of these theological examples are apparently Matthew's interpretations of what Jesus taught, if in fact, Matthew reported it that way. Therein lies the problem, for those who believe that every word is true or that the written verses were divinely inspired.

As I saw this and other examples from the viewpoint of a preponderance of evidence, New Testament reporting was often double hearsay, and often, beyond that, tweaked by mortals through the years. If we were to test the New Testament reporting according to the rules of evidence in English jurisprudence, we would exclude it as not credible. If you are seeking the truth, at what point do you doubt the evidence? How many inconsistencies must there be?

How many tweaks can you accept? How many must you defend to give a deity justification?

I was concluding that the New Testament in conjunction with the Old Testament, or standing alone as the case may be, was based in condemnation, prejudice, and judgment seeking enforcement through fear of retribution, but I stopped and told myself to take time and be more forgiving. For all the failings of these verses, I knew that the New Testament had the concept of love through the man called Jesus. After all, the Sermon on the Mount stood for that. Stories of healing, service to the poor, and even birth, death, and everlasting life set him apart from anything else in the Abrahamic religions. With such paradigm-shifting philosophy, it does seem strange that the Gospels of Mark and John ignore the sermon altogether as do Apostles Paul, Peter, and John. But Luke, who intersperses sayings from the sermon, says in Luke (6:24-25), "But woe unto you that are rich! For you have received your consolation. Woe to you that are full for ye shall hunger."

Then, I ran across some treatises on a Jewish sect called the Essenes. If you divided the Jewish people, at the time of Jesus, into three major sects, you would see they parted along three different political groups, the Pharisees, the Sadducees, and the Essenes. The intriguing thing about the Essenes is the parallel that can be drawn to Jesus. They were called "healers" and "doctors." They were praised for their honesty, justice, reason and temperance, and they were talented Prophets and healers. The New Testament never refers to the Essenes by name, but at times there were words that had to come from them: "the Spirit of the Lord is upon me, because He hath anointed me to preach the gospel to the poor, He has sent me to heal the brokenhearted, to preach deliverance to the captives, and of recovering of sight to the blind, to set at liberty them that are bruised" (Luke 4:18).

This sect took a vow of poverty, dressed in white robes, and by the time of Christ, worked against the codification of the Levites. The Essenes viewed the Levites as having left the true path of the teachings of Moses and misdirected their people as a result of an obsession with wealth and elitism. In the view of the Essenes, the Levites were not the priests from centuries before. The Dead Sea Scrolls indicated that there were many separate, but related religious groups which shared similar mystic, eschatological, messianic, and ascetic beliefs. It seemed that many of these could fit under a broad umbrella of Essene. But it also seemed, even as in today's Christianity, that each group believed it had the answer to questions of the unknown and the infinitude of death.

I decided that if I took a close look at how the New Testament talked about Jesus' birth and looked for consistency in comparing what it told of his death, perhaps I would find a seed of insight that could help answer my questions. The four chapters of the New Testament, Matthew 1 and 2, and Luke 1 and 2 purport to tell the story of Jesus' birth, and the six chapters, Matthew 28, Mark 16, Luke 24, John 20, 21, and 1 Corinthians 15 purport to tell the story of Jesus' resurrection. For anyone seeking consistency, they soon feel like a ping-pong ball. Exaggeration can quickly be identified, historical eras as pointed out by scholars, and what appears to be mutually exclusive religious traditions, all cobbled together by a series of books. Unfortunately, it raises the possibility that none of the gospel writers (Matthew, Mark, Luke, and John) were correct in the literalness of their assertions, even as Luke is saying that he wrote the correct version. All of this gives people like me, who are looking for straight answers to end-of-life questions, a pause in consideration.

For the Jesus story, it all begins with the beautiful fable of that first Christmas. It is the most familiar part of the Bible, and we celebrate it each year with an extended holiday. Scenes in our neighborhood yards from the narratives of the birth of Jesus, lighted and unlighted, are everywhere. Remindful Christmas carols play in every store and mall and on every radio station, while every television channel has a Christmas special. The tunes of "O Come, All Ye Faithful" and "Hark! The Herald Angels Sing" flow across the nation, while Macy's announces the start of the season with a massive parade.

I have observed that in the many years of hearing and singing the Christmas carols I am not truly aware of the meaning of their words. It is a rote memory, but it seems that the warm melodies attract me. I suppose this occurs with many others as, by osmosis, the content slips into the subconscious. Of course, we have the American advertising picture of little Bethlehem, a star in the East, angelic choruses, shepherds, wise men, and the baby Jesus. It all looks so clean and neat, and we have viewed it in the same way every year of our life.

How could we not like the show, when we see the yearly Currier and Ives pictures of winter and Christmas? They bring out a warm feeling that probably hasn't surfaced in a while. By choice, we remain either blissfully unaware or blatantly ignorant of the problems of logic, not to mention untruth, in the narrative. Mythical cosmology plays an integral part. The assumption presented in the Biblical story is that blue sky separates God's dwelling place in heaven from the mortal habitat on earth. This is understandable for Jesus' time, because back then people could only know what they see, and what they could see was not only limited, but also mysterious and unexplainable. Consequently, they would make up a story of mythic primacy.

It is said that he who writes history creates history. Bethlehem was a little town, filled with small-town gossip. In fact, since most people could neither read nor write, and there was no such thing as a printing press or news media; the main modes of communication were word-of-mouth and gossip. Let's suppose that it literally occurred that a star led three exotic Eastern magi on their camels to the door of a little house or barn, where they dismounted and presented gifts of gold, frankincense, and myrrh to an infant. Would have everyone living miles around remember that house? There would have been no way to keep it secret. It would have been a massive crowd. As to that star, navigation by the stars for dead reckoning had been used by travelers and sailors for centuries to find a land mass destination. However, GPS pinpoint identification had not been developed.

Why was Matthew the only gospel writer to relate this account? This is the inception of the great story of the life of Jesus. What happened to the other gospel writers on these details? Even more peculiar in Matthew's later tale that Herod did not seem to know either the location of the house or the identity of the infant, and so he killed all the Jewish male babies up to two years of age to remove the newborn King. Yet, the official records of King Herod as described in historical archives in Rome do not refer to such a massive act, and no other biblical source or gospel seems to be aware of it.

When one takes this massacre of children into account, as part of the nativity scene, it seems that our celebration should be one of mourning as much as glee over the birth of a newfound king. The parade of Jesus' birth never seems to care about the casualty rate of innocent Jewish babies who were murdered. This is as much a part of the wise men story as the birth itself, the star in the East or the gifts of gold, frankincense, and myrrh. When I think about it, omission can be as much a lie as fabrication in the presentation of our rituals. We establish this denial and omission as an element of our belief.

I sat down with the writings of several scholars who had cross-referenced the discrepancies between each of the Gospels in the Nativity story. It was revealing. Luke says the announcement (Annunciation) by the Angel Gabriel that Christ would be born occurred before conception (Luke 1:26 – thirty-one). Matthew says it happened after Mary had conceived Jesus (Matt 1:18-21). Matthew says the announcement was to Joseph (Matt 1:20). Luke says it was made to Mary (Luke 1:28).

In the Sheppard story in Luke, we read that the shepherds journey into Bethlehem and somehow find Joseph, Mary, and the baby in the stable. How did they do that? With the help of a star? Perhaps not. We make that assumption, but Luke does not know anything about the star. Should we just say that Luke forgot to mention that? I don't think so. If a star suddenly sat down on your house or barn, it would be big news. It would not be the type of news one would forget to mention, and if it did occur everyone in town would show up.

On the other hand, Matthew doesn't seem to know anything about shepherds. He doesn't mention them. Luke isn't very clear about it. He only says that the shepherds went to Bethlehem and found the child. Matthew says that following the birth, Jesus, Joseph, and Mary flee to Egypt (where they stay until after Herod's death) to avoid the murder of Jesus, as Herod slaughters all the male infants two years old and under (Matt 2:13 – 16). Luke, however, says that Joseph, Mary, and baby Jesus remain in the area of Jerusalem for the presentation of Jesus at the Temple for about forty days and then return to Nazareth without ever going to Egypt (Luke 2:22 – 40). It quickly becomes evident that to make the overall story work one must do some editing and patch supernatural miracle upon historical enterprise excerpting from different books, but even if you accept the unexplained supernatural, it is impossible to do the same with the inconsistencies and deletions of the telling.

It was a time when superstition was all people could rely on to explain what they saw in the sky and on earth. No one had ever been beyond the blue of the sky, flown in an airplane, or met other civilizations in remote places that had different myths. Even though they were fascinated by the stars and used them for basic navigation, they knew nothing of the solar system, let alone the universes. To them, the sun magically rose and when it set the moon and the stars magically took its place. Just as magically, God could hang a star in the air to guide magi or shepherds to a specific spot on the ground. The more I researched, the more problematical the story of Christmas became.

One night, later in my years of reflection, deep in the sanctity of my writing room, I sat back in my chair and wondered what it would be like to write a book about superstition. I had the feeling that we humans really like it, and it would be fun just to see in American culture, alone, in the midst of this informational, technological and scientific age, how many superstitions we have. I wondered, "is there a difference between superstition and myth," or "are they the same?" I had known many athletes in various sports. I suspected that ballplayers are the most distinct group which relied on superstition. Yet, when I thought of it, we rely on superstition every day. It's that persistent feeling that the unexpected happened by supernatural design. From there, we usually lapse into a false premise of cause, called by the experts, sympathetic magic, a close relative to motivated thinking.

Christians live once a year in a happy state of unsupportable myth, and it's great fun. Of course, there is nothing wrong with that, just as there is nothing wrong with a child being told and believing in Santa Claus just for the fun and excitement of it. It seems to me, however, that when people accept it as a foundational truth with the admonition, subtle or otherwise, the lack of questioning poses a problem.

If I were to believe in an after-life described in the Gospels, the starting point for any reasonable believer would have to be in the consistency of the beginning. There has to be a preponderance of evidence of reality. For one to come to earth as a deity with knowledge of other worlds and with the intent to show people how to get there, there has to be something other than a mysterious, inconsistent beginning. Why would any deity or its progeny wrap it in confusion? For what purpose to humanity?

Matthew knew nothing of shepherds, or he would have told us about them. Luke apparently knew nothing of wise men. In my part of the country, the Christmas pageant follows Luke's storyline about Gabriel's announcement to Mary that she's pregnant with Jesus, the journey to Bethlehem, birth, angels, shepherds, and the ultimate, dramatic conclusion with the shepherds kneeling before the crèche in the stable. In these Christmas pageants, Matthew may or may not be used by adding the story of wise men, and conveniently no two-year-old children are murdered by King Herod's troops, but therein lies the inconsistency, the fallacy between the two stories. There was no manger in Matthew's story of the wise men, no stable, and no journey by Joseph and now pregnant Mary from Nazareth to Bethlehem for a taxation enrollment. Even if Luke thinks his is the real story, as he states at the beginning of his book, he has several serious differences with Matthew.

In Matthew's Gospel, Mary and Joseph lived in a house in Bethlehem over which a star could stop. They were not traveling from a distant place to Bethlehem. According to Matthew, Joseph and Mary went to live in Nazareth only because Herod's brother Archelaus had taken the throne in Judea and might continue to try to find and kill the newborn King.

If you read Matthew and Luke with a critical eye regarding the nativity scene, you see that the underlying motivation is to get Mary to Bethlehem, so that it can be said that Jesus was born there, because that was the Old Testament prophecy of a Messiah. It is interesting that each writer took a different path with different timing, but found it crucial to get her there, to fulfill this specific prophecy. For credibility, writers of these two Gospels decades after Jesus' death had to follow the Old Testament prophecy of Micah 5:2, which had led Jews to expect that the long-awaited Messiah would be born in Bethlehem. So each author sought their solution on how to get Mary there for the birth of her child.

Luke says that in the time of the Cyrenius (Quirinius), governor of Syria, Caesar Augustus decreed a census for taxation purposes, and each person had to go to their own city. Someone's "own city" was, allegedly, the city of a person's lineage from centuries ago. Historians have pointed out that no one would know that or have any idea of how to keep up with lineage to that extent. Luke claims Joseph was of the House of David and therefore he had to go to the city of David, which is called Bethlehem. When you look at that, it is quite ridiculous. It might make the story fit with Micah but David, if he existed, and that is a whole different question, lived nearly 1000 years before Mary and Joseph. I suspect Joseph had no idea who was his grandfather a thousand years earlier. I sure don't know who mine was a millennium ago. Besides, why would Romans have required Joseph to go to the city where someone had lived a thousand years earlier? That makes no sense. Historians combing actual documents have shown that Luke's attempt to date this event is off. There was indeed a census under Governor Quirinius, but it was a local census, not one decreed by Caesar Augustus for the Empire as a whole, and it was long after Herod's death, A.D. 6. Historically, Luke's story is just impossible. The writer pushed too hard to fulfill the prophecy of Micah.

Inconsistency doesn't stop there. Luke chronicles that on the eighth day of his life Jesus was circumcised (Luke 2:21) and that on the fortieth day was presented to the Temple in Jerusalem, as required by law, but then they returned into Galilee "to their own city of Nazareth" (Luke 2:39). After they performed these religious acts in Jerusalem, Joseph, Mary, and Jesus returned peacefully to their home in Nazareth, but according to Matthew, they were fleeing for their lives into Egypt, and only after Herod's death years later were they able to risk returning to Bethlehem. Even then, they felt it too dangerous, so they journeyed on into Galilee to settle in Nazareth. One thing is clear from this inconsistency. One cannot be in Jerusalem, Galilee, and Egypt, all at the same time.

Most Christians believe or just accept the notion that the Chronicles of Matthew, Mark, Luke, and John are the original text. They often feel that God inspired every original word. However, through the centuries biblical scholars and archaeologists, following separate disciplines of research have uncovered many signs that point to the composition of the narratives as deliberate attempts to retell stories in the Hebrew tradition. It would seem that the story of the wise men in Matthew was crafted on the basis of the Hebrew account of Balaam (22 – 24), a diviner in the Torah with his story occurring in the Book of Numbers.

The Shepherd narrative in Luke may well have been composed on the basis of Micah (4, 5), while the Bethlehem story had to be created to meet the messianic expectation of Micah (5:2).

Herod's murder of the innocent children, while not historically based on the documents of Herod, is evidently a retelling of the Pharaoh – – Moses infancy story from the Hebrew tradition, in which a wicked king sought to destroy God's chosen deliverer by killing the children.

Even the star in the East is present in the rabbinic interpretations of other references in the Torah, as a phenomenon which marked the birth of Isaac. We also know that the character of Joseph to whom God frequently spoke in dreams was patterned on the patriarch model in the Book of Genesis, and the similarities of God's chosen people escaping from Egypt to that of the story of Joseph, Mary and Jesus escaping from the despot of that time. Thus, the stories of Jesus' birth are not made out of whole cloth, but they do give vibrancy to myths of old and bring them all together to focus on one man, Jesus.

I joined many scholars by asking whether the writings of the Gospels were simply a forcing of the historical context aimed at developing a myth of the Messiah. The numerous inconsistencies seem to indicate the existence of a small religious sect ("Christians") attempting to grow and establish credibility within the Jewish and Hebrew tradition that had been told for centuries and to do so with new writings. Later, we shall see that the writers of these Gospels were writing to different audiences at different times, but always with the motivation to gain credibility. And remember, there was no Bible at this time. It came centuries later, as a human compilation.

Chapter 10

Who Wrote the New Testament and Why

MY ORIGINAL GOAL was not to pick out every discrepancy in the New Testament that I could find. My goal was to compare what each Abrahamic religion had to say about death, but with the Qur'an and the New Testament, it was impossible to conduct that study without confronting unexplained supernatural occurrences and inconsistencies in the storytelling. In studying the New Testament with emphasis on what happens when we die, and comparing it to the Qur'an or Old Testament, I touched on the core principles of Christian faith, the immaculate conception of the baby Jesus as the Son of God, and the belief in events surrounding and after his death. But as I worked through these core principles, I found that it was also necessary to delve into the history of each of the Gospels. To know what was happening in the writer's community at the time of the writing would give better insight into the paradigm of the community and the writer's goal. After all, a gospel is speaking to an audience. It is not there as a static writing. If you know the audience of the time, you have a better understanding of what is being said and how it might apply in today's world.

To answer my simple questions of how we die and what happens to us afterwards, I felt that these core principles and the chroniclers who tell the stories of Jesus' birth and death must maintain credibility through consistency. Having looked at some of the paradigms expressed in the Torah, Old Testament, and New Testament, I turned my attention to death and the after-death. I started researching the other important annual Christian celebration, indeed where the Christian movement had originated – – Easter.

It was already clear to me – – again, from the earlier study – – that there were contradictions, though not for those Easter Christians who come to church once a year to hear excerpts of the gospel and sing the hymn, "He is Risen." Errors become evident when we compare all the resurrection accounts of the gospel writers. They exist even after many changes by the scribes who copy the texts in an attempt to make more compatible Gospels.

Anyone who studies the sources of the New Testament soon learns that the text has been changed many times, aside from the fact that the scribes never had originals to work from in the first place. Sometimes scribes changed their writings because they thought the text contained a factual error. For example, at the beginning of Mark, the author introduces his gospel by saying "just as is written in Isaiah the Prophet, 'behold I am sending a message before your face... Make straight his paths...'" The writer of Mark was mistaken, however. The quotation is not from Isaiah at all, but it's a combination of passages from Exodus 23:20 and Malachi 3:1. Subsequent scribes recognized the mistake and changed the text to read "just as is written in the prophets..." I found several historical sources pointing this discrepancy out.

It is a small thing, but this and numerous other examples of glitches in the Gospels become cumulative and shake one's confidence in their accuracy. At other times, a scribe would attempt to correct a perceived error that was not a factual mistake by the gospel writer, but an interpretive one. In Matthew 24:36, where Jesus is predicting the end of the age (a theme that had become popular in the pre-Christian time) he says that "concerning that day and hour, no one knows – – not the angels in heaven, nor even the Son, but only the Father." It, in the mind of the scribes, apparently did not fit the picture they wanted to portray of an all-knowing Jesus. How could the Son of God not know when the end will come? So, they modified the text by taking out the words "nor even the Son." Now the angels may be ignorant, but the Son of God isn't. The scribes always attempted to protect the deification of Jesus.

As I use the word "scribe," it is essential to understand what that title entails. A scribe at the same time acts as a copyist who makes a mistake or two, and as a forger, and the one attempting to copy the script he is copying from exactly right. It is a painstaking work done by hand, and the format was not in the form we see today in the Bible. This was a world without electronic means of publication. There were no photocopy machines, carbon paper, or printmakers.

The copyist never had an original to anything in what we now call the New Testament. A typical copyist would work from a copy of a copy and would copy not just the words of the original, but also the mistakes his predecessor made in copying the original copy. Whoever came after him copied his mistakes and the errors of the predecessor and then would introduce mistakes of his own. And so it went, year after year, century after century, but always with the motivation to make it fit. This was the existence of the most dedicated copyist. Sometimes mistakes were insignificant. Other times, they were significant and changed the meaning. But then, some copyists changed or added to the script either for some ulterior motive or because they just thought they could improve the text they were copying.

Take for example the famous story found in later manuscripts of the Gospel of John about the woman who was caught in the act of adultery and brought to Jesus for judgment. This is the account of the famous saying:

"Let the one without sin among you be the first to cast a stone at her."

This story, however, is not found in the oldest manuscripts of the Gospel of John. Even the writing style in Greek is significantly different from the writing style of the rest of the gospel. When you look at it, it doesn't take a literary editor to see that this story inter-

placed in the way that it breaks the flow of the narrative of John 7 – 8, where it is found. If you take the story out of John, the context makes much better sense when the story immediately before the account flows directly into the story immediately after it.

What was going on with the scribe who dreamed up this story at the time he placed it in the Gospel of John? It would be interesting to know. It's a great story and makes an excellent point on comparative sin, but John didn't write it, and there is no other evidence that the event happened or Jesus uttered these famous words.

Much later after my sabbatical, actually in my retirement, as I was preparing to write this book, I ran into the works of the scholar Bart D. Ehrman. He makes the point that most of the apostles were illiterate and couldn't write. Nevertheless, after Jesus' death, writing started to appear that claimed to be written by apostles, but contained all sorts of bizarre and contradictory views. Ehrman points out:

"In many instances, the authors of these writings could not actually have been who they claimed to be… But why would authors claim to be people they weren't? Why would an author claim to be an apostle when he wasn't? Why would an unknown figure write a book falsely calling himself Peter, Paul, James, Thomas, Philip, or even Jesus?"[6]

Professor Ehrman poses an answer appropriate for the time and place, after the death of Jesus:

"The answer should seem fairly obvious. If your name was Jehoshaphat, and no one (other than, say, your parents and siblings) had any idea who you were, and you wanted to write an authoritative Gospel about the life and teachings of Jesus, an authoritative letter describing what Christians should believe or how they should live, or an inspired apocalypse describing in detail the fate of souls after death, you could not very well signed your own name to the book. No one would take the gospel of Jehoshaphat seriously. If you wanted someone to read it, you called yourself Peter. Or Thomas. Or James. In other words, you lied about who you really were."[7]

As the struggle for dominant Christian theology progressed after Jesus' death, the scribes sometimes altered the Gospels for selfish theological reasons. An example of this was Christian motivation to show, indeed insure, Christian superiority to Judaism reminiscent of my study of Islam and its motivation to be superior to Christianity. I could particularly see this motivation once Emperor Constantine took over.

In the second century, many Christians firmly believed that the salvation brought by Christ was an entirely new thing and superior to Judaism. In essence, the old religion of the Jews had become outdated. The parable that Jesus tells of new wine in old wineskins seems to cause a problem with this view, however.

"No one places new wine in old wineskins... But new wine must be placed in new wineskins. And no one who drinks the old wine wishes for the new, for they say, 'the old is better.'" (Luke 5:38 – 39)

To the scribes, the parable is Judaism v. Christianity. How could Jesus indicate the old is better than the new? So, they eliminated the last sentence.

Many books and treatises have been written with substantial documentation on variations, deletions, and additions to what we call the New Testament. Through the centuries, especially the first three after Jesus' death, scribe manipulations of texts and theological battles raged for supremacy. Ultimately, in the mid-1500s the first edition of the Greek New Testament was published which divided the text into verses, the form in which it now exists. Not only did scribes alter texts through the centuries, but also no originals had existed, only copies of hand-written copies. We should also remember that other books of the gospel floated around from early on, and human scribes and ultimately the Dutch scholar, Desiderius Erasmus, produced an accepted compilation, the Greek New Testament. Books which were left out were deemed not worthy. Still, one wonders how many Gospels were written that were never found, those that never made it out of antiquity. Preservation of written material in antiquity was neither organized nor efficient.

Christendom settled into complacency with its Greek New Testament, which it reproduced again and again. These reproductions provided the form of the text that the translators of the King James Bible eventually used, and the passages in the King James' version became rote memorization from 1611 onward, until new translations came about with more modern language in the twentieth century.

However, a man by the name of John Mill (1645 – 1707), a fellow of Queens College, Oxford, and chaplain to Charles II, published a ground-breaking edition of the Greek New Testament in 1707, the year of his death. At the time, it caused serious questions regarding the Greek New Testament research, acceptance, and publication. I stumbled upon writings about Mill and his work, and even before him, there were others in the field of New Testament criticism. The term so often used by these researchers was their examination of "extant" literature. I found that for scholars "extant" refers to texts that have survived, but that does not necessarily mean original. The term encompasses original manuscripts, their copies, quotations and paraphrases of passages of non-extant texts contained in other works and translations of non-extant works into other languages.

Mill spent an intense thirty-year effort accumulating materials and then published his text. It was shocking. He had identified some 30,000 places of variation, 30,000 places where different manuscripts and versions had different readings for passages of the New Testament. He died soon after its publication, but later studies of what he had accomplished indicated he had found far more than 30,000 places of variation. Mill did not cite everything he had discovered, leaving out variations such as those involving changes of word order. I saw the importance of how meaning could easily be changed by word order as pointed out by other researchers. The adage of "give me a comma, and I can change the meaning of anything" definitely applied to word order in the transcription of New Testament documents. This, of course, applied equally as well to earlier versions in languages such as Syrian and Coptic, which differed very much from the Greek.

Of course, once Mill's work was out, the battle of the defense of the Greek New Testament by traditionalists was on. His work shook the comfort of their life's belief. But there were also academics who took Mill's work as a springboard to go further. The English deist Anthony Collins, a friend and follower of John Locke, wrote in 1713 a pamphlet called "Discourse on Free Thinking." It urged the primacy of logic over mystic revelation in the Bible and claims of the miraculous.

Today, more than 5700 Greek manuscripts have been discovered and cataloged ranging from just a few words to a few that contain a complete copy of the New Testament. Scholars differ in the number of variants in these manuscripts from 200,000 to over 400,000. One thing is for sure. Consistency is not primary. While that may have had a temporary effect on believers in the 1700s, the strength of belief in the New Testament, in its current compilation and in spite of lack of consistency, has not shaken New Testament believers. In fact, it would be fair to say that most have never heard of John Mill or that an original of the Gospels does not exist, or that there are 200,000+ variations. Think for a moment of all the fundamental sermons that have been given based on one verse out of the King James Version, attesting that it was the divine word of God.

Those preachers, priests, and evangelists are not Bible scholars. Real Bible scholars don't just read and interpret the book we call the Bible. Scholars learn Greek, Coptic, Syrian, and Aramaic and work on translations and pour over the more than 5700 Greek manuscripts that have been discovered and cataloged, as well as the Coptic copy of Matthew's Gospel, called the Scheide Codex, and the Codex Sinaiticus. They couple such study with disciplines found in archaeological academics and some 10,000 manuscripts of the Latin Vulgate. It is no wonder that the work of such scholars is a lifetime calling, but as far as I could tell, New Testament criticism did not take traction, particularly not to the extent that its defense did. I could not have known at the time of my study that the ethos of criticism would be revitalized in the 1990s and on into the twenty-first century, but fortunately for me, the 1990s for some reason reinvigorated the criticism of the lack of consistency and the truthfulness of the New Testament. I say that it was fortunate for me because the scholars of the late twentieth and early twenty-first century enhance my research project long after my earlier sabbatical.

While the Nativity is a beautiful story, it is the moment of Easter that is the real origin of the Christian movement and its drawing power. No one wants to die, to be straightforward about it, and if we must, every person wants to reunite with their loved ones. The Easter narratives of the New Testament give us hope. Jesus is the risen Lord, and he tells us we can do the same. This is the source of power, the centrality, in the life of the Christian believer.

In spite of historical inconsistency and taking the current compilation of the New Testament at face value, numerous writers have noted variance in the telling of Christ's resurrection from death. "Risen" in most people's mind is a physical rising. We would call it a resuscitating of the body. Apparently, it was more than that, as Christ can appear and disappear at will, as if out of or into thin air (Luke 24:15, 31). There are several examples, using mysterious words, which we could interpret in different ways. For example, Christ appears in a room where the doors were shut "for fear of the Jews" (John 20:19). He apparently was able to move through matter such as walls or a door. In another instance, Christ says to Mary Magdalene, "touch me not for I have not yet ascended to my Father" (John 20:17), yet in another passage, he says to Thomas, "Put your finger here and touch my wounds and take your hand and thrust it into my side" (John 20:27). To me, these are very strange attempts at quoting words purportedly spoken by Jesus, and I find it odd that a deity must seek to establish credibility that he has returned from death. This seems to be a mortal attempt at overcoming a burden of proof regarding a specific allegation.

Scholars like Bart D. Ehrman and numerous others get into the complexities, actually inconsistencies, of who, what, when and where in the Gospels covering the crucifixion. Their work gives the feeling that everyone around the crucifixion was guessing at what happened. If your group leader were killed, it would only be natural to have questions and to attempt to find answers. We still do that today with President Kennedy's assassination. Jesus, as a spiritual leader would, of course, create a plethora of questions and competition for the answers among believers. Mark's account is that Jesus is crucified and then buried by Joseph of Arimathea on the day before the Sabbath (Mark 15:42 – 47). "On the day after the Sabbath, Mary Magdalene and two other women come back to the tomb to properly anoint the body (Mark 16:1 – 2). When they arrive, they find that the stone has been rolled away."[8] I suppose this is for convincing possible doubters since we learn later from John that Jesus can move through closed doors, but it seemed to me He did not need the stone removed from the tomb. Based on what John says, Jesus could have just been sitting outside without the removal of the stone.

"Nevertheless, entering the tomb, Mary and the other women see a young man in a white robe, who tells them, 'do not be startled! You are seeking Jesus the Nazarene, who has been crucified. He has been raised and is not here – – see the place where they laid him?' He then instructs the women to tell the disciples that Jesus is preceding them into Galilee and that they will see him there 'just as he told you.' But the women flee the tomb and say nothing to anyone, 'for they were afraid.' (Mark 16:4 – 8)."[9]

But then Jesus, himself, appears to Mary Magdalene, who goes and tells the disciples, but they don't believe her (Mark 16:9 – 11). He then appears to others (Mark 16:12 – 14), and finally to the eleven disciples who sit at a table. "Jesus upbraids them for failing to believe, and then commissions them to go forth and proclaim his gospel 'to the whole creation.' Those who believe and are baptized 'will be saved', but those who do not 'will be condemned.'

This is Mark's basic story, but then his words become even stranger:

'And these are the signs that will accompany those who believe: they will cast out demons in my name; they will speak in new tongues; and they will take up snakes in their hands; and if they drink any poison, it will not harm them; they will place their hands on the sick and heal them.' (Mark 16:17 – 18)."[10]

Everyone writing about the Resurrection seems to have a different story. We could overlook it if it were a human event like a car wreck or a big explosion, but this was a godly event. One would expect God's revelation to his people to be clear and consistent, not so muddled, and one has to ask, why to this little group of people? Why here? Does not this omnipotent God reveal Himself in some other part of the earth, why not to a broader base of humankind?

Even Jesus seems confused about what is happening as he asks, "My God, why hath Thou forsaken Me?" He has spent a lifetime believing in and teaching about heaven and life after death. Did he perceive that this might not be the case? To be fair, it is clear that each witness to the resurrection was sure that something had happened with Jesus, but as you read there recounts, it is impossible to reconcile the Gospels. The question arises, if you have spent a lifetime as a follower, learning a religious and philosophical group of beliefs based upon pre-existing precepts, do you not urge the end to be self-fulfilling? Of course, you do. How depressing and personally destabilizing it would be if you questioned the veracity of your beliefs and the ending as it occurred.

As to who went to the tomb at dawn on the first day of the week, Paul said nothing about anyone going. This seems very strange for an evangelist. "Mark said that Mary Magdalene, Mary the mother of James, and Salome went. (The Pauline Epistles, Chapter 16). Luke said that Mary Magdalene, Mary the mother of James, Joanna, and some other woman went (24:10). Matthew said Mary Magdalene and the other Mary only went (1:28). John said that Mary Magdalene went (20:11)."

"What did the women find at the tomb? Since Paul made no reference to a tomb visit, he has nothing further to contribute to this section of the narrative. Mark, however, said that the women found a young man dressed in white garments who gave the resurrection message. Luke said it was two men clothed in dazzling apparel. Matthew said it was nothing less than "an angel of the Lord" who descended in an earth-quake, put the armed guard to sleep, rolled back the stone, and gave the resurrection message. John began with no messenger at all, but on Mary Magdalene's second visit she confronted two angels, although they were speechless. Finally she confronted Jesus himself, whom she mistook for the gardener. From Jesus she received the resurrection message."[11]

Christendom argues about whether the women saw the risen Jesus in the garden at dawn on the first day of the week; while Mark and Luke said no, Matthew said yes. John said yes, but that it was later. Likewise, there is disagreement as to where Jesus appeared to his disciples. Paul did not talk about a location. Mark recorded no appearance stories, which is strange since he usually weighs heavily on the supernatural and the superstitious. He does hint that there would be a meeting between the risen Jesus and the disciples in Galilee. Matthew wrote that the only time Jesus appeared to the disciples was in Galilee on a mountaintop, at which time he gave what he called the Divine Commission. Luke disagreed with Mark and Matthew, he interpreted that the risen Jesus ordered the disciples to remain in Jerusalem until the Holy Spirit empowered them; they were not to go to Galilee as the angelic messenger in Mark had ordered. Luke asserted that the only resurrection appearance took place in the Jerusalem area.[12]

As scholars delineate these variances, one attempting to maintain a focus on critical thinking wonders what was going on with the writers of the Scriptures and why a deity would muster such confusion. If you make columns of these comparisons within the New Testament, it looks something like this:

(Matthew = MT)

(Mark = MK)

(Luke = LK)

(John = JN)

MT 27:55, MK 15:40, LK 23:49: The women looked on from afar.

JN 19:25 – 26: They were near enough that Jesus could speak to his mother.

MT 27:62 – 66: A guard was placed at the tomb the day following the burial.

MK 15:42 – 16:8; LK 23:50 – 56; JN 19:38 – 42: No guard is mentioned. The rumor had it that Jesus' body was stolen and the Resurrection feigned.

MK 16:1 – 3; LK 24:1: it would seem there could not have been a guard, since the women were planning to enter the tomb with spices. Though the women were aware of the stone, they were unaware of a guard.

MT 28:1: the first visitors to the tomb were Mary Magdalene and the other Mary (two people).

MK 16:1: Mary Magdalene and the other Mary, plus Salome (three people).

LK 23:55 – 24:1, 24:10: Mary Magdalene, Joanna, Mary the mother of James, and "other women."

JN 20:1: Mary Magdalene only.

MK 16:1 – 2: the women came to the tomb to anoint the body.

JN 19:39 – 40: the body had already been anointed and wrapped in cloth.

MK 16:5, LK 24:3: the women entered the tomb.

JN 20:1 – 2, 11: they did not.

MT 28:1: it was toward dawn when they arrived.

MK 16:2: it was after sunrise.

LK 24:1: it was early dawn.

JN 20:1: it was still dark.

MT 28:1 – 2: the stone was still in place when they arrived. It was rolled away later.

MK 16:4; LK 24:2; JN 20:1: the stone had been rolled or taken away.

MT 28:2: an angel arrived during an earthquake, rolled back the stone, then sat on it.

MK 16:5: no earthquake, only one young man sitting inside the two.

LK 24:2 – 4: no earthquake. Two men suddenly appear standing inside the tomb.

JN 20:12: no earthquake. Two angels are sitting inside the tomb.

MT 28:8: the visitors ran to tell the disciples.

MK 16:8: they said nothing to anyone.

LK 24:9: they told the eleven and all the rest.

JN 20:10 – 11: the disciples returned home. Mary remained outside. Weeping.

MT 28:8 – 9: Jesus' first Resurrection Appearance was fairly near the tomb.

LK 24:13 – 15: it was in the vicinity of Emmaus (7 miles from Jerusalem).

JN 20:13 – 14: it was right at the tomb.

MT 28:9: on his first appearance to them, Jesus lets Mary Magdalene and the other Mary hold him by his feet.

JN 20:17: on his first appearance to Mary, Jesus forbids her to touch him since he has not yet ascended to the Father.

JN 20:27: a week later, although he has not yet ascended to the Father, Jesus tells Thomas to touch him.

MT 28:1 – 18: the order of Resurrection appearances was: Mary Magdalene and the other Mary, then the eleven.

MK 16:9 – 14: it was Mary Magdalene, then the others, then the eleven.

LK 24:15 – 36: it was to, then Simon (Peter?), Then the eleven.

JN 20:14 – 21:1: it was Mary Magdalene, then the disciples without Thomas, then the disciples with Thomas, then the eleven disciples again.

1 Corinthians 15:5 – 8: it was Cephas (Peter?), then the "twelve", but which twelve because Judas was dead by now? Then 500+ brethren, then James, then all the apostles, then Paul.

MK 16:14 – 19: the Ascension took place (presumably in a room) while the disciples were together seated at a table, probably in or near Jerusalem.

LK 24:50 – 51: it took place outdoors, after supper, at Bethany (near Jerusalem).

Acts 1:9 – 12: it took place outdoors, after 40+ days, at Mount Olivet.

MT 28:16 – 20: Ascension is not mentioned, but if it took place at all, it must have been from a mountain in Galilee since Matthew was there.[13]

(… And on and on it goes with discrepancies, inconsistencies, and deified confusion.)

It gets more confusing when we hear from Paul in Corinthians. He goes along with the first-day-of-the-week tradition for the first Easter appearance, but he stretches the time in which these manifestations occurred so as to include his own conversion moment. His "seeing" of the risen Jesus did not differ from the other appearance narratives, except for the allegation that his was the last (1 Corinthians 15:8). The effect of that is that it opens the timeframe to a span of from one to six years after the events of the first Holy Week and Easter. This, in spite of the chronology of Luke that suggests no more than fifty days marked the time of the Resurrection Appearance and that no resurrection occurred after the Ascension (Acts 1:3).

Chapter 11

The First Four Books
of the New Testament

HISTORIANS AND ARCHAEOLOGISTS place the initial writing of each of these first four books of the Bible at the end of the first century, which would indicate that each of the disciples would have either been dead or too old to be writing anything themselves. The disciples were named Andrew, Nathaniel, James the elder, James the younger, John, Philip, Jude, Judas, Matthew the tax collector, Peter, Simon, and Thomas.

The word "According" in the title of the Gospels is interesting to me. I assume it is used because of variances and inconsistencies between each book, as well as Paul writing Corinthians having a bit of a different story. Numerous scholars have researched and written about the environment in which each of these gospel writers wrote. It is essential to learn this to understand what the writer was trying to do in producing the gospel.

Evidence suggests that the Story originated in a Jewish –
Christian community in Roman Syria. The Story is Jesus gathering
an inner circle of disciples, being rejected by the Jews, being
crucified, and making a post-death resurrection at which time he
commissioned his disciples to take his message of salvation to the
Gentiles and Jews who would accept. The investigation further
shows that the writer of Matthew wrote towards the end of the
first century A.D. and that the writer was and remains anonymous.
Interestingly, though the Book of Matthew is placed first in the New
Testament, we now know that it was not the first book written. The
Books of the New Testament are not in chronological order. Many
research scholars indicate this now, such as John Shelby Spong
who succinctly states this in his book, Rescuing the Bible from
Fundamentalism:

"Matthew knew of the Gospel of Mark and used it extensively.
Mark had been circulating among the various Christian
communities for 15 to 20 years. Matthew had no difficulty with
the framework of demonic powers that was assumed by the First
Gospel. That was the unquestioned wisdom of the day. But he also
did not regard Mark as either Holy Scripture or as literally inerrant,
for Matthew altered Mark's text frequently to suit his agenda, his
writing task, his audience, and his theological perspective. But
Matthew wrote after Mark, so the need to define Jesus had had
more time to develop, had more challenges to meet and more false
ideas to confront. The way Matthew changed Mark's text made this
clear."[14]

Scholars such as Spong point out that the author of the Gospel According to Matthew appears to be a Jew living in perilous times. The history of the period records the city of Jerusalem had been destroyed by the Romans more than a decade earlier. "In the year 66 A.D. the Jews of Judea rebelled against their Roman masters. In response, the Emperor Nero dispatched an army under the general Vespasian to restore order. By the year 68, resistance in the northern part of the Providence had been eradicated, and the Romans turned their full attention to the subjugation of Jerusalem. That same year, the Emperor Nero died by his own hand, creating a power vacuum in Rome. In the resultant chaos, Vespasian was declared Emperor and returned to the Imperial City. It fell to his son, Titus, to lead the remaining army in the assault on Jerusalem."[15]

Roman legions marched in formation with drums making a fearful sound as they surrounded Jerusalem and started destroying the Jewish stronghold. There was no need to hurry. Both water and food were cut off. In fact, slow strangulation added to the intensity of punishment for the Jews' attempted rebellion. By the year 70 A.D., the Romans broke Jerusalem's defense and began its systematic ransacking. As the city slowly died, so did the Temple, the center of Judaism and the Jewish faith, as it burned and fell to destruction. The Temple was the cohesive center of Jewish identity and was no more. There was death and devastation everywhere and a feeling of loss that the Temple could never be replaced, let alone Jerusalem. These were the Jews of the diaspora, the dispersed Jews, and would remain so; now, Jerusalem, the Temple, the symbol of their unity was gone. It is here, in the middle of this desperate sense of defeat and loss, that Matthew was writing and was offering a reunification of the diaspora with a new belief, one founded in the prophecy of the Old Testament, albeit by forcing historical references sporadically into the story.

While the Temple structure of the Pharisees and Sadducees was destroyed and tribal descendants dispersed and diminished, Jewish Christians also had to feel the intensity of destruction and occupation by a foreign power. For Jewish Christians, however, this new belief provided a sense of unity and hope, and therefore, they could work toward reconnection. There was no way to escape the memories of the persecutions under Emperor Nero, and how first-generation Jewish Christian leaders like Peter and Paul had perished under the torture of Rome. But it wasn't just the Romans that isolated the Christians. Their Jewish brothers and sisters rejected them for breaking ranks with the Orthodox Judaism. So, you had this Jewish group with a consolidated faith developing a historical story supporting that religion, which was pressured by Roman torture from one side and excluded from tribal ethnicity and communal religion on the other side. The author of Matthew almost certainly lived in and experienced life in this competing vulnerability. He was a Jew of the diaspora, deeply devoted to tradition, a conservative, trained in legal disciplines and interests popular among the Levites. However, the tribal priests of the Levites had drifted somewhat from Abrahamic teachings. Now, in this environment, he could write in a way that takes countervailing pressures as a molding force for connection and reunification in a new story, a new faith. But, you can also see why Matthew, whoever he was, would not use his real identity. He would become a target.

The Second Gospel, known to us as "Kata Marcus" or "According to Mark" is a book of ghosts, goblins, and the supernatural. This was not unique to Mark or other gospel writers. It was the prevailing wisdom of the day, as I mentioned before. Such explanations of events were common, unquestioned, and popular in the Judaism of the first century, as well as non-Jewish communities. Superstition was an accepted method of explanation. Biblical scholars describe Mark not as a scholar, nor as a great philosophical thinker, but more of a person who accepted the street-version mythology without questioning. To Mark, what could not otherwise be explained, needed no explanation beyond the supernatural one. No-one knew that most often germs, bacteria, and viruses cause sicknesses. No-one knew that washing hands could prevent most diseases or that a microscopic world lay beneath the range of the unaided human eye. People didn't know that there were vast reaches into the universe; so, causes emanating from any of those sources were explained with demons and the supernatural. This was not only Mark's audience of the time, but it was also his own understanding and explanation. Even a quick reading of Mark, without referring to biblical scholars and historians, brings one to this conclusion.

The Gospel according to Luke appears to be a composition dated to the early 60s A.D. This is according to traditional Christian scholarship. It is possible that this same author wrote the Acts and the Apostles, but there is much debate among scholars about that. Nevertheless, the author(s) is unknown, though it is known that he was a Gentile, and again as with the other Books, there was an important historical context in which the author wrote. The Jewish rebellion had brought disaster on the Holy Land. In the ensuing warfare, Judea was conquered and Jerusalem destroyed. In the ancient Mediterranean world near the end of the first century of the Common Era, the gods of the Olympus were dead. No viable unifying religious system rose to take their place, creating a vacuum at the religious heart of life.

History has proven that although there may be periodic laps or gaps, humankind must have religion, and this was a period in which a new religion, like Christianity, had a chance. In this environment, even though there was a wide variety of cults, mystery religions, and superstitions, many Gentiles found themselves drawn to the God of the Jewish tradition. It was bookish, monotheistic, and had a history of prophets who offered hope. The Gentile worshipers were known officially among the Jewish people as "proselytes," but they seldom became converts. It is among these that Paul found his most enthusiastic response, as the Book of Acts exemplifies.

But the world that Luke experienced changed significantly in the 15 to 20 years since Mark's Gospel achieved written form. Christianity grew in strength in numbers in this spiritual vacuum. There was tension in the Empire and a rising fever of persecution. The persecution under Nero was devastating and resulted in death of many Christians, and this history would plant a seed in Christian theology of being the persecuted ones that would last forever. We see it in every sermon preached today. But about the year 80 CE, Emperor Diocletian came to power, ruling until the year 96. With his ascent to the throne, there was a great fear of a Nero redux, intense persecution. It was in this context that Luke decided the time had come to write a public document addressed to a Roman official, "most excellent Theophilus" to counter the rising tide of hostility. He took on that task of showing that Christianity was not subversive, but was a natural development within a recognized and respected Jewish religious tradition. He asserted that it grew past Jewish limits and became a worldwide religion.

One can see that since Luke was arguing for official Roman recognition of the Christian movement, he wrote kindly of Roman officials in his narrative. The story was that Jesus was pronounced innocent by the Roman Procurator Pontius Pilate, and he only acquiesced in Jesus' execution to placate Jewish religious leadership, the Pharisees. In Luke, it was Herod's soldiers, not Roman soldiers, who scourged Jesus, while a Roman soldier, a centurion, at the cross pronounced Jesus the Son of God. Luke made a good point of how Jesus would turn his back on a political revolution, in favor of a revolution of the spirit and proclaimed that His kingdom was not of this world. Luke was arguing that there was no threat here to the political establishment.

Who was Herod? Was Luke writing this letter to Herod? Herod was born 73 BCE – – died March/April, 4 BCE in Jericho, Judea. "He was the Roman-appointed king of Judea, who built many fortresses, aqueducts, theaters, and other public buildings and generally raised the prosperity of his land but who was constantly the center of political and family intrigues in his later years. The New Testament portrays him as a tyrant, into whose kingdom Jesus of Nazareth was born."[16] Jesus was born in his kingdom at a time when Herod ordered the murder of all Jewish children two years and younger. Until his final years, Herod was not a tyrant but quite progressive, as mentioned before. But the birth of Jesus was in the final years of Herod's life when he was deranged and could well have issued such an order. Would the Roman legions have followed it? Probably not. By this time, shortly before his death, Herod mandated numerous bizarre orders, but had lost his influence as the "king of Judea" due to loss of mental stability and murders in his own family.

"Herod was born in southern Palestine. His father, Antipater, was an Edomite (a Semitic people, identified by some scholars as Arab, who converted to Judaism in the second century BCE. Antipater was a man of great influence and wealth who increased both by marrying the daughter of a noble from Petra (in southwestern Jordan), at that time the capital of the rising Arab Nabataean kingdom. Therefore, Herod was of Arab origin, although he was a practicing Jew.

When Pompeii (106–48 BCE) invaded Palestine in 63 BCE, Antipater supported his campaign and began a long association with Rome, from which both he and Herod were to benefit. Six years later Herod met Mark Antony, whose lifelong friend he was to remain. Julius Caesar also favored the family; he appointed Antipater procurator of Judea in 47 BCE and conferred on him Roman citizenship, an honor that descended to Herod and his children. Herod made his political debut in the same year, when his father appointed him governor of Galilee. Six years later Mark Antony made him tetrarch of Galilee.

In 40 BCE the Parthians invaded Palestine, civil war broke out, and Herod was forced to flee to Rome. The Senate there nominated him king of Judea and equipped him with an army to make good his claim. In the year 37 BCE, at the age of 36, Herod became the unchallenged ruler of Judea, a position he was to maintain for 32 years."[17]

"Herod endowed his realm with massive fortresses and splendid cities, of which the two greatest were new, and largely pagan, foundations: the port of Caesarea Palaestinae on the coast between Joppa (Jaffa) and Haifa, which was afterward to become the capital of Roman Palestine; and Sebaste on the long-desolate site of ancient Samaria. At Herodium in the Judaean desert Herod built a great palace, which archaeologists in 2007 tentatively identified as the site of his tomb. In Jerusalem he built the fortress of Antonia, portions of which may still be seen beneath the convents on the Via Dolorosa, and a magnificent palace (of which part survives in the citadel). His most grandiose creation was the Temple, which he wholly rebuilt. The great outer court, 35 acres (14 hectares) in extent, is still visible as Al-Ḥaram al-Sharīf. (…) Herod undoubtedly saw himself not merely as the patron of grateful pagans but also as the protector of Jewry outside of Palestine, whose Gentile hosts he did all in his power to conciliate."[18]

Herod had ten wives and 14 children. However, he developed mental instability which was fed by the intrigue and deception within his family. "In his last years Herod suffered from arteriosclerosis.

GLEN AARON

He had to repress a revolt, became involved in a quarrel with his Nabatean neighbors, and finally lost the favor of Augustus. He was in great pain and in mental and physical disorder. He altered his will three times and finally disinherited and killed his firstborn, Antipater."[19]

So, who was "The Most Excellent Theophilus" to whom Luke was writing? No one knows. There are several different theories:

1. "The name 'Theophilus' literally means 'loved by God,' but carries the idea of "friend of God." This has led some to believe that "Theophilus" is just a generic title that applies to all Christians. However, from the context of Luke and Acts, it seems clear that Luke was writing to a specific individual, even though his message is intended for all Christians in all centuries. While both the Gospel of Luke and the book of Acts have applications for all Christians, they were probably written to a specific individual whom Luke addresses as 'most excellent Theophilus' (Luke 1:3).

2. Since it seems clear that Theophilus was an actual person, we will look at what we do know about him from the Bible and then discuss a few of the many theories as to who he might have been. First, it is important to note that Luke addresses him as 'most excellent,' a title often used when referring to someone of honor or rank, such as a Roman official. Paul used the same term when addressing Felix (Acts 23:26; Acts 24:2) and Festus (Acts 26:25). Therefore, one of the most common theories is that Theophilus was

possibly a Roman officer or high-ranking official in the Roman government.

3. Another possibility is that Theophilus was a wealthy and influential man in the city of Antioch. There are second-century references to a man named Theophilus who was 'a great lord' and a leader in the city of Antioch during the time of Luke. Such a man would fit the description, as many scholars believe that Theophilus could have been a wealthy benefactor who supported Paul and Luke on their missionary journeys. That would account for Luke's wanting to provide an orderly and detailed account of what had happened."[20]

4. According to another theory, Theophilus was a "Jewish high priest named Theophilus ben Ananus. Theophilus ben Ananus was high priest in Jerusalem in AD 37 – 41. He was the son of Annas and the brother-in-law of Caiaphas. While less popular, this theory seems to be gaining popularity among some groups. Still another theory is that the Theophilus Luke was writing to was a later high priest named Mattathias ben Theophilus, who served in Jerusalem in AD 65 – 66.

5. Yet another theory about the identity of Theophilus is that he was a Roman lawyer who defended Paul during his trial in Rome. Those who hold this theory believe that Luke's purpose in writing Luke and acts was to write a defense of Christianity, somewhat akin to a legal brief. If this theory is correct, Luke's writings were designed to defend Paul in

court against charges of insurrection and, at the same time, to defend Christianity against the charge that it was an illegal, anti-Roman religion.

While each of these theories holds possibilities, it seems most likely that Theophilus was a high-ranking or influential Gentile for whom Luke wanted to provide a detailed, historical account of Christ and the spread of the gospel throughout the Roman Empire. Whether this Theophilus was a wealthy relative of Caesar, an influential government official, a wealthy benefactor who supported Paul or Paul's Roman lawyer does not matter. We cannot know for sure who Theophilus was, but we can know what Luke's intentions for writing were. His stated reason for writing to Theophilus was 'that you may have certainty concerning the things you have been taught' (Luke 1:3 – 4). Luke wrote a historical account of the life, death, and resurrection of Jesus Christ and detailed the spread of Christianity throughout the Roman Empire. His intention was to give Theophilus certainty that the 'things he had been taught' were indeed true and trustworthy."[21]

To read any of these Books, one should understand the environment in which the author(s) wrote. Luke in his attempt to appease Rome showed Paul protected by such Roman officials as Felix, Festus, and Agrippa and even delivered him from hostile mobs and Jewish imprisonment by his Roman citizenship. Interestingly, the fact that Paul was put to death under the Roman Emperor Nero was never mentioned when he wrote the Book of Acts. When you read Luke and place him in his time, you see a writer who is a defender of the faith and forever the evangelist.

The Gospel according to John is again written by an unknown author, apparently at a time in a small community where there was a substantial tension between the massive Jewish religion and the smaller Christian faith cult. It seemed to be written at different times between 90 and 100 A.D., according to the most reliable scholars, but it was in the second century that the book began to be referred to as the Gospel According to John.

Historically, as Luke had worked on his gospel writing to placate Rome, John wrote in an attempt to ease the religious divide between Jews and Christians and offer an alternative pathway for Gentile Jews. In the years between the life of Jesus and the writing of the Fourth Gospel of Luke, the Christian movement took hold and was successfully launched. In the fifth and sixth decades of the Common Era, Christianity made inroads into the Gentile world, primarily as a result of Paul's work. Paul apparently died in 64, and Christianity was still a Jewish movement. Christianity began to grow quite apart from Jewishness, and the tension that divided Jew and Gentile, also divided Jewish Christians and Gentile Christians.

The Jewish reaction to the destruction of Jerusalem and the Temple was to tighten the screws of Jewish orthodoxy, which also meant moving the Jewish Christians out. The writer of John made his appeal to those Jews who were torn between their faith in Jesus and their deep emotional desire not to leave Judaism. John placed heavy emphasis on Jesus as the Messiah; Jesus as being the Temple but not made with hands; Jesus as the new meaning for Jewish feasts. This was designed to encourage those who might be forced to withdraw or be expelled from the synagogues.

It helps to know what was going on as the writer John wrote. With his work, Christianity had matured and developed theologically. New concepts and nuances interpreting both spirit and the mandate of faith couched within Jewish histology provided a light of understanding for both Jew and Gentile. The writer of the Book made bold claims that were clearly born out of decades of contemplation on the meaning of Jesus and how it could become a religion.

Paul in his writings of the two books of Corinthians was a doctrinaire catalyst of what one should believe within the Christian faith. He was both an organizer of churches and a persistent proselytizing preacher in the new faith and seeking new converts, many of whom were Greek.

Finally, from a historical context, it is important to realize that most of the disciples were illiterate and could not write. In this sense, I use the term "disciple" referring specifically to the Twelve Apostles. I recognize that the Gospels and the book of Acts referred to varying numbers of disciples that range between 70 and 122.

There is no way the disciples could have left an authoritative writing. Therefore, apostolic writings must be based upon verbal hearsay by definition. The problem is that numerous writings began to appear, claiming to be written by an apostle, but as we have seen, were written by anonymous writers. If you were in a court of law, required to follow tested rules of evidence admissibility, how would you get such writings into evidence for the purported truth of what they say when you tell the judge:

"Your Honor, we offer the following writings as evidence of veracity and for the truth therein on the following basis:

1. Matthew, Mark, Luke, and John writings are purported writings on life and death of Jesus which are known to be verbal hearsay. The length of the hearsay line of communication is not known, nor upon whose original statement is the hearsay based.

2. The individual writers, Matthew, Mark, Luke, and John are not, in fact, who they say they are but someone undisclosed.

3. Further, Your Honor, we must mention that certain parts of these books are known to have been altered and forged by subsequent copiers."

And, perhaps you should point out to the judge in considering the evidentiary admissibility that both before and after the books were written, there were divergent Christian beliefs and stories, each one claiming to be the truth. For example, a powerful and influential sect in the second and third centuries maintained that there is not just one God, but two Gods. A Christian sect called Gnostics, the knowing ones, said there were thirty divine beings, while others said 365. Each group from the death of Jesus had their own documents, claimed they were right, and that the others were wrong. Each group claimed to be uniquely correct in their view, which represented the Divine truth, and that Jesus himself taught their theology and shared it through the Apostles. It took four centuries of Christian sect battles and fundamental theological differences to produce finally a human winner for a compilation of books.

But aside from fighting among themselves with their varied beliefs, they were all under constant pressure from the Jews as essentially outcasts. Then there were the Romans with their persecution of the same sects. The first recorded official persecution of Christians on behalf of the Roman Empire was in 64 A.D. According to the Roman historian Tacitus, Emperor Nero blamed Christians for the great fire of Rome. Most historians, however, doubt that the Roman government at the time distinguished between Christians and Jews, but there is no doubt about the overall Roman persecution.

Christians suffered from sporadic and localized persecutions over a period of the first two and a half centuries after the death of Jesus. But in 312 A.D. at the Battle of the Milvian Bridge where Constantine claimed the Emperorship of the West, Christianity became the dominant religion of the Roman Empire by decree. Stories vary as to whether an epiphany or Constantine's mother, who was a Christian, caused him to become a Christian at age 42. Some historians give the conversion a more geopolitical base as needing more soldiers for this battle and finding them among Christians. Whatever the reason, it appears to me that the two driving forces that put the messianic Gospel in the position of a significant world religion were Paul's early leadership and Emperor Constantine's mandate, despite the inconsistent evolution of its New Testament story.

Chapter 12

Josephus

WHILE IT IS useful to follow the writings of those navigating the creation of a new religion, it is just as important to note writers of the same time, experiencing the same political events that simply don't mention that which was so important to the religious creators.

Josephus was a Jewish historian born in A.D. 37 to a priestly Jewish family. He was well educated and followed the Pharisaic form of Judaism. As you can see from his birth date, he was born not too long after the death of Jesus and was a mature man by the time of the Jewish revolt against the Romans (A.D. 66 – 70). In fact, he commanded a Jewish force in Galilee with some success.

Obviously, this was also the time that the writings of the New Testament were surfacing and the destruction of Jerusalem by the Romans, as they choked the city to death. Besieged at Jotapata, Josephus was captured by the Romans. He then devoted his energy to helping the Romans persuade the remaining Jews to come to terms. He went to Rome and lived there until his death about A.D. 100. He did all of his historical writing in Rome, such as The Jewish Wars and The Antiquities of the Jews (which tells the story of the Jews from creation to the fall of Masada.)

Josephus gives very valuable information from the Maccabean revolt onwards, and he provides most of our knowledge of the New Testament background. The Antiquities of the Jews includes two short references to Jesus in Books 18 and 20 and a reference to John the Baptist in Book 18.

What is the most impressive is not that a few words were said about Jesus or John the Baptist or what they say with the lack of any recognition of the claims surfacing as to what was ultimately included in the New Testament, particularly Matthew, Mark, Luke, John, and Acts.

What is clear is that these references or certainly a part of them were interpolation, meaning that a writer later inserted these words into the original script. Regardless, there is nothing in the history of Antiquities of the Jews, the most complete history of the time, which would support the life of Jesus as reflected in the New Testament.

Most scholars of antiquity agree that Jesus existed, but scholars differ on the veracity of specific episodes described in biblical accounts of Jesus. The only two events with almost universal scholarly agreement are the moment when John baptized Jesus and when, between one and three years later, the Roman Prefect Pontius Pilate ordered Jesus' crucifixion.

Those New Testament stories whose authenticity is disputed include two accounts of the activity of Jesus the miraculous, turning water into wine, walking on water and the resurrection, and certain details of the crucifixion.

While nothing was written about Jesus before his death, "the Synoptic Gospels are the primary source of historical information about Jesus and of the religious movement he founded. These religious gospels – – the Gospel of Matthew, the Gospel of Mark, and the Gospel of Luke – – recount the life, ministry, crucifixion and resurrection of a Jew named Jesus who spoke Aramaic. There are different hypotheses regarding the origin of the texts, because the gospels of the New Testament were written in Greek for Greek-speaking communities, and were later translated into Syriac, Latin, and Coptic. The fourth Gospel, the Gospel of John differs greatly from the Synoptic Gospels. Historians often study the historical reality of the Acts of the Apostles when studying the reliability of the gospels, as the Book of Acts was seemingly written by the same author as the Gospel of Luke.

Historians subject Gospels to critical analysis by differentiating authentic, reliable information from possible inventions, exaggerations, and alterations. Since there are more textual variants in the New Testament (200 – 400 thousand) than it has letters (c. 140 thousand), scholars use textual criticism to determine which gospel variants could theoretically be taken as 'original.' To answer this question, scholars have to ask who wrote the gospels, when they wrote them, what was their objective in writing them, what sources the authors used, how reliable these sources were, and how far removed in time the sources were from the stories they narrate, or if they were altered later. Scholars may also look into the internal evidence of the documents, to see if, for example, a document has misquoted texts from the Hebrew Tanakh, has made incorrect claims about geography, if the author appears to have hidden information, or if the author has fabricated a prophecy. Finally, scholars turn to external sources, including the testimony of early church leaders, to writers outside the church, primarily Jewish and Greco-Roman historians, who would have been more likely to have criticized the church, and to archaeological evidence."[22]

The preserved books of Josephus are an example of examining other writings of the time.

Chapter 13

The Essenes and the Purported Letter from Jerusalem

ADDING TO THE perception of inconsistency covering the story of Jesus is any discussion of the Jewish sect, the Essenes. At the time of Jesus, the Jewish people could be divided into three main sects, as they split along political lines with very different religious perceptions of the "Kingdom." The largest two groups and the most powerful within the diaspora were the Pharisees and the Sadducees, but the smallest and least understood in the historical sense was the sect sometimes called the Essenes. However, the Essenes did not call themselves by that name, but went more by labels such as "healer" or "Doctor" or "teacher."

Some scholars see the Dead Sea Scrolls community as Essenes, who were led by a high priestly leadership. Their mission was service in humility among the Jews. Why the New Testament does not mention them is a bit of a mystery. But, it is thought that the label "Essene" is not used partly because that label was used by others as well, not to be confused with the third Jewish sect, and partly because the New Testament and the Jewish Bible comprise about 60 etymologies, involving Greek, Hebrew, Aramaic, Syrian, Persian Avestan, Sanskrit, Akkadian and many others. What is known is that there was a well-organized group, which was hailed for their honesty, temperance, reasoning, and justice, as well as their knowledge of healing and talent for prophecy.

It is clear that both John's and Christ's followers were familiar with Essene teachings. They washed their bodies, as well as their hearts. They studied and meditated (what today has evolved into "prayer") on the issues of man and God, and they believed in divine revelation and that it was essential to understanding the relationship between God and man. Though several groups made up this sect coming out of the Second Temple Judaism, they shared similar mystic, eschatological, messianic, and ascetic beliefs. It would be difficult to separate the Jesus' character portrait in the New Testament from that of the Essenes.

I had at least some reference to the Essenes from my courses at Baylor, but some years later, I ran across the most interesting purported original Latin manuscript, called a letter, which it was, but it was so epic it was almost like a book. It was translated by a German translator, but claimed to be originally discovered in Alexandria in an ancient house that supposedly had been owned and occupied by the Order of Essenes. The Order of Free Masonry claimed historical connection to the early Essenes and participated in saving the manuscript with the help of influential Abyssinian merchants and Pythagorical Societies. I say "saving" the manuscript because the story is that the Jesuits tried to destroy it, but were not successful. The original is supposedly guarded in the Masonic fraternity in Germany.

As far as I know, no scholars have been allowed to examine the document and no one performed carbon dating, but allegedly, this is a very old document written in Latin of the time. More on that in the following pages. Mostly, however, I have not been able to find much writing about the document, but the tale it tells is quite fascinating and shows knowledge of the Essenes.

The letter purports to be answering a request by a "Terapeut" (elder) of the Essene in Alexandria wanting to know about the life and death of Jesus. A "Terapeut" in Jerusalem writes the account as known to him and sends it to his friend, an Essene Brother, in Alexandria. He affirms that "Jesus was born in Nazareth, by the entrance to the beautiful valley into which the river 'Kisson' rushes down 'steep declivities of the Mount Tabor.' He was put under the protection of the Order by a member of our Brotherhood, by whom his father and mother found a refuge on their flight to Europe."[23] He then says that Jesus was admitted to the Order simultaneous with John (I assume referring to the apostle John) when they were young. Jutha was the place of his initiation. John baptized Jesus in Jordan, near the shore of the Dead Sea, as part of the sacred institution of the Order, and both men followed the Order rituals of baptism, breaking of the bread and passing on the wine.

The letter refers to rumors of miracles performed by Jesus as "... You ought to know that the rumor is like a wind. When it commences it drives the pure air far ahead, but in its progress it receives all vapors and mist from the earth, and when it has traveled some distance it creates darkness instead of clear pure air of which it was first composed, and at last consists solely of the particles it has received during its progress."[24]

The Terapeut writer describes Jesus as living a holy life, who had learned the secrets of the kingdoms of nature; that his parentage should be held in high esteem though he was delivered to the Essenes as an infant for raising. Mary, however, is described as an excitable woman "given to imaginings, delving into the supernatural and the mysteries of life, and she found deep interest and pleasure in the things she could not explain."[25]

The writer verifies some of the stories of the New Testament but tells them differently, and poses different backgrounds to some of the stories. The letter tells the tale of the rearing of Jesus, interaction between the Essenes responsible for raising and protecting Jesus and their communication with Joseph and Mary, and the conflicts in this environment with the rabbis of the Temple and the Pharisees. But without exception, the letter gives a more human picture of the man, Jesus.

The writer tells of how Jesus was called to preach, teach, and heal as he grew and how the writer and the Brotherhood in Jerusalem witnessed this process. Then the writer, while praising Jesus for His martyrdom in standing for his beliefs, states that he is now going to resolve the rumors that had already reached Rome. However, the translator makes a note at this point that the attempted destruction of the document had made it impossible to translate this segment of the parchment.

From there, the letter describes the procession of Jesus and the two thieves winding their way from Jerusalem to Golgotha, the place of execution, the setting of the crosses and the men upon the crosses. He describes the "sounds of anguish and lamentation were drowned out by the noise of horsemen advancing to the scene. This was the high priest 'Caiaphas' with a large escort of servants, who came to mock and deride the crucified son of God."[26]

The author describes the day and the night and an earthquake, but then refers to a reproach by the Alexandrian Brethren that the Jerusalem Essenes had failed to save Jesus by secret means. What you learn in the following pages is that they did save Him – when they took Him down from the cross that night he was unconscious, but not dead. They knew that because the spear wound in his side was still flowing blood, so the heart was pumping. They took him to the tomb, dressed his wounds and resuscitated his lungs, using healing methods, oils, and herbs known for their healing properties. Nicodemus is thought to be a significant part of this. They dressed Jesus in a white robe of the Essenes, which many of them wore. As the earth quaking weather continued in its terrifying manner, Jesus gained consciousness. The attending Essenes told him that this was not a good place to remain because of the High Priest, so they took him to a home owned by the Order that was close to Calvary, because Jesus was weak and could make it no farther.

A lot of confusion and rumor arose there, as on one occasion Jesus was seen in a garden as he recuperated, and on another a young Essene in a white robe who was attending him was apparently mistaken for Jesus. Mary, his mother, saw him but thought he was the gardener, and even when he spoke to her in his weak and suffering condition, "she did not know him,"[27] but then he convinced her but told her he could not embrace her because of his wounds.

Ultimately, the Brotherhood moved Jesus away from the Jerusalem environs to another area described in the letter with the caveat:

"Thou art not safe in this country, for they will search after thee. Do not, therefore, go any more among the people to teach, for what thou hast taught will live among thy friends forever, and thy disciples will publish it to the world. Remain, I pray thee dead to the world. The Brotherhood has brought thee back to life through its secrets, therefore live henceforth for our Holy Order to which thou art bound. Live in seclusion of wisdom and virtue, unknown to the world."[28]

The writer then explains:

"But Jesus, in the ardor of his sacred enthusiasm, said: 'The voice of God is more powerful within me than is the fear of death. I will see my disciples once more, and will go to Galilee.'"[29]

Jesus set forth on his journey with the help of the Essenes, and the writer describes encounters with his disciples as reported later by his Essene escort. After his journey and again with the aid of the Essenes, Jesus returned to Massena and finally arrived at a place in a valley controlled and protected by the Essenes, the same Valley where he had wandered with John, "his beloved companion, and with whom he had been initiated into our Holy Order."[30]

Finally, the Terapeut describes Jesus' condition both psychologically and physically:

"And Jesus meditated on that John, who, as a physician, had founded the school and had baptized, had been slain by the enemies, while he had been saved by the hand of God, wherein he saw the command of God that he should not rest, in that his body had been restored to him for some purpose."[31]

Again, Jesus journeyed to see the disciples and other followers, but he was constantly in danger from both the High Priest and Pilate, and the Essenes struggled to secret Him. The writer, however, describes Jesus through this as weak, struggling with his broken health and often speaking of death. He implored the Essenes to dissolve their vows of secrecy, and like him, become more open and teach publicly.

"But Jesus was accompanied on his way by the elders of the Brotherhood, likewise by Joseph and Nicodemus; and in the night time they procured a beast of burden for Jesus, who grew more faint. His mind was greatly moved at leaving his friends, and he felt that his death would soon come."[32]

"His soul longed for his disciples, and he was anxious that nothing should be neglected. His restless mind found no consolation in the solitude, and anxiety consumed his vital powers."[33]

"The Eternal Spirit had gently burst the clay, and tranquil as his life was his death.

And he was buried by the physician close by the Dead Sea, as bids the regulations of our Brotherhood."[34]

"Here, my dear brethren, you have the only true account of our friend, whom God had called to teach wisdom and virtue to the people through parables and noble deeds."[35]

There is much more within this letter, but I think this gives the basics. According to this letter, the Resurrection was a rumor, and the author criticizes the disciples for not countering the rumor:

"But in the city there arose a rumor that Jesus was taken up in a cloud, and had gone to heaven. This was invented by the people who had not been present when Jesus departed. The disciples did not contradict this rumor, inasmuch as it served to strengthen their doctrine, and influenced the people who wanted a miracle in order to believe in him."[36]

This is a real Easter buster.

But in all honesty, I later read that scholars had examined the text as published, although not the original, and were confident that this was written in the mid-nineteenth century as a hoax. Indeed, that might well be, but isn't it interesting how such a tale, fiction or not, could have happened, as easily as the tales we have received from the Gospel writers. I suppose this was the author's purpose in writing the spoof.

True investigative scholars of religion are professionals using their knowledge of ancient languages, archaeology, parchment or paper or ink dating procedures, and contemporary storytelling and writing styles and writing equipment of a certain time. I like to call them investigative historical detectives. With their knowledge base that takes many, many years to acquire and the aptitude for learning, they apply critical thinking, and as real professionals, avoid motivated thinking.

Early on in my search and to this day, I hold them in high esteem and weigh heavily on their opinions. This is to be distinguished from those who are called PhDs in theology. My experience is that their doctorate is from a seminary of their faith, which is nothing more than a procedure for learning how to defend the way the accumulated Bible we have today reads.

Chapter 14

From Rumor to Fabrication

TRADITIONAL BIBLE INTERPRETATION places John and James as cousins of Jesus, and their mother Salome as the younger sister of Mary, the mother of Jesus. John and James were the first disciples of John the Baptist, their second cousin. Both John and James are considered to have ranked high among the 12 apostles, not only because they were the first of the disciples but also because of their kinship with Jesus. According to the Book of Mark, Peter, James, and John were the only witnesses of the raising of the daughter of Jairus. This is the story immediately following the exorcism at Gerasa, where Jairus, a patron of the synagogue, asks Jesus to heal his dying daughter. However, according to Matthew, his daughter is already dead, not dying. As they travel to Jairus' house, a sick woman in the crowd touches Jesus' cloak and is immediately healed. This is called the miracle of Christ healing the bleeding woman. Meanwhile, the daughter dies, but Jesus continues to the house and brings her back to life.[37]

John, James, and Peter witnessed the Transfiguration of Jesus as well. That is the episode in which Jesus is metamorphosed and became radiant up on a mountain. Jesus and these three apostles go up there, and Jesus begins to shine bright rays of light. Then, the prophets Moses and Elijah appear next to him, and he speaks with them. Jesus is called "Son" by a voice in the sky, assumed to be God, just as His voice spoke when James was baptized.

Then, the same three witnessed the agony of Jesus at Gethsemane, the garden at the foot of Mount of Olives in Jerusalem. This is where Jesus and his disciples are said to have prayed the night before he was arrested and the day before his death.

Jesus sent only John and Peter into the city to prepare for the final Passover meal, the Last Supper. During the meal, the "disciple whom Jesus loved" sat next to Jesus and leaned on his chest. The tradition says that it was John (John 13:23-25). After Jesus' arrest, Peter and the "other disciple," again John according to tradition, followed him into the palace of the high priest, Caiaphas, the Roman-appointed Jewish high priest. (John 18:15). It is said that Caiaphas organized the plot to kill Jesus, and that he also participated in Jesus' trial.

It was John alone who remained near Jesus at the foot of the cross of Calvary and followed his instruction from the cross to take Mary, the mother of Jesus, into his care. After Jesus' ascension, when he was taken up to heaven in the resurrected body and an angel told the waiting disciples that Jesus' second coming will take place in the same manner as his ascension, and after the descent of the Holy Spirit on Pentecost where the Apostles were instilled with the Spirit of God, John, together with Peter, took a prominent part in the founding and guidance of the Christian church. John was with Peter at the healing of the lame man in the temple. He was also thrown into prison with him.

Some scholars believe that John wrote the Letters of John and the Book of Revelation, and although some scholars agree in placing the Gospel of John somewhere between A.D. 65 and 85, the scholar John A. T. Robinson (1919 – 1983, Cambridge) has proposed an initial edition by 50 – 55, with a final edition by 65, due to the narrative similarities with Paul. Other critical scholars think that the Gospel According to John was composed in stages, yet there is a strongly held view amongst contemporary scholars that the Gospel was not written until the latter third of the first century BC, and some say it couldn't have been written until close to the beginning of the second century.

I have used John to relate the traditional understanding of the life of Jesus and purportedly his closest friend, to compare it with the story of the crucifixion of Jesus in the previous chapter. I can't help but find it interesting that the Gospels never mentioned the sect of the Essenes, and yet we see so many similarities in the teachings of Jesus and the ways of the Essenes.

"The loss of the Temple, which had been the inspiration of the new Judaism, was a great grief but with hindsight it seems that the Jews of Palestine, who were often more conservative than the Hellenised Jews of the diaspora, had already prepared themselves for the catastrophe. Various sects had sprung up in the Holy Land, which had in different ways dissociated themselves from the Jerusalem Temple. The Essenes and the Qumran sect believed that the Temple had become venal and corrupt; they had withdrawn to live in separate communities, such as the monastic-style community beside the Dead Sea. They believed that they were building a new Temple, not made with hands. Theirs would be a Temple of the Spirit; instead of the old animal sacrifices, they purified themselves and sought forgiveness of sins by baptismal ceremonies and communal meals. God would live in a loving brotherhood, not in a stone temple."[38]

In 1947, in a cave west of the Dead Sea and just 13 miles east of Jerusalem, the Dead Sea Scrolls were first discovered. Researchers searched other caves and found 11 manuscripts. Authors of all of them were the Essenes, living at roughly the same time and place as John the Baptist and Jesus. These books covered numerous subjects including the Essenes, apocalyptic views of the world and its approaching end, their worship and liturgical life, as well as copies of the Hebrew Scriptures 1000 years older than any previously found.

Wearing white robes, seldom marrying, washing and purifying in baptism, breaking of bread and passing of wine, professing knowledge in the healing arts and joint belief and teaching that all were living at the end of the age and that God would soon intervene in a cataclysmic act of judgment – this is all connected to the Essenes, but also to Jesus. I am well aware of the warning that "fools rush in where angels fear to tread," which may well apply to me, but there are clearly similarities between Jesus and the Essenes.

"The majority of the Dead Sea Scrolls are in Hebrew, with some fragments written in the ancient paleo-Hebrew alphabet thought to have fallen out of use in the fifth century B.C. But others are in Aramaic, the language spoken by many Jews — including, most likely, Jesus — between the sixth century B.C. and the siege of Jerusalem in 70 A.D. In addition, several texts feature translations of the Hebrew Bible into Greek, which some Jews used instead of or in addition to Hebrew at the time of the scrolls' creation."[39]

A gap between factual history and faith formed early, but fictions of the life of Jesus were mostly written throughout the eighteenth and into the nineteenth century, showing the consternation of analytical thinkers as to how discrepancies could be resolved. These writers included K. F. Bahrdt (1792), K.H. Venturini (1809), and H. Paulus (1828). Venturini claimed that Jesus was just a member of the Essenes, who staged his miracles, and who was crucified but did not die. Paulus took a rationalistic approach and attempted to give natural explanations for the miracles, and David F. Strauss (1808 – 1874) wrote "The Life of Jesus Critically Examined" in 1835, and he was the major figure to suggest the Gospels are mostly fictitious because of the miracle claims. He claimed that the Gospels were designed to teach trans-central moral truths to the followers.

In my opinion and from what I have seen, there is no evidentiary basis for any of these positions. They merely boil down to one's opinion. Each is possible, but none can produce a preponderance of evidence any more than the Gospels themselves.

Chapter 15

Hebrew and Jewish History

I LEFT MY study of the New Testament and my frustration with its inconsistencies and claims of miraculous supernatural events and turned my attention to the last group in my comparative Abrahamic study, albeit the oldest, the history of the Hebrews and Jews.

The kingdom of Israel was on the north with its southern border touching the north shore of the Sea of Galilee and bordered on the west by the Mediterranean Sea. The Kingdom of Judah was smaller geographically and bordered Israel on the south with its eastern border being the Sea of Galilee. These two kingdoms were surrounded by the Assyrian Empire on the northern flank and from north to south on that east border of the Kingdom of Aram-Damascus, Aramean tribes, the Kingdom of Amon, the Kingdom of Moab, and to a distance the Mmabatho tribes. To the west of

Judah were the Philistine states, and on the south of Judah were the Arab tribes and the Kingdom of Edom.

Up to this point, for my informative study, I used archaeological finds, epigraphy (the study of inscriptions or epigraphs) and the unbiased writings, to the extent that I can determine a lack of bias or ulterior motive, and works by archaeological and historical scholars. What I have reviewed here is by no means academic or complete, but an attempt to view pre-existing and outside influences on the history as reported by the Torah, the Jewish Bible, and the Old Testament.

We can broadly divide the sources for the history of ancient Israel and Judah into the biblical narrative (the Hebrew Bible), deuterocanonical works and non-biblical works of later, all of which become problematical as to dating because these sources give no dates. Archaeological records can be divided between epigraphy, the written inscriptions, both from Israel and importantly Mesopotamia and Egypt and the material record, which is the result of archaeological digs and interpretation. The real problem is not only the difficulty in dating biblical history, due to the Bible's lack of datable events and its unreliable chronology, but also that the Israeli government and religious sects have been less than ethical. They attempt to force influence, sometimes successfully, on archaeologists seeking access to digging sites, in order to substantiate their historical view to support their religion.

Nevertheless, it became clear by the 1920s that the archaeological record did not support the idea of an Israelite conquest of Canaan, the story in the book of Joshua. The evidence shows that the Israelites were indigenous Canaanites. There was no need for conquest, even though in a later period Israelites took on a different ethnicity for themselves. This meant that while the Bible had depicted the Israelites as monotheists from the beginning, they were not. They were polytheists who harbored a small but ultimately successful group of monotheistic revolutionaries. No material remains have been found which can reliably separate Israelite from non-Israelite, i.e. Canaanite, sites in the earliest period.

The nation of Israel today and Judaism still treat the post-conquest biblical story as real history. Fundamentalist Christians who believe the history is literal also contest the independent scholars and scientists who have worked the area. At the far extreme on the other side is the theory that the Jews originated as a "mixed multitude" of settlers sent to Jerusalem by the Persians, where they concocted a past for themselves.

"Israel's southern neighbor, the Kingdom of Judah, emerged in the eighth or ninth century BCE and enjoyed a period of prosperity as a client state of first the Neo-Assyrian Empire and then the Neo-Babylonian Empire before a revolt against the latter led to its destruction in 586 BCE. Following the fall of Babylon to the Achaemenid Empire under Cyrus the Great in 539 BCE, some Judean exiles returned to Jerusalem, inaugurating the formative period in the development of a distinctive Judahite identity in the province of Yehud Medinata."[40] Jumping to the second century B.C.E., the Judaens revolted against the Hellenistic Seleucid Empire, which had followed conquests by Alexander the Great, and created the Hasmonean Kingdom. This lasted until 63 BCE when Roman conquest took it over.[41]

"Israel had clearly emerged by the middle of the ninth century BCE, when the Assyrian king Shalmaneser III named "Ahab the Israelite" among his enemies at the battle of Qarqar (853). At this time Israel was apparently engaged in a three-way contest with Damascus and Tyre for control of the Jezreel Valley and Galilee in the north, and with Moab, Ammon and Damascus in the east for control of Gilead; the Mesha Stele (c. 830), left by a king of Moab, celebrates his success in throwing off the oppression of the 'House of Omri' (i.e., Israel). It bears what is generally thought to be the earliest extra-biblical Semitic reference to the name Yahweh. (…) French scholar André Lemaire has reconstructed a portion of line 31 of the stele as mentioning the 'House of David'."[42]

The word "Yahweh" is used, today, interchangeably with "Jehovah" or "the Lord" or "God of Israel." Yahweh was not a Canaanite God, and modern scholars see him originating in concept in Edom, the region south of Judah. Initially, the goddess Asherah may have been Yahweh's consort, but the main God of the Iron Age kingdoms of Israel and Judah as being Yahweh became entrenched in Judaism in their exile and the Persian periods, when Judaism was developing their concept of one God.

There are several archaeological leads as to where the idea of Yahweh originated. The first probable record of that name is in two inscriptions from the fourteenth and thirteenth centuries B.C., as the name of a place. YHW was in the region of Edom, an area associated with Shasu-Bedouins. The Edomite God YHW could have been brought up north to the Canaanite Hill country and the early Israelites by migratory Edomite desert tribes. The Bible tells a story in which the Israelites escaped from Egypt, wandered in the wilderness, and met Yahweh on a mountaintop in the wilderness. They agreed to become his chosen people and with his help conquered Canaan. This doesn't match with all of the archaeological evidence.

Nevertheless, a century after the Kingdom of Israel fought for control of the Jezreel Valley and Galilee, "it came into increasing conflict with the expanding Neo-Assyrian Empire, which first split its territory into several smaller units and then destroyed its capital, Samaria (722). Both the biblical and Assyrian sources speak of a massive deportation of people from Israel and their replacement with settlers from other parts of the empire – such population exchanges were an established part of Assyrian imperial policy, a means of breaking the old power structure – and the former Israel never again became an independent political entity."[43] Of course, not until current time with its placement by the international community of the Western world in the twentieth century.

Jerusalem, of course, was in Judea, and Judea emerged somewhat later than Israel. During the rule of Hezekiah, between C. 715 and 686 B.C.E, the Judean state grew significantly stronger. An example is the Broad Wall, a defensive city wall for Jerusalem, Hezekiah's Tunnel, an aqueduct designed to provide Jerusalem with water during the siege by the Assyrians, and much more. In the seventh century B.C.E. Jerusalem grew to contain a population many times greater than ever before and achieved clear dominance over its neighbors. Interestingly, this happened at the same time that Israel was being destroyed by Syria, and was most likely the result of a cooperative arrangement between Judah and the Assyrians to establish Judah as an Assyrian vassal controlling the valuable olive industry. But in the last half of the seventh century B.C.E, Assyria suddenly collapsed. That collapse started a competition between Egypt and the Neo-Babylonian Empires for control of Palestine, which led to the destruction of Judah.

"The Babylonian conquest entailed not just the destruction of Jerusalem and its temple, but the liquidation of the entire infrastructure which had sustained Judah for centuries. The most significant casualty was the state ideology of "Zion theology," the idea that the god of Israel had chosen Jerusalem for his dwelling-place and that the Davidic dynasty would reign there forever. The fall of the city and the end of Davidic kingship forced the leaders of the exile community – kings, priests, scribes and prophets – to reformulate the concepts of community, faith and politics. The exile community in Babylon thus became the source of significant portions of the Hebrew Bible: Isaiah 40–55; Ezekiel; the final version of Jeremiah; the work of the hypothesized priestly source in the Pentateuch; and the final form of the history of Israel from Deuteronomy to 2 Kings. Theologically, the Babylonian exiles were responsible for the doctrines of individual responsibility and universalism (the concept that one god controls the entire world) and for the increased emphasis on purity and holiness. Most significantly, the trauma of the exile experience led to the development of a strong sense of Hebrew identity distinct from other peoples, with increased emphasis on symbols such as circumcision and Sabbath-observance to sustain that distinction."⁴⁴

To accept the history of the Hebrews, one can only rely on what was written as the Hebrew Bible in exile in Babylon and then somehow juxtapose it on to archaeology, as opposed to the other way around. Also, this should be done without date chronology, since there is none in the Jewish Bible, only event chronology, even though dating was used in the Babylonian Empire and before, as found on inscriptions in many places. From the early Babylonian poem, "Enuma Elish," celebrating the victory of Gods over chaos, to man's creation of Apsu (identified with sweet waters of the rivers), his wife, Tiamat (the salty sea), and Mummu, the Womb of Chaos, to new Gods emerging such as Lahmu and Lahamu (silt, water and earth) or Anshar and Kishar (horizons of sky and sea) and Anu (the heavens) and Ea (the earth), or Marduk, the Sun God, mindset of the humankind had evolved entrenched and hard-wired for the conceptual need of a God. Simultaneously throughout the world beyond the Mediterranean, this same evolution was happening, only with different expressions.

The myth of Marduk and Tiamat, which was very similar to the story about Baal-Hadad, the God of storm and fertility, influenced the people of Canaan. This story of Baal's battle with Yam-Nahar, the God of the seas and rivers, exists on tablets that date to the fourteenth century B.C.E. There is a long mythical history of Baal, the Storm God, and how he dies and his father, the High God – El Elyon, comes down off his throne to mourn. These are rich, sexy mythical stories, and a lot of them exist. The death of a God and a return to the divine sphere was consistent and recurring in religions and even reoccurred in the One God worshiped by Jews, Christians, and Muslims, as in Jesus, Son of God, dying on earth and returning to His father in heaven.

In her book, A History of God, the 400-year quest of Judaism, Christianity, and Islam, Karen Armstrong says that the biblical story is attributed in the Bible to Abraham. We are told that Abraham left Ur which, as we know today, would have been in ancient times a city at the mouth of the Euphrates on the Persian Gulf (Iraq), and that he settled in Canaan sometime between the twentieth and nineteenth centuries B.C.E.

"We have no contemporary record of Abraham but scholars think that he may have been one of the wandering chieftains who had led their people from Mesopotamia towards the Mediterranean at the end of the third millennium BCE. These wanderers, some of whom are called Abiru, Apiru or Habiru in Mesopotamian and Egyptian sources, spoke West Semitic languages, of which Hebrew is one."[45]

These tribes were not regular desert nomads like the Bedouin:

"Their cultural status was usually superior to the desert folk. Some served as mercenaries, others became government employees, others worked as merchants, servants or tinkers. Some became rich and might then try to acquire land and settle down. The stories about Abraham in the book of Genesis show him serving the King of Sodom as a mercenary and describe his frequent conflicts with the authorities of Canaan and its environs. Eventually, when his wife Sarah died, Abraham bought land in Hebron, now on the West Bank."[46]

Armstrong digests with admirable clarity the Hebrew immigration, which I have re-verified from my reading of the Jewish Bible:

"The Genesis account of Abraham and his immediate descendants may indicate that there were three main waves of early Hebrew settlement in Canaan, the modern Israel. One was associated with Abraham and Hebron and took place in about 1850 BCE. A second wave of immigration was linked with Abraham's grandson Jacob, who was renamed Israel ('May God show his strength!'); he settled in Shechem, which is now the Arab town of Nablus on the West Bank. The Bible tells us that Jacob's sons, who became the ancestors of the twelve tribes of Israel, immigrated to Egypt during a severe famine in Canaan. The third wave of Hebrew settlement occurred in about 1200 BCE when tribes who claimed to be descendants of Abraham, arrived in Canaan from Egypt. They said that they had been enslaved by the Egyptians but had been liberated by a deity called Yahweh, who was the god of their leader Moses. After they had forced their way into Canaan, they allied themselves with the Hebrews there and became known as the people of Israel. The Bible makes it clear that the people we know as the ancient Israelites were a confederation of various ethnic groups, bound principally together by their loyalty to Yahweh, the God of Moses. The biblical account was written down centuries later, however, in about the eighth century BCE, though it certainly drew on earlier narrative sources."[47]

Here, again, the difficulty lies in historians writing history centuries after the fact, with no Divine intervention to correct or perfect it.

Chapter 16

My Early Look at the Old Testament

TO STUDY JUDAISM is to have a delightful relationship with the history of the area known as the Levant. The Levant is a geographical and multi-cultural region of the Eastern Mediterranean littoral between Anatolia (the westernmost protrusion of Asia or Turkey) and Egypt. It includes most of modern Lebanon, Syria, Jordan, Israel, and the Palestinian territories.

In this area in the late second millennium BC, serious political instability hit the Middle East and the Eastern Mediterranean. The main casualties were the Mycenaean Greek kingdoms and the Hittite Empire. "Writing fell out of use and Greece entered the 400-year-old Greek Dark Age."[48] At almost the same time, the dominant Hittite Empire of Anatolia collapsed, probably destroyed by invaders from southeast Europe.

Waves of migration caused chaos throughout Mediterranean and Middle East; Mycenaean civilization centers destroyed by unknown invaders, writing fell out of use and Greece entered dark age (lasted 400 years), Hittite empire collapsed, Babylonia attacked by nomads from Arabian desert, Egypt attacked by mysterious group of migrating people (Sea Peoples).

Mesopotamia, the area from Anatolia to what we call today the Persian Gulf also suffered invasions by the Aramaean and Chaldean nomads of the Arabian Desert. The decline of the region's great powers favored the foundation of small kingdoms in the Levant, the most influential of which was the Hebrew kingdom founded C. 1020 BC. Also, instrumental in this period were the Phoenicians, a seafaring people, who began to create a Mediterranean trading network. This was the beginning, established by both written documents and tablets that have survived, as well as archaeological discoveries.

The foundation of the Hebrew kingdom went unnoticed by the troubled great powers of the region, as they warred with each other and grappled for survival over internal strife. However, this was an event of fundamental importance to the development of Jewish, Christian and Islamic religions. By making Jerusalem his capital, the Hebrew king David ensured its lasting significance as a holy site for all three faiths.

Historical documents show that the Hebrews were closely related to the Canaanites, and the Canaanites were the first people to write using an alphabetic script. This allowed for a bookish evolution and an essential element for survival. Around 1100 BC, the neighboring Phoenicians devised their own alphabet based on the Canaanite original, and because of their seafaring activities disseminated their script around the Mediterranean.

One of the documents that survived this pre-Hebrew period was the Epic of Gilgamesh. I found it most interesting, as it spoke of my critical question. This is the epic point in Mesopotamia dating back to the eighteenth century BC, with later versions through following centuries. The story centers on a friendship between Gilgamesh and Enkidu. "The latter half of the epic focuses on Gilgamesh's distress at Enkidu's death, and his quest for immortality. In order to learn the secret of eternal life, Gilgamesh undertakes a long and perilous journey to find the immortal flood hero, Utnapishtim. He learns that 'The life that you are seeking you will never find. When the gods created man they allotted to him death, but life they retained in their own keeping.'"[49]

But for Abrahamic religions, it was the seventh and six centuries BC that were among the most important. It was then that the Hebrew kingdoms were conquered first by Syria and then by Babylon. Large numbers of Jews, as Hebrews were starting to be called, were deported to Mesopotamia. It was among these Jewish exiles that the key books of the Old Testament were written in approximately their present form, and Judaism emerged as a definitively monotheistic religion. It is interesting how the Old Testament shows an understanding of Mesopotamian mythology. This within itself would be a fantastic comparative study, as would be an investigation of the extent of influence upon the Old Testament by the Iranian prophet Zoroaster, who espoused monotheism and cosmic dualism. The idea of one God was not original to the Hebrews.

If you read the Old Testament with a realistic view, the Hebrews were an arrogant marauding band of looters, killers, and destroyers. They utilized their monotheistic God as an excuse to make claims on the land of others. God appears in some passages to be a nationalistic deity, even a sadistic one who delighted in killing firstborn in every Egyptian household (Exod. 11:4-6) (Reminiscent of Herod in the later New Testament?). Obviously, the mindset of retribution was firmly established, but the writer of Exodus said that this murder was so "that the Lord makes a distinction between the Egyptians and Israel" (Exod. 11:17). The Torah said "do not steal," but Moses commanded in the Exodus from Egypt to rob the Egyptians of their jewelry, silver, gold, and clothing (Exod.12:35-36). What you see throughout the Old Testament is a vicious code of ethics that internally prohibits the behavior which is encouraged in dealing with outsiders.

Parts of the Hebrew Scriptures extol tribal hatreds as virtues. If captive people were spared from death at all, they were reduced to slavery, or if a captive person was a woman, she was used for sexual sport. Judah treated his daughter-in-law, Tamar, as a prostitute and then proposed to kill her when she became pregnant (Genesis 38). While bearing false witness was prohibited by the 10 Commandments, Moses didn't seem to have a problem with it in his conversations with Pharaoh, but then you get into inconsistencies even within the Torah. Aside from two creation stories that vary in detail and contradict each other in order (Gen. 1:1-2:4 and

Gen. 2:5ff), Moses contradicted himself radically in the first two chapters. There are three separate and distinct versions of the 10 Commandments that cannot be reconciled (Exodus 20, Exodus 34, and Deuteronomy 5). Either God couldn't stay consistent, or Moses just couldn't get it down. Again, at the very outset of my study, I was faced with Deified inconsistency.

I can understand from a historical sense why the Hebrew were so war-like, but not from a Deist standpoint. The Levant was an area of persistent tribal war with constant pillage, marauding, and slaughter, but if God made humankind and he was a loving God, why constant retribution taken in His name? In actuality, because the Hebrews won the ancient struggle, their point of view rather than that of the Canaanites became dominant and prevailed in the biblical record.

The Torah, the first five books of the Jewish Bible as the law given by God to Moses, is the foundation of the Old Testament. Slavery was assumed, and the master could beat this lady unmercifully because the Law said, "the slave is his money" (Exod. 21:21). The child who struck or cursed a parent shall be executed (Exod. 21:15,17). Anyone who sacrificed to a God other than Israel's God "shall be utterly destroyed" (Exod. 22:20). Menstruation was unclean, and whatever the menstruating woman touched was unclean (Lev. 15:19ff). A man who had a wet dream "shall be unclean until the evening" (Lev. 15:16). You could not be a priest if you were blind or lame or had a mutilated face or were a hunchback or a dwarf or had a body defect or an itching disease or scabs or crushed testicles (Lev.22:16-22). If you blasphemed

God you were to be executed (Lev. 24:16). "When a man causes a disfigurement in his neighbor, as he has done, it shall be done to him, fracture for fracture, eye for eye, tooth for tooth, as he has disfigured a man he shall be disfigured" (Lev. 24:19-20). If a "spirit of jealousy" came upon a man, it was his wife's fault. He could force her to drink a poisoned potion. If she died, her guilt causing his jealousy was assumed. If she survived she was presumed to be innocent (Num. 5:11ff).

Indeed, suppressive womanhood is present in verse after verse of the Torah. The woman is thought to be incompetent to make a decision, so her father is given veto power (Num. 30:1-5). Later in her life, her husband has to approve her utterances if they are to have any force (Num. 30:8). The subjugation of women permeates the Old Testament, while at the same time mandating fervent nationalism. Non-Israelite groups, such as the Midianites, were ordered to be destroyed by God (Num. 31:1,2). Israel obeyed: "they warred against Midian as the Lord commanded Moses and slew every male" (Num. 31:7). They spared the women and children and took as booty all their cattle, flocks and goods (Num.31:9). Then they burned Midianite cities (Num.31:10). Moses was angry that they had let the women live (Num. 31:15). He then ordered all male children to be killed (Reminiscent of Herod in the Jesus birth story in the New Testament?). Finally, Moses ordered the murder of all women who were not virgins, and allowed the Israelite men to keep all the virgins for themselves.

Sexuality was always a problem for the Hebrew mind, and of course, for those who wrote the New Testament. Not only did this religion subvert women, but it was also homophobic with great fear. The law stated: "you shall not lie with a man as with a woman; it is an abomination" (Lev. 18:24ff). To do these things is to be cut off from the people of Israel (Lev. 18:29). Later in the Torah, death is called for as the penalty for homosexuality. If a man lies with a man as with a woman, both of them have committed an abomination; they shall be put to death" (Lev.20:13). Interestingly, the writer must not have contemplated a woman lying with a woman, so perhaps they escape God's wrath.

Finally, I turned to the Jewish tradition and religion to see what foundation, if any, there was for life after death. Several sources in Judaism are on a par and complement each other, and I found that one cannot approach a sole source for an answer without going to the interrelated sources for guidance. Since Judaism is the oldest of the Abrahamic religions with the longest history of interpretive chronicles and philosophical debate, the amount of text is massive. That is not to say the same is not true for Christianity and Islam, but it becomes overwhelming when approaching Jewish religious history. It is no wonder that so many individuals in each of these religions begin their study early in life and never complete the process before death, though they spent every day attempting to do so.

The Torah is the first five books of the Jewish Bible. These are the purported laws given to Moses by God, part on the mountain but mostly in the tabernacle. The word Torah in English means to guide or teach or provide a system for doing so.

The Tanakh is the Hebrew Bible, a canonical collection of Jewish texts that covers such issues as Jewish thought of gathering the exiled diaspora together, the coming of a Jewish Messiah, afterlife and the revival of the dead, as well as how to conduct daily life.

The Talmud is the seat of Jewish scholarship written and compiled over many centuries. It holds within it the oral scholarship before written works as handed down through generations, then followed by the Rabbinic Period in which all scholarship was scribed. Rabbis expounded on and debated the laws expressed in the Hebrew Bible, sometimes resulting in consensus, sometimes not, but covering a wide variety of laws and statements on principles, as it sequenced them by subject matter instead of Biblical context. These Jewish religious teachings and commentaries grew and evolved over centuries, at times redacted and changed.

My interest, my search, was to see what jewels of knowledge might exist about the end of life, not so much eschatology, the theology of final events in the history of the world, though that might give some insight. Zohar is a work in the literature of Jewish mystical thought known as Kabbalah. So esoteric as to be difficult to reduce to an understandable hypothesis, it is nevertheless is a set of teachings meant to explain the relationship of the eternal with the mortal or finite. It forms the basis for mystical religious interpretation.

These works taken together, the Torah, the Tanakh, the Talmud and Zohar, cross-referenced when available, are the concept of the Jews. A single statement or derived conclusion made from these works can be up for debate, and centuries of debate among the Jews and their Rabbis have proven so. Nevertheless, I thought I would trudge on.

Solomon states in the book Ecclesiastes: "for what happens to the sons of men also happens to animals; one thing befalls them: as one dies, so dies the other. Surely, they all have one breath; man has no advantage over animals for all is vanity. All go to one place: all from dust, and all returned to dust. Who knows the spirit of the sons of man, which goes upward, and the spirit of the animal, which goes down to earth?" (Ecc. 3:19-21).

Later, Solomon reflects further, "but for him who is joined to all the living there is hope, for a living dog is better than a dead lion. For the living know that they will die; but the dead know nothing, and they have no more reward, for the memory of them is forgotten. Also their love, their hatred, and their envy have now perished; nevermore will they have a share in anything done under the sun." (Ecc.9:4_6).

Psalms 146:2 – 4 states: "do not put your trust in princes, nor in a son of man, in whom there is no help. His spirit departs, he returns to earth; in that very day his plans perish." Then, in the book of Job is stated: "but man dies and is laid away; indeed he breathes his last and where is he? So man lies down and does not rise. To the heavens are no more, they will not awake or be roused from their sleep... If man dies, shall he live again?" (Job 14:10, 12, 14a).

I found these passages refreshing in that they seem to be asking the same questions I was asking and did not take a circular course and giving an answer. It seemed honest. They questioned. I wondered if the Talmud followed in the same vein or did what the New Testament and the Qur'an did – – fabricate Heaven, Hell, life hereafter, and the rules for getting there.

Turning to treatises written by Rabbis considered historical experts on the Talmud, Jewish oral traditions of mysticism, the Zohar, and the commandments and stories of the Torah, it appeared not only that the Talmud was limited to the subject of life after death, but also that Jewish oral traditions entertained it in some form of reincarnation. The doubt, as expressed in the above citations, as to what happens upon death seems to be an outlier.

The Zohar was written by Rabbi Shimon bar Yochai 2000 years ago at a time when Christian thoughts of the afterlife were peaking. He makes frequent and lengthy references to reincarnation and that there was a world to come. Other Rabbis rose to refute the idea of reincarnation as a non-Jewish belief. There came a philosophical divide within the various sects of Judaism and the broad umbrella of the religion, as to whether there was life after death, and today, you find some Jews believe that there is, while others see no support for it.

While I covered various Jewish texts, I could find nothing definitive about afterlife – neither a belief in an afterlife, nor its denial. I did read the treatises of several learned Rabbis who seemingly tried to force an interpretation of afterlife from the Torah, while at the same time admitting that the Torah is mostly about its emphasis on the immediate, concrete, physical rewards and punishments rather than abstract or mythical future ones.

At a later time, I asked a Jewish friend of mine what she thought of this, and I felt comfortable with her answer. In her view, it was an open question, or rather a question with an open answer. Unlike some religions, Judaism is not focused on the issue of how to get into heaven; it is focused on life and how to live it. Some say Judaism believes in an afterlife but has little dogma about it; some say Jewish afterlife is called Olam Ha-Ba or The World to Come; some say resurrection and reincarnation are within the range of traditional Jewish belief, and some say that for the wicked there is temporary, but not eternal punishment after death.

I was impressed that no matter how every Jew chooses to believe they are not excommunicated for their belief. That dogma followed in the later Abrahamic religions.

Chapter 17

The End of My Comparative Study

WHILE SOME OF what I learned in the last chapter, I gleaned from periodic studies at various times in my life, the foundation was that earlier sabbatical in New York. I left the sabbatical for a new life in the oil business. I used my knowledge of legal research only collaterally, as needed. I stored my notes and pushed questions revolving around the end of life to the rear of the bus. Schatzie would just have to wait for me to find out the answers. I had not saved sufficient time to study Judaism, and I wanted to know the historical basis of that great religion. This was a time before computers, so I took all notes by hand, and I must say, not with the best practice of writing down complete references to my sources. Nevertheless, the process would go on for the next four decades during periods in which I would seek solitude and research, sometimes retracing earlier research with new, at other times breaking new ground.

The time in my life of the first sabbatical, my early 30s, was an exciting time, and I was now looking forward to getting on with it. I felt that I had given my best attempt at using critical thinking and reading the works of those scholars, historians, and archaeologists that relied on logic and questioning in evaluating the religions of Islam and Christianity. I knew that I had fallen short because of time limitation in doing the same with Judaism. I knew that I was very fortunate to be able to afford and take this time of study and reflection in my life, to search for answers to questions which first arose as a child when my dog died, a search that continued in my college days at Baylor, and now in this sabbatical.

But my time for departure had come, and I felt the frustration that I was no further along the path to finding answers covering and affecting the process of dying, dying, itself, and what if anything happens to a person after death. I had read a lot of postulation, tendentious motivated thinking, and I had read demands for belief, using fear of loss or condemnation as the motivator. I did admire the gospel writers for their attempts to establish direct evidence on behalf of Jesus, but their use of distant hearsay and lack of consistency made the end of life story questionable. The Abrahamic religions have spent thousands of years trying to give what Mediterranean peoples asked for and desperately wanted – – a God. From that came the age-old desire for immortality, and the religions attempted to provide that.

The idea of immortality raised a difficulty for the religions and how to explain it. At times, there was an obsession with the body. Could it just rot in a grave and that was the end of it? What would this vision of immortality look like? A garden? A material community of mansions? What would we look like? Was a soul the same as a body? If not, what did it look like? Each religion, Islam, and Christianity in particular, tried various explanations of resurrection, place, end of the world in a cataclysmic sense but with a New World coming for a chosen few, and bodies rising to meet approval and inclusion by one God, a deity orchestrating the transference.

But always in the back of my mind in each Book of each religion was the question of who wrote this, what was their source, and what was going on in their life when they wrote it. In spite of the "he said – she said" aspect, the ultimate source was always "God." I wanted to ask "who was God" and what was the evidentiary basis that there was a God. Indeed, what was His beginning? Where did He come from and how? It always seems to circle back either to someone's personal revelation that others must accept or a mythic story of the supernatural which has its foundation in tribal stories told throughout centuries and later captured to make a religion.

The Apocrypha is a group of 14 books, which are not considered Canonical, and which are included in the Septuagint and the Vulgate as part of the Old Testament. These were various religious writings of uncertain origin regarded by some as inspired, but rejected by most authorities, and herein lies the persistent problem, particularly for Christianity and Judaism. All the writings are questionable as to who wrote them, and the texts of all three Abrahamic religions presupposed the existence of a God. The only proof was myth layered upon myth. Clearly, Man created God. God did not create Man.

I was disappointed because I had hoped that in this small time gap in my life between jobs and marriages I would find original, credible answers to questions surrounding the end of life. I was well aware of the spoon-feeding every religious leader and zealot, and indeed, every fundamentalist believer was willing to offer in each of these three religions. The preacher, the rabbi, the imam were each there to lead the flock. That's not what I wanted. I wanted to find the answers for myself, straight on, without assumption or manipulation.

While I failed in my quest, I met the writings of great philosophers and scholars from each religion. I gained respect for humankind's search and the faiths that served that search. They were each the product of the cultures from which they had come. That, I could understand, but the success of the propagation into the leading religions of the world was difficult to understand, unless I coupled religion with a geopolitical drive for power.

I had a deep-seeded fear at this point in my early 30s that, as I ran out of time on this sabbatical, I may never be able to return to a study of the Abrahamic religions. That left me with a feeling of loss, yet at the same time, I felt this commitment that one day I would return to the study again. It is said that the key to writing successful fiction is to bring the reader to a suspension of disbelief. I did not reach that point in reading the great books of the Abrahamic religions as each told of the existence of its God, so I could not accept projections of end-of-life or end-of-world, as stated.

Perhaps, the next time I got a chance to study I would find something new, something revealing.

PART II

MY COMPLETED STUDY OF ABRAHAMIC RELIGIONS

Chapter 18

Building upon Earlier Learning

BY THE TIME of my retirement from the practice of law, there were periods in my life when I would study religions other than Abrahamic, and I was forever picking up a book by some scholar and reading it while on vacation. However, a focused in-depth review of my notes from that early sabbatical and an attempt to bring together all that I had experienced and learned in my life did not come about until retirement.

For people who spend every waking moment going through the stages of life, working and making a living, which is most of us, it is impossible to focus on questions of religion or commit ourselves to independent study. It is true not only for religious issues but the very nature of our lives. Because we do not have time to be experts in every field, we naturally delegate our inquiries to "experts." When we have a medical problem, we rely on a doctor; a legal issue, a lawyer; and, on matters of religion we rely upon the interpretation of the religious sect to which we belong. Beyond that, the average person, even when given the opportunity, would not care to be an expert but just wants a credible answer to their question, as it arises.

My quest had always been a bit different from that, especially when it came to the credibility of religion and answers to questions about the end-of-life. I didn't want to rely on someone else. I wanted to dig out the truth for myself, and doing this required pulling together not only what the great Abrahamic religious books said, but reading various disciplinary fields that did not rely upon those books – – archaeology, evolutionary psychology, anthropology, physics and so on. Such an approach takes a lot of time reading, note taking and cross-disciplinary questioning.

The freedom of retirement gave me this opportunity, so I return to share what I found. Not to convince or persuade you for any ulterior purpose but to just tell you the story of my quest and to tell you that the conclusions reached are my own. If I had a goal outside of that, perhaps it would be to encourage others to think independently, but without predetermined bias. It is not easy to do, but doable.

Chapter 19

Movement through the Levant

IN THE 90s, before retirement, I fell under the influence of Karen Armstrong when I read her book, A History of God, the 4000-year Quest of Judaism, Christianity, and Islam. I had not known of Karen Armstrong before, but suddenly, right there before my eyes was a succinct comparison of the Abrahamic religions and their origins. She traced the history of how men and women perceived and experienced God, from the time of Abraham to the present and how the Jews evolved and transformed pagan idol worship in Babylon to a monotheism concept. She showed how both Christianity and later Islam rose out of this Jewish idea but refashioned "the One God" religion to suit the social and political needs of their followers. I was amazed at what she had accomplished and immediately ordered most of her books and began reading.

The writings of Karen Armstrong piqued my interest in the prehistory of the Hebrews – how did they come to be and how was the concept of a God created? I became fascinated with the archaeological history of the Levant, and in my spare time would check out books on the archaeology of the Levant or acquired books I wanted to study through the interlibrary loan program.

A picture began to evolve out of the Paleolithic or Old Stone Age era, which brought the technological division of human prehistory, extending from the first appearance of tool-using ancestors c. 2.6 million years ago to the end of the last glaciation c. 11,500 years ago. This is a long extended period through which the human species evolved. Early human migrations around the world brought about a proliferation of different cultures and groups that split from one another and adapted to various environments. Much of that early migration, perhaps at two different periods out of Africa, came through the Levant. By the end of the last Ice Age, approximately 14,000 years ago, the best calculation is that the population of the entire world was only about 4 million people.

But what interested me was the area of Levant, that region of the Eastern Mediterranean. If you spent your life going to church, at some point you got the feeling that the Hebrew were there at the beginning of time. It turns out that, as prehistory goes, they were latecomers, as was their creation of God. Before the Hebrews, there was the Natufian culture, and before them, there were other humans.

Radiocarbon dating of their archaeological finds places the Natufians' existence from 12,502 to 9500 BC. While they hunted such animals as gazelles, they mainly ate cereals, fruits, nuts, and other edible plants. The Levant during this period of the Natufian was not the dry, barren, and thorny landscape of today, but plush and full of woodland. One of the leading researchers of the Natufian culture and their era is professor Ofer Bar-Yosef of Harvard. This area that we know today as Palestine, Israel, Jordan, Lebanon, and part of Syria was quite different. It comprised the Levant, and humans passed through it on their way to populating the world, slowly, over thousands of years. I rely heavily on the writings and research of professor Ofer Bar-Yosef regarding the Natufians.

I found it interesting that the Natufians are the earliest archaeological evidence for the domestication of the dog. At a site, Ain Mallaha in Israel, dated to 12,000 BC, an elderly human and a four-to-five-month-old puppy were found buried together. At the cave of Hayonim, humans were found buried with two dogs. But I found it interesting that of the many archaeological sites establishing the culture of the Natufians, there is no evidence of religion, though there is evidence of Shamanism. However, even with the earth-dwelling Natufians, who lived in the Levant long before there was a Hebrew, there must have been thoughts of an afterlife. Their burial places not only had their pets with them but had the things that one might like to take with them on an afterlife journey. Or, at least, some of their burial sites might be interpreted in that way. •

Of course, Paleolithic men and women could leave no written record of their myths, but ethnologists and anthropologists tell us they were conscious of the spiritual dimension in their lives. Even before they began to develop stories of another world and archetypal beings, they had to be impressed by the rejuvenation,

187

death to life, of objects in their life. A tree would die but in time be reborn and come to life, the moon and the sun would die and rise the next day again, plants would do the same. Many of their myths were there to explain these occurrences, and many would survive, in fragmented form, in the mythologies of later literate cultures.

Archaeologists named the time following the Paleolithic Period as the Neolithic Period and divided it into three categories beginning around 9500 BC. There is the Pre-Pottery Neolithic A (PPNA) dating approximately 9500 to 8500 BC; the PPNB and the PPNC which has the following dating classifications:

Early: 7500 – 7200 BC

Middle: 7200 – 6500 BC

Late: 6500 – 6000 BC

It appears that Levant development occurred in the north and spread south, though much of this is still a matter of archeological debate. While initially, the inhabitants were hunter-gatherers, they evolved into nomadic herders and then herders and farmers started coexisting. But it appears that through the Neolithic Period of the Levant major climate changes affected the inhabitants, how they lived and how they thought. One has to assume that the primary goal of any inhabitant was subsistence and survival. During the PPNB, it has been established that the southern Levant would have experienced substantial summer and winter rainfall, but by the post-PPNB, there was a warming trend and acidification with hot, dry summers and rainy winters.

Early cultivation evolved near water resources such as springs, lakes or rivers in places like Jericho, Tell Aswad, Netiv Hagdud, and Mureybet. The Natufians were the early people, but by the PPNB the population increased 16 times that of the Natufians. Some of the larger excavations exceed 24 acres in area, which could have housed between 1000 and 2000 people, which included central places that probably performed community and religious roles.

This period was a notable period of evolution before the area became more populated and the ancestral tribes developed, such as the later tribes of Israel. The very first rectangular buildings occur in this period (PPNB), in which some were partitioned. House plans varied considerably, often depending on location in the Levant. In the arid areas, people still preferred the circular dwelling. Plaster came into use and even foundations of stone.

After 1000 B.C.E., we could characterize the PPNB as regional episodes of resource shortfall due to land degradation, increased importance of domestic animals and legumes, and increasing specialization of sheep and goat pastoralism. There was apparently an extensive exchange of information over a wide area across Southwest Asia during this period. Communication and trade links are indicated by the presence of Mediterranean shells from the East and West Anatolia and asphalt, the latter used as glue for hafting stone tools. Archaeologists find increasing uniformity in arrow and spear points with other regions that would indicate interregional communication.

People started establishing specific informal traditions during this time, representing a significant change from previous customs.

Burials, sometimes communal, became common. In many cases, the head was removed, and in some cases, the skulls were modeled in plaster. Sometimes shells replaced the eyes, all of which may have represented an ancestor cult. Painted plaster seems a popular use that had risen. As to the skulls, 72 have been found without mandibles, modified by the application of plaster, clay, collage, as well as shells and paint decorations on the heads. Young men, children, and women are all represented.

While the Natufian left animal art, the people of PPNB were especially known for their painted plaster statues – usually either female or genderless, but the skull detachment and adoration are the most interesting. It would seem to indicate an increasing interest in "ancestors," as does the behavior of communal burial. Interest in ancestors correlates with the existence of lineages. In turn, lineages correlate with concepts of ownership of defined pieces of food-producing land. If the idea of land ownership was developing, tensions between cultivators and hunters could have existed, as hunters began finding access denied to lands which formed part of their seasonal hunting that they had done for generations.

The period of the inhabitants was a period of increasing size of settlements, even amounting to small towns, which would provide the opportunity to seek partners and for the very first time become "settlement – endogamous," that is giving rise to marrying within a particular social order or the development of tribal systems. Life was beginning to be quite different from nomadic or hunter-gatherer life. With the increasing size of settlements, internalization would be encouraged, increasing identification of individuals and families with specific settlements and the land they worked, building up extended families in defined areas. As closeness developed, no doubt the concentration of belief systems developed within a village mentality.

While I have focused on the Natufian culture as a starting point in the southern Levant in order to lead up to the beginnings of the Hebrew culture, one should not think that I am suggesting the Natufians were the first inhabitants of the area. Before the Natufians, the Kebaran culture appeared in southern Palestine showing clear connections to the earlier microlithic cultures using bow and arrow and even grinding stones to harvest wild grains, the knowledge of which had been developed by the Halfan culture of Egypt from c. 24,000 – 17,000 and then that process came from a still earlier Aterian tradition of the Sahara. The Kebaran culture was quite successful and may have been ancestral to the later Natufian culture of 10,500 to 8500 BC, which extended throughout the whole Levantine region. It all depends on just how far back one desires to go to try to get a handle on Hebrew establishment. For example, anatomically modern Homo sapiens existed in the area of Mount Caramel during the Middle Paleolithic dating from about c. 90,000 BC, and there are many layers of humanity between that and the Natufians.

Thus, in a broad brush view, it appeared to me that the tribal development of the Hebrews in the Levant was a natural evolution of the human species. Until about 10,000 years ago, the inhabitants were groups of nomadic hunter-gatherers and moved from campsite to campsite. Then the first nomadic pastoral society developed, defined as a mixed economy with a symbiosis within the family in the period from 8500 – 6500 BC in the southern Levant, as well as the beginnings of Semitic languages in the region of the Ancient Near East.

But also during this period as the first nomadic pastoral society developed, the pre-existing Natufian society of the southern Levant in Jericho (modern-day West Bank) was using and becoming dependent upon domesticated grains and farming that included cattle and pigs, the establishment of permanently or seasonally inhabited settlements, and the use of pottery.

The study of archaeological finds in the writings of renowned archaeologists covering the area was refreshing. It gave me the insight that human development was slow and evolved over thousands of years. Nothing happened quickly. Even the use of tools was a slow process. I now wondered how religious history fit with the archaeological picture.

Chapter 20

From Many Gods to One

𝕿HE STUDY OF the beginning of the Abrahamic religions is the search for a historical understanding of Israel and Judah, the related Iron Age kingdoms of the ancient Levant. The history of Israel and Judah is a picture of war. Because of this, it is essential to have some idea of the timing of the Iron Age in the Levant. The start of iron production appears to have begun as bronze fell out of favor because of its lack of hardness (Bronze Age Collapse), and this beginning of the iron production seems to have commenced around 1200 BC in Anatolia, that area we know as Turkey, today.

In the Levant (as a reminder, modern Syria, Lebanon, Israel, Palestine, and Jordan), the Iron Age is believed to have begun about 930 BC from carbon dating of the earliest furnace that has been found at Tell Hammeh, Jordan. This will become important as we look at the Kingdoms of Israel and Judah, as Israel became a significant local power by the ninth century BCE. The Iron Age is significant not only for tool making but also for the making of weapons of war. A war from Mesopotamia, the "Cradle of Civilization" of the Tigris – Euphrates basin (now Iraq), through the Levant to Egypt washed back and forth for centuries.

That is not to say that humankind waited on the Iron Age to wage war. They fought with each other long before that. It's just that weapons of iron were stronger and were more deadly. Plato said "only the dead have seen the end of war," and indeed, through evolution, the human brain became hard-wired for war. The rise of the first cities in Mesopotamia is dated ca. 5300 BC, but their real growth period was between 3500 and 3400 BC. "With these towns, ties of religion began to replace ties of kinship as the basis for society. During the Uruk phase, colonists and traders from Southern Iraq established important quarters in settlements throughout the northern part of the Levantine region (e.g. Amuq)."[50]

For my study of the beginning of Hebrew development, Mesopotamia (greater Iraq) and later Babylonia (Southern Iraq, Euphrates cradle region with Syrian border), is essential in seeing how God myths developed. With the development of cities came advances in technology such as the wheel and development of writing. Between 3200 BC and 2400 BC pictographic record-keeping was created, later signs were used to write in Sumerian, and by the end of that period, signs became cuneiform. There was a constant ebb and flow, rise and fall of empires, caused more often than not by war and conquest.

Gods played important roles in conquest both for rulers and sandals on the ground. Typically, a conqueror would accommodate conquered people by allowing or assimilating their gods. There would be the State gods and then those of the people, giving rise to a more polytheistic religion. This was enhanced by different gods being responsible for different things – – fertility, war, etc. Through this history, I observe that War created God, the need for a God, some higher power that could consolidate the psychology of the people as being special and winning against adversaries; or, in the event of defeat, creating a psychology of survival.

"In the second millennium BCE, when the Mesopotamian scribes conducted a divine census, listing the gods in various Mesopotamian cities, they came up with nearly two thousand names. The pantheon typically included lots of nature gods (sun, moon, storm, fertility and so on). Much like in the Catholic faith with saints for different vocations and purposes, so in that ancient state; there were gods for farmers, scribes, merchants, and craftsmen. (...) Like the gods of prehistory, these gods expected goods and services from humans, and dished out rewards or punishment accordingly. So everywhere people made sacrifices to the gods, flattered – that is, worshipped – them, and tended to their needs in other ways. (...) Everywhere the upshot was a symbiotic relationship between people and gods, with each having something the other needed. And everywhere – as in chiefdoms – the political leaders took the lead in mediating that relationship, and indeed defining the relationship; everywhere, religion was used by the powerful to stay powerful."[51]

This process ended with the development of the first empires around 2300 BC. People called the Akkadians invaded the Euphrates

Valley under their King, Sargon I. They established supremacy over the Samarians who lived there, and the Akkad Empire extended into Syria as far as the coast. Archaeological finds in the ancient Syrian city of Ebla produced a massive archive of tablets in the Samarian cuneiform script, which predated the Semitic languages of Canaan, like Ugaritic and Hebrew. The tablets all date a period between ca. 2500 BC and the destruction of the city ca. 2250 BC.

By the twenty-second century BC, the Sargon period had faded and the Empire of Ur developed. Elamites and Amorites destroyed Ur around 2000 BC. Their distinct groups participated together in trade, governing and war with outside forces. By 1900 BC, Akkadian became the main spoken and written language. Mesopotamia during this period covered a vast region greater than current Iraq but was tribal and segregated. Between 1800 BC and 1700 BC, Hammurabi united much of Mesopotamia under his dynasty.

But between 1600 BC and 1500 BC, this began to fall apart, and the Hittites raided Babylon. The Hittites had evolved in the Anatolia (Turkey) and become mighty warriors in the Bronze Age with expert use of chariots. During this period, most of the older centers had been overrun and were weak. By 1400 BC, Babylonia was conquered by the Kassites. The Kassites were a warring people, possibly out of the mountains of Iran and during this period controlled South Mesopotamia. Then, by 1200 BC the Assyrians conquered much of Mesopotamia, but by 1100 BC Aramean became the main spoken language of the Near East during this time and for centuries to follow.

Coming back to the Levant, it is important to remember its location as wars and cultures ebbed and flowed to its North and East; Assyria, Mesopotamia, and Anatolia. To its South and West was the Egyptian Empire and the Levant could be seen as a strategical bridge between the two geographical areas with their various kingdoms of expansionism. While war culture surges and counter-surges were occurring throughout Mesopotamia through these millennia, parallel developments were happening in Egypt, which by the thirty-second century BC had been unified to form the Old Kingdom of Egypt. From 1550 BC until 1100 BC, Egypt conquered much of the Levant, which in the latter half of this period was contested by Syria with the Hittite Empire.

But in 700 BC Assyria conquered Egypt, while in 600 BC the Chaldeans destroyed Assyria. The Chaldeans were Semitic tribes that had evolved from the tenth century BC and only briefly ruled, being replaced by the Persian Empire. Looking back, the destruction at the end of the Bronze Age left many tiny kingdoms and city-states behind, which my broad-brush approach does not take into consideration. "A few Hittite centres remained in northern Syria, along with some Phoenician ports in Canaan that escaped destruction and developed into great commercial powers. In the twelfth century BC most of the interior, as well as Babylonia, was overrun by Arameans, while the shoreline around today's Gaza Strip was settled by Philistines."[52]

In summary, although the millennia history of the Levant affected the ultimate evolution of the Hebrew culture, the most direct effect happened from the tenth century BC onwards, as the Levant Bridge saw conquering armies and culture changes. "During the ninth century BC the Assyrians began to reassert themselves against the incursions of the Aramaeans, and over the next few centuries developed into a powerful and well-organized empire. Their armies were among the first to employ cavalry, which took the place of chariots, and had a reputation for both prowess and brutality. At their height, the Assyrians dominated all of Syria-Palestine, Egypt, and Babylonia. However, the empire began to collapse toward the end of the seventh century BC, and was obliterated by an alliance between a resurgent New Kingdom of Babylonia and the Iranian Medes."[53] Over the next few decades, they annexed the realms of Lydia in Anatolia, Damascus, Babylonia, through the Levant to Egypt.

As we turn to look at the Iron Age kingdoms of the ancient Levant, Israel, and Judah, we see the Kingdom of Israel emerging as a significant local power by the ninth century BCE, before it fell to the neo-Assyrian Empire in 722 BCE.

Chapter 21

The Sifting of Gods and Religion

THROUGHOUT THE 90s, much of my pleasurable reading evolved around Karen Armstrong's works and on occasion going to her note references and reading her sources. This was in the midst of a very active law practice, but at times I was able to escape into the question of the origin of Abrahamic religions.

It became clear that the seventh and sixth centuries BC were among the most important ever in the history of religion and ideas throughout the world. Before that, there had been numerous concepts of deities and even, on occasion, a belief in a one God, though quite different from Yahweh and the way He evolved. Of course, war and conquest was a consistent ingredient in forcing the belief of a God, even as separate ideas of a deity developed.

As we have seen, in the eighth and seventh centuries BC, the Hebrew Kingdoms had been conquered first by Assyria and then by Babylon. The Hebrews were beginning to be called Jews, though Hebrews were an amalgamation of ethnic tribes, and large numbers of Jews were deported to Mesopotamia (Iraq). Among these Jewish exiles, the central books of the Old Testament were written in approximately their present form, and Judaism emerged as a monotheistic religion. It is clear that Mesopotamian mythology and probably the Iranian prophet Zoroaster's espousal of monotheism and cosmic dualism had an influence in the writing of the Old Testament by the exiles.

But in the same period, there were important religious developments in other parts of the world. In India, the composition of the philosophical Upanishads was a major step in the development of classical Hinduism, while the ritualistic nature of Hinduism was challenged by the religious ascetic Mahavira, founder of the Jain religion, and Siddhartha Gautama, the founder of Buddhism.

In China, the same period saw the life of the sage Confucius, who emphasized respect for legitimate authority, social order, the family, ancestors, tradition, and education, all of which became seeded in Chinese thought. Lao-Tzu, the mythical founder of Taoism, may also have lived during this period. Further, the sixth century BC saw the beginning of the Greek scientific tradition in the works of the mathematicians Thales of Miletus and Pythagoras, a seminal path to higher thought beyond myth. Even in the scientific beginning, however, people did not lose their love of myth, as the foundation of the drama Festival in honor of the God Dionysus at Athens became an important moment in the development of theater. Greek culture spread widely around the Mediterranean and the Black Sea through colonies founded by the growing Greek city-states, but without as much intensity as in the Levant. With new paradigm, Athens introduced a form of democracy and 509 BC and gave birth to one of history's most potent political ideas countering traditional kingdoms and tribal thought.

Ultimately, of course, the multitude of religions throughout the world would begin to narrow and to a few leaders, as this process would evolve over centuries. The Americas would take a different and later path in religion beginnings with the Toltecs and Mayans, somewhere around the first century BC and ultimately fall to Christianity by war and conquest.

As I approached retirement in the first decade of a new century, I looked back over a lifetime of interest in the evolution of religion and the search for answers to what had seemed like a simple question. Although wide gaps of time followed the short periods of study, I have followed this quest with a characteristic investigative approach which I use in my profession, that of backward evaluation. Instead of beginning chronologically with Hebrew history, I began with the more recent religion of Islam and worked backward. While I am not a theologian, historian, or archaeologist, I did rely heavily on those independent disciplines, and I felt that I had at least found a preponderance of evidence that the man made the God, not the other way around, regardless of the perpetual forcing by religious leaders for their purposes.

Clearly, by a preponderance of evidence, God is the creation of humans in order to serve sundry purposes. Such a Man does not exist.

But what about Jesus? If we assume that Jesus actually said all that the Apostolic Gospels attribute to Him, which is a leaky assumption, then we know Jesus referred to God as His father in heaven. Unfortunately, Jesus was operating from a limited base of information. He could not have known of the human evolution, geopolitical shifts and archeological evidence that came before Him for 20,000 years, or that other major world religions were evolving on earth at the same time. He was speaking on the basis of His beliefs. What He knew was what the Torah, as it came out of Babylon, told Him. That is the history that was verbally taught in the temple. Therein laid the assumption, the "belief," i.e. reliance on facts yet to be proved, that there existed a God in heaven.

As beautiful as some of the teachings of Jesus are, they in no way support that He was the son of God, because "God" was a mental creation. As for Mark and other tellers of mystical ascendancy and transference, it is pretty clear that these were embellishments to make the new religion more popular and more converts a century after Jesus' death.

PART III

SCIENCE AND ATHEISM

Chapter 22

Myth and the Development of the Brain

EARLY IN MY life, about college time, my mind would periodically surface the thought: "this is all just myth – – this religion thing…"

Then I would think: "well, some of it has to be true. Why else would religion be here; why else would so many people follow it?"

I would wonder what part of religion was made up, what part false. Admittedly, there must be other explanations for those tales of rising from the dead, curing blindness and so on. When I would initiate discussion about my doubt with my fellow Baylor classmates, they would shun and back away subtly. I would counter:

"I'm not saying there isn't a God, or Jesus isn't my Savior, but there are things here I don't understand."

I asked:

"What is a myth anyway?"

For a long time, I confused myth with superstition. I wasn't sure whether God fitted into either category. I often heard through my life that God was there because I could feel it inside. I could feel that He was there. I could talk to Him. And it was right, I did feel a presence within me, and like so many others, there were times that I could do something or an event would occur that I was sure was not by my hand alone, something beyond me, something that could only have happened through an intervening hand. It felt that way, and I knew that others felt the same thing.

How many times have I watched an athlete point to the sky in gratitude to God for the successful athletic act or play he/she has just completed? How many times have I seen people shocked by grief, fear or joy sink to their knees in supplication of prayer for strength, forgiveness or gratitude in response to something that has just happened? They felt what I felt. There had to be something there.

But in time I came to realize that while sentience has its place and is the function of a neurological system, it is not necessarily based on fact, but on feeling, which can quickly lend itself to superstition. I came to understand that superstition, myth, and "old wives' tales" can be overcome and clarified with the scientific method, statistical analysis, or critical thinking for truth and greater exactness. However, I also observed that unless you are a scientist or philosopher you are too busy with daily life to utilize the tools of these disciplines, and it's easier just to feel or guess. It could be possible in our busy daily lives to use the principles of critical thinking; however, most people don't know how to think critically, even many professional people, strange as that may be. But then, people are born in religious myth and raised in worldly illusion. It's not difficult to see why they lack reason.

In time, I learned to distinguish between myth and superstition. Neither was factually based, but they had a different purpose. I made lists to distinguish between them:

Superstition:

Prayer (praying to ask for something; praying to get what I want; praying to exceed, or to win, or to protect.)

Higher power

Believing in someone or something that can give me what I want.

Believing in a supernatural power that can make me perform beyond my capabilities.

Believing in a guardian angel.

Having a lucky icon.

Believing in an icon to heal or bless.

Personification of sun, moon or solstice.

Believing in luck at cards, because there is a force leading you.

Believing in luck as a specialty; you believe that some power makes you luckier than others.

Believing in coincidence for coincidence sake, in other words, magical thinking.

Myth:

A non-factual story or explanation of:

The Beginning

Creation

Birth

Death

Life after death

End of times

End of the world

Personification of sun, moon or solstice, as an answer.

All religion is a myth and has a historical mythical basis. It seems to me that the mythical story has to come first and then superstition can follow, or not.

The great historian and myth investigator, Joseph Campbell, saw God as a thought: "God is a metaphor for a mystery that absolutely transcends all human categories of thought, even the categories of being and non-being. Those are categories of thought. I mean it's as simple as that. So it depends on how much you want to think about it. Whether it's doing you any good. Whether it is putting you in touch with the mystery that's the ground of your own being. If it isn't, well, it's a lie. So half the people in the world are religious people who think that their metaphors are facts. Those are what we call theists. The other half are people who know that the metaphors are not facts…"[54]

Heinrich Zimmer, Indologist and historian, taught Campbell that "myth (rather than a guru or spiritual guide) could serve in the role of a personal mentor, in that its stories provide a psychological roadmap for the finding of oneself in the labyrinth of the complex modern world."[55]

Zimmer relied more on the meanings of mythological tales (their symbols, metaphors, imagery, etc.) as a source for psychological realization than upon psychoanalysis itself. Campbell later borrowed from the interpretative techniques of Jung and then reshaped them in a fashion that followed Zimmer's beliefs – interpreting directly from world mythology. This is an important distinction because as it serves to explain why Campbell did not directly follow Jung's footsteps in applied psychology.

Campbell spent 12 years studying the myths and rituals of both the East and the West. While there was a commonality in both critical timing and evolution of the world's myths and often similarities in rituals, prayers, temples, gods, sages, definitions, and cosmologies, Campbell found in the Indian Upanishads, the Chinese Tao Te Ching, the Vedic sage, or the Buddhist text an open introspection. But in the breadth of Western mythological thought and imagery, whether in Europe or the Levant, he found a Creator personified from the outside. In the Western sense, a historical myth was God and Man standing against each other, with God in judgment and Man giving up to God, as exemplified through the type of piety recognized in Zoroastrianism, Judaism, Christianity, and Islam.

Joseph Campbell had a theory that all myths and epics are linked in the human psyche, and they are cultural manifestations of the universal need to explain social, cosmological, and spiritual realities. In interviewing and referring to Campbell about his vast work on myth, Bill Moyers said:

"He imagined that this grand and cacophonous chorus began when our primal ancestors told stories to themselves about the animals that they killed for food and about the supernatural world to which the animals seemed to go when they died. 'Out there somewhere,' beyond the visible plain of existence, was the 'animal master,' who held over human beings the power of life and death…"[56]

Karen Armstrong in her Short History of Myth states: "Finally, all mythology speaks of another plane that exists alongside our own world, and that in some sense supports it. Belief in this invisible but more powerful reality, sometimes called the world of the gods, is a basic theme of mythology. It has been called the 'perennial philosophy' because it informed the mythology, ritual and social organisation of all societies before the advent of our scientific modernity…"[57]

Myths have been around since early man. There is no exact way of knowing when the human brain evolved to rudimentary storytelling. One can easily envision an early hunter ancestor, who without the advent of spoken language, sits down at the evening fire and tries to tell a family member by hand gesture and symbol, what he had seen that day, an animal or a bird that might be taken for food and where it might be tomorrow.

We are sure from evolutionary principle, that such a condition existed for thousands of years, 100,000 years more or less, and while archaic, symbolic and straightforward it was, nevertheless it was functional at the beginning of storytelling. Survival needs were basic – – food, water, and warmth. Reproduction was basic and as with other animals revolved around the hormonal drive. Whatever caused the "Big Bang," eons later, whether protein diet or learning to transport water in order to wander far farther, there had to be a brain change, a brain expansion.

The Middle Stone Age began around 250,000 years ago and ended 50 – 25,000 years ago. Apparently, there were two sources of early humans according to archaeological evidence. While Neanderthals and Homo sapiens were distinguished from one another by various visible anatomical features, archaeologically they were very similar. The Middle Stone Age hominid of Africa, Homo sapiens and their contemporary Middle Paleolithic Neanderthal of Europe had artifact assemblages that indicate important similarities as to where they were in brain development and usage:

* Little variation in stone tool types, with a predominance of flake tools that are difficult to sort into discrete categories.

* Over long periods of time and wide geographical distances there was general similarity in toolkits.

* A virtual lack of tools fashioned out of bone, antler or ivory.
* Burials lacked grave goods and signs of ritual or ceremony.
* Hunting was usually limited to less dangerous species and evidence of fishing is absent
* population densities were apparently low.
* No evidence of living structures exist and fireplaces are rudimentary.
* Evidence for art or decoration is also lacking.[58]

However, about 40 – 50,000 years ago the picture changed. Modern humans began to appear out of what was before. This change was abrupt and dramatic as it pertains to subsistence patterns and symbolic expression. The cultural adaptation was not only quantitative, but there was a significant departure from all earlier human behavior. It was a "creative explosion" exhibiting "technological ingenuity, social formations, and ideological complexity of historic hunter-gatherers."

There was significant innovation:

* A remarkable diversity in stone tool types.
* Tool types showed substantial changes over time and space.
* Artifacts were regularly fashioned out of bone, antler, and ivory, in addition to stone.
* Burials were accompanied by ritual or ceremony and contained a rich diversity of grave goods.
* Living structures and well-designed fireplaces were constructed.

* Hunting of dangerous animal species and fishing occurred and there were higher population densities.

* Abundant and elaborate art as well as items of personal adornment were widespread.

* Raw materials such as flint and shells were traded over some distances.[59]

Homo sapiens became modern in appearance and behavior. Precisely how this occurred is not well understood, but apparently it was restricted to Homo sapiens and did not happen with the Neanderthals, as they became extinct.

As one studies the history of myth, its beginnings and evolvement, the myth is always a story with an underlying explanation about a phenomenon that was not understood – – birth, death, rising sun, the waxing moon – – and out of those stories came the natural human correlative thought that some human-like being must be responsible and in control. The stories became varied and creative and evolved into religions.

While the myths were stories that took different paths with different cultures but always addressing those subjects relevant to the human mind, they were followed by superstition. The basis of superstition was to have faith in some aspect of the mythical story, most often relying on the supernatural. It seemed that the dynamic was that the mind would believe in the story, and then start having faith in the superstition, so the two must be connected by a power greater than both.

Today, we look back and laugh at the basic explanations of the stories, or wonder how a certain culture came up with such bizarre tales of battles and sex between gods, or observed with horror the sacrificial rituals used to placate an angry God. Then, on Sunday, we drive to a church, synagogue, mosque, or temple to replicate a milder form of what existed before.

Chapter 23

The New Atheists

WITH THE ADVENT of my retirement, I began to read books by outspoken atheists. I knew that religion wasn't going anywhere. People needed relief from their fear of daily events and fear of human death not to mention having a mystical or superstitious place to go for their want list, sometimes called "prayer." I already knew this, and I knew that my study of Abrahamic religions had established that picture of religion for me.

My knowledge of atheism was no knowledge. I grew up and lived in Texas where there was a hated atheist, Madelyn Murray O'Hare, who mysteriously disappeared or died. One thing I knew for sure from the way the media treated her and the preachers harangued her was that if you wanted to be isolated in your Texas community while at the same time killing your business, just say that you were an atheist. So, that was enough for me. I didn't question or speak out.

So, I admired writers that stood up and started questioning. There was a rush of publishing between 2004 and 2007, and authors such as Richard Dawkins, Daniel Dennett, Sam Harris, Christopher Hitchens, and Victor J. Stenger broke new ground with intelligent, direct questions. Some of this, perhaps a good deal of it, I had already discovered on my own, but the notes from my studies were not as concise or as clear in writing as what these authors wrote.

What initially rang out to me from these authors was the brave stance that "religion should not simply be tolerated but should be countered, criticized, and exposed by rational argument wherever its influences arise."[60] It was something that had been in the back of my mind for some time. I had even dipped my toe in the water of countering blind faith in one-on-one conversations in my hometown of Midland, Texas. I quickly found that blind faith controlled the population of my community from the highly educated to the intellectual slaves of the labor force. It became clear that to try to expose that blind faith would be a choice of social and professional martyrdom. This realization made me admire more those new atheists, those that had come out, who were brave enough and intellectually strong enough to counter popular thinking, but I also realized that it was one thing to write from a distance and quite another to speak up in the face of the community submerged in religious dogma.

I was impressed that the New Atheists wrote mainly from a scientific perspective. It was in this period, the 1990s and the early 2000s that physics made great strides as to how the universe, indeed the universes, was formed, and theories in astrophysics made progress in viewing other planets and galaxies. The scientific revelations and clarity were beginning to seep out into the public mass. To me, the difference between science and the mythology of religion, any religion, was clear. Science and particularly physics was based upon mathematical logic to reach what a lawyer would call a preponderance of evidence. Religion used none of this but called upon human imagination for the creation of supernatural stories without evidence of logical fact and then mandated blind faith for a following.

Victor Stenger proposed that the personal Abrahamic God could be looked at as a scientific hypothesis that can be tested by standard methods of science, but frankly when you do that God fails the tests. Dawkins argued somewhat the same thing in pointing out that a God created the physical universe is like any other hypothesis. It can be tested, verified or falsified. Both Dawkins and Stenger concluded that the hypothesis fails such tests. They argue that "naturalism is sufficient to explain everything we observe in the universe, from the most distant galaxies to the origin of life, species, and even the inner workings of the brain and consciousness"[61], as we are now seeing with great strides in brain mapping. "Nowhere, they argue, is it necessary to introduce God or the supernatural to understand reality while upholding the possibility of one."[62]

Victor Stenger argued that God, having omniscient, omnibenevolent and omnipotent attributes, which he termed a "3O God," cannot logically exist. Rebecca Newberger Goldstein in her book 36 Arguments For The Existence of God goes a step further and sets forth in syllogistic fashion the 36 most popular arguments for the existence of God and then shows where each argument fails for one or more faulty premise, often, one fallacy built upon another. Michael Martin and Ricki Monnier proffer a series of logical disproofs of a God in their The Impossibility of God, the logical conclusion being that God cannot exist.

Stephen Hawking, the astrophysicist, takes on the whole concept of creation with astrophysical proof that God is not needed in order to create. In his The Grand Design written with physicist Leonard Mlodinow, he makes an argument that invoking God is not necessary to explain the origins of the universe and that the Big Bang is a consequence of physics alone. The book examines the history of scientific knowledge about the universe and explains 11 dimensions of what is called "M – theory," which is supported by a majority of physicists.

To discount or ignore science in the search for God or end-of-life answers makes no sense. To refuse to use the proven elements of logic and ask questions about God, or to refuse to ask questions at all, takes one back to the dark ages of suppression and ignorance. Where I live, and from what I can see as the predominant paradigm in America, there is a widespread problem concerning the conscious inquiry. I have long thought that it might relate to our overall educational system, and the failure to teach and learn higher math. Mathematics and physics can logically answer so many questions, as opposed to making up unfounded mythical stories for explanations about the natural world. It is not the purpose of physics to disprove

God. In fact, the scientific process never purports absolutism but distinguishes the greater probability. In short, as Hawking pointed out, the consideration of whether there is a God is not a necessary element in understanding creation.

Today, a major quest in search of a scientific answer has made a breakthrough, and it is exciting to see it. There's been for some time what is termed the Standard Model, a reigning theory of elementary particles and the forces with which they influence each other. Though mathematically these particles could be identified, what gave them their mass was not found. Logically, there had to be a particle that connected the particles. The clue was there, but where was it? The known particles exerted forces on each other. That could be seen through the symmetry between the forces. For example, the electromagnetic force, as well as the weak nuclear force, provides the first step in a chain of reactions that gives the sun its energy.

As Professor Steven Weinberg (Nobel Prize recipient in physics) of the University of Texas points out "you could interchange the photon, the particle of light that carries the electromagnetic force, with some combination of the W and Z particles that carry the weak nuclear force, and the equations would be unchanged. If nothing intervened to break this symmetry, the W and Z, like the photon, would have no mass. In fact, all other elementary particles would also be massless."[63] In layman's terms, there would be no "us"; there had to be an identifiable connecting particle.

Since the mid-60s, physicists have been looking for it, but they didn't have the necessary physical facility to make this exploration of the outer front tier of nature. It requires a massive governmental financial investment of building what is called a "supercollider." The federal government in Texas started constructing such a facility at one point, but local resistance and politics caused its abandonment. Fortunately, the Swiss picked up from there and built the supercollider in Switzerland and established the CERN laboratory in Geneva.

Without going into how the supercollider works by making protons collide by accelerating energy to over 3000 times larger than the energy contained in their own masses while they go many times around a 27-kilometer circular trail, the exciting news is that the particle, called "Higgs Boson," has now been identified. We know through science why we are here. The identifier for mass has been discovered.

Does this disprove God? No, because that is not its purpose, but if you take together "M – theory" in astrophysics and the Higgs Boson in particle physics, you know how the universe was created and how mass was created to give us and our environs existence. A religious fundamentalist would say "and yes, all of this was done by God's process," but there is absolutely no evidence or logic to back that up. The scientific fundamentals are there without the need for the existence of a God, and these fundamentals are not built upon made up stories handed down through tribal myth. These fundamentals are self-standing in logical truth.

Chapter 24

The Scientific Inquiry and the Preponderance of Evidence

I HAVE OBSERVED that the elements of critical thinking go beyond intuition for the long haul. Surely, the years that I spent investigating and presenting both civil and criminal cases proved that premise to me. Perhaps for me, the seed of logical resolution began with the use of the Socratic Method for teaching in law school, to get beyond memorization and regurgitation.

Education and experience have taught us that every issue should begin with a question, one question. It is all right to have many of them, but clarity can only be acquired by taking them one at a time in identifying the causal relationship of each to follow. Ambiguity, vagueness and arguments and propositions of jumping from a well-founded conclusion to a completely different syllogism as evidence of proof are techniques of motivated thinking, not logic. Although it often sounds convincing, if the premise does not support the conclusion, it is simply a faulty equation.

Within such a framework, the critical and connecting element is evidence, and it has to be tested. Obviously, the best method for testing evidence is the use of scientific method. The scientific method is a body of techniques for investigating what purports to be evidence. It is a method of inquiry based on empirical and measurable possible evidence. If the "evidence" does not lend itself to data compilation, observation, and experimentation, it cannot be subjected to the scientific method. A purely scientific investigation lets reality speak for itself while making no conclusion other than when a theory's predictions are confirmed and challenging a theory when its predictions proved false.

In presenting cases to a judge, judicial panel, or a jury, there would be delightful occasions in my career when an element of a case could be clarified by theory substantiated by the scientific method. More often, however, the process for determination of the existence of a factual basis would have to be evaluated in the light of logic and critical thinking. For example, in a car, truck, or train wrecks distances can be determined by mathematical coefficient formulas relating to the surface upon which the vehicle was traveling. Whether the driver/operator was maintaining a proper lookout, however, must be evaluated in light of circumstantial evidence.

Frequently, there are facts alleged that seem true by intuition but can't be substantiated. This is usually where juries get into trouble by guessing. In a civil case, the proponent of a fact must prove that fact by a "preponderance of the evidence" so that the fact can be accepted. Recognizing that every fact cannot be subjected to the rigorous testing of the scientific method, this "preponderance" balancing is used by the courts. It means that by looking at all parts of the evidence with critical reasoning, a more convincing evidence is that which is accurate within a range, more likely to be than not be; or, the reverse, more likely not to be than be.

As an example, one knowledgeable witness may provide a preponderance of the evidence, while a dozen witnesses with hazy testimony does not.

Black's Law Dictionary, 7th ed., defines "preponderance of the evidence," as follows:

"the greater weight of the evidence; superior evidentiary weight that, though not sufficient to free the mind wholly from all reasonable doubt, is still sufficient to incline a fair and impartial mind to one side of the issue rather than the other."[64]

The term is also used alternatively as the preponderance of proof or the balance of probability.

Connected to the act of weighing evidence is the nature of evidence, itself. Black's defines evidence as:

"something (including testimony, documents, and tangible objects) that tends to prove or disprove the existence of an alleged fact."[65]

To weigh evidence, or submitted facts for consideration, it follows that the facts being weighed must be valid, correct, to conclude the truth. If the facts are fabricated and with no logical foundation, then false conclusions will naturally be the preponderance. In a court of law, that's where cross-examination comes in – – to test the validity of the fact submitted.

One can quickly see in asking the questions, "is there a God; or, is there a heaven; or, did Jesus rise from the earth to heaven and then reappear on earth; or, did the Angel Gabriel come to Muhammad in the cave and through dreams speak the words of the Qur'an to him," that there are going to be many categories of evidence that must be tested and weighed:

* Character evidence is evidence regarding someone's personality traits; evidence of a person's moral standing in a community, based on reputation or opinion. My question is how do we test the character of the writers of the Gospels when we don't even know who wrote them. You might create your own character evidence question about Muhammad.

* Circumstantial evidence. This is evidence that relates to a physical act without actually seeing its occurrence. You wake up in the morning and there is snow on the ground. Circumstantially, it snowed last night. Circumstantial evidence is not testimonial evidence. As a matter of fact, the only circumstantial evidence relating to the Bible or Qur'an is either epigraphy or archaeological discoveries. Many, if not most, counter the stories of the Abrahamic religions.

* Corroborating evidence is evidence that may differ from but strengthen or confirm other evidence. Inconsistency is not, by nature, corroborative. As we have seen, the gospel tales of Jesus are more inconsistent than anything else, not to mention the documented forgeries and insertions made by later writers.

* Fabricated evidence is false or deceitful evidence which is created, usually after the relevant event. Throughout the history of the Abrahamic religions and particularly Christianity and Islam, scholars have wrestled mightily with deciphering what is and is not fabricated.

* Forensic evidence in the legal sense is evidence that has been tested, especially evidence arrived at by scientific means, such as ballistic or medical evidence. From a scientific basis, physics for example, there is no way to test the myths of the Abrahamic religions. You cannot produce forensic evidence for something that does not exist. The forensic evidence that Abrahamic religions do have is in support or refutation, as the case may be, of their history from archaeologic excavations.

* Relevant evidence is evidence tending to prove or disprove a matter by being both probative and material. In listening to an evangelist preach, or an imam speak, as I have many times, one observes the constant habit of mixing premises so that they are not common, or using an unfounded conclusion as one premise to reach yet another unfounded

conclusion. Thus, the proffered evidence is mixed with irrelevance. Such motivated speaking often follows:

*   rhetorical tautology – "a series of statements that comprise an argument, whereby the statements are constructed in such a way that the truth of the proposition is guaranteed, or that the truth of the proposition cannot be disputed, by defining a dissimilar or synonymous term in terms of another self-referentially."[66]

*   Circular reasoning – the premises stated as the conclusion in an argument, instead of deriving the conclusion from the premise with arguments.

These are nothing more than well-practiced speaking tricks to convince an audience. Nevertheless, we allow ourselves to be affected every day by these techniques in statements and misleading statements, misdirected information, disinformation and motivated thinking and speaking.

In a quest for validation of religion's answers to the end-of-life questions, I think it is important to use the mental tools that modern humans have developed – – the scientific method where possible, critical thinking principles at all levels, and at the very least, the test of the preponderance of evidence for the likelihood of validity. Our brain evolution, thankfully, has brought us these tools, and we must use them.

In the chapters covering each of the Abrahamic religions, I have sought consistency in what was being portrayed, because inconsistency portends the possibility of fabrication. By preponderance, if a presentation or an allegation is inconsistent, it isn't a fact. When it came to theory, I have tried to weigh in on the logic of the proposition and look for verifiable evidence. This becomes most difficult when dealing with mythical stories coming down through verbal tribal history of many centuries of how things were created or who saw what, and when, as later reported by those who had been told.

I have wrestled with the issue of hearsay. Returning to Black's for a definition, hearsay is:

"traditionally, testimony that is given by a witness who relates not what he or she knows personally, but what others have said, and that is therefore dependent on the credibility of someone other than the witness."[67]

Biblical or Islamic scholars deal with hearsay every day because direct testimony has never been found. Jesus did not use scribes, Muhammad could neither read nor write, and Hebrew history predates script.

In every instance, scholars must rely on double hearsay, and indeed, many layers of it amounting to much more than a double. Nevertheless, double hearsay is defined by Black's, as:

"a hearsay statement that contains further hearsay statements within it."[68]

This, of course, applies to both oral and documentary testimony, as the case may be.

In a court of American or English law, the fundamental hearsay rule is that no assertion offered as testimony can be received (oral or document), unless it has been open to testing by cross-examination or scientific process.

In the following chapter, all of these elements must be weighed, as I enter what I called my "scientific Inquiry Period." Fortunately for me, in the 90s and the first decade of 2000s scientists wrote many books for laymen, in just about every discipline from astrophysics to evolutionary psychology. Through much of this period, a writer, a reviewer, by the name of Dennis Luttrell took it upon himself to review every book published on Amazon on evolution. It was a monumental undertaking by a critical thinking individual that provides great insight. The name of his book is Understanding Evolution and Ourselves.

Chapter 25

Evolution v. Intelligent Design

I GREW UP in West Texas in the 50s where we didn't learn about the science of evolution. The curriculum was silent on the subject. We students didn't have to ask a question or even think to ask, of how we got here, in this place, at this school. We knew – – God placed us here – – the preacher said so.

In 1959, I graduated from high school and went to Baylor University for my college education. In the second semester, I took geology 101. It seemed the thing to do since I came from oil country and a second generation oil family. In one of the classes, a student asked the professor if his presentation of paleontology was evolution. He cautiously responded that "we are told that 'evolution' is God's way of doing things." At the time, I had never heard of the term but did make a cursory review of Darwin and his theory at the library. His theory seemed fine to me and didn't rattle my faith one way or the other at the time, as my period of research had not yet commenced.

With the advance of the last 20 years of the twentieth century, a resurgence of Christian fundamentalism and proponents of creationism erupted, and a battle for control of school boards and textbooks settled in throughout Texas from local levels to state headquarters. While this movement was sourced by both Christian fundamentalists and Catholics in Texas, it didn't seem to affect the major research university, the University of Texas, or established academic universities like Rice University, but it did permeate lesser colleges and schools preparing teachers for the educational system. In time, intelligent design (ID) was being given at least lip service in junior high, high school and junior college science classes, often with an emphasis on its validity. As for control of textbooks and what they say, the fundamentalists eventually won.

By the time of this roiling and prolonged battle, I had completed my humble, personal, comparative study of the Abrahamic religions and quickly understood that ID was based on blind supernatural faith, without application of scientific, critical thinking. I could see how you can teach it in a comparative religion class, or at least the principle of ID, but for the life of me, I could not see what it was doing in science classes. Beyond that, I began to wonder about the constitutional basis of separation of church and state, i.e., establishing a religion through a governmental school system, when I thought the founding fathers had established a secular government to protect freedom of religious belief or nonbelief for all.

I could see that this movement was creating layers of problematical issues that needed to be addressed, but it was difficult to take time to inquire and debate, as the movement was so well financed and organized. It was forcing its way into government like a cataclysmic mudslide. In time, I discovered that the core of the attack was in the framework of biology. Literalists of the Christian Bible could not accept the theory of evolution. It threatened their belief that God created everything just the way Genesis said it did, and it turned out, that a majority of Texans were literalists. So, the spear point of the attack was in the field of biology and the thrust of change must be at the junior high, high school, junior college, and hopefully college level. If young minds could turn away from evolutionary teaching, what followed in colleges would not make that much difference, because most students wouldn't be taking college biology, anyway.

It wouldn't be until 20 years later that physicists would write in layman's terms about discoveries in the universe that would confound notions of intelligent design based upon mathematical logic and scientific evaluation through observation. This never seemed to concern the ID movement very much, however, because again most students will never tap their toe into physics, astro or otherwise.

The battleground was evolution, and the greater mass of Christian religion wanted no part of evolutionary theory. So, naturally, I had to ask the question, what was the theory of evolution? Had the theory developed further in the 150 years since the publication of the Origins of Species? If so, how and to what extent?

A person who is just beginning to look at evolutionary theory should take time for both simplicity and humor. They can do that by reading books by Richard Miller and enjoying with delight his tongue-in-cheek numerous and dramatic visual portrayals of evolution from A to Z. Richard Miller is an Associate in Anthropology at the American Museum of Natural History and a Fellow of the Linnean Society of London. It is nice to begin a study with presentations that are fun and do away with predetermined contentiousness.

You learned that Darwin, himself, insisted that uncertainty is part of science. If there were no uncertainty, there would be no need for science. In an Oxford meeting in 1860, Thomas Huxley asked his listeners to suppose they were lost in the countryside on a dark night, with no clue to the road. If someone came along offering a flickering lantern "...should I refuse it because it shed imperfect light? I think not – I think not."[69]

Evolution, like any science, is a continual quest of posing the question and then through logical enterprise seeking the answer. It is not based on a tribal story or a premise that it is the truth because someone once said it was true. Like all science, it is under continuous examination from multiple fields of science. Through a century and a half of study, Darwinism, natural selection, "survival of the fittest" (that, I notice even the fundamentalists like), and other key concepts kept evolving through examination and testing. Even Darwin, in those early stages, tinkered with his theory from one edition of Origin of Species to the next, and no one has since left it alone. History has seen it evolve into Neo-Darwinism and later the Modern Synthesis, or Synthetic Theory of Evolution, and in the 1970s brought a view of a significant and wide-ranging shift in emphasis regarding rates and pattern of change known as the theory of Punctuated Equilibrium (or "Pink Eek"). Indeed, the history of science is as fascinating as the science, itself, but by scientific nature, it is never static. Enlightenment is not static. Repression is.

Today, numerous other scientific disciplines such as archaeology joined and supported evolutionary theory, and now with the advent of DNA testing for further substantiation of evolutionary hypotheses. From DNA sequences to stone artifacts, from skeletal morphology to agent artifacts to carbon-13 measurements in bones, we know that Homo habilis emerged in Africa about 2.5 million years ago and that Homo ergaster was the first hominid to migrate out of Africa approximately 1.5 million years ago. We know about the "second great expansion of the human brain" 150,000 years ago and another "out-of-Africa" migration.

But for me in the quest for answers to my early questions, the evolution and development of the human mind to entertain the supernatural and the contemplation of immortality, as seen through what several scientific disciplines call the mind's "Big Bang" between 90,000 and 50,000 years ago is of a powerful interest. It didn't just happen in the Pleistocene; it evolved, albeit with some acceleration over more recent millenniums as the brain group. These are scientific, proven facts, not myths, though out of this evolving brain grew creative myths, tribal stories, even poetry, various ideas, accessing and receiving information mentally and then memorizing and reciting.

Artifact history makes it evident that once symbolic language develops, people can evolve slowly mentally. Could it be that as the symbolic language evolved, the process hard-wired our brains to rely on deep-seeded meanings of symbols, even as we do today? Nevertheless, at this early beginning, humans started demonstrating stories of events by symbols that stood for actual objects they had seen or thought they had seen, or the use of symbols for events that had happened. They could even tell stories. Simplistic as the stories may have been, the early human's innovation developed and evolved slowly, as evidenced by the differences between the Late Stone Age culture and the Middle Stone Age culture, between the Upper Paleolithic and the Mousterian. How fascinating it is to see how one person might craft a net for catching birds or fish, while others would develop a strategy for stampeding wildebeests over a cliff. Equally interesting is to observe the lapse of time between one idea to another. Of particular evolvement was when the human arm learned to throw a spear. An early problem, however, was that travel to hunt or migrate was limited without water. In time, they discovered that scans or watertight baskets could hold water and extend their maneuvering, and on and on and the progression and evolvement went.

As fascinating as the development of the hominid brain is, equally amazing are the findings of evolutionary microbiology and how mutation after mutation has affected the cell, the DNA, the genes in all living things. The data through 150 years of study and enhanced by the advance of technology is overwhelming. Oddly, because of the scientific mass, I have heard the fundamentalist argument that it is just too complicated to be true. However, I have found that you can segregate any part of the scientific evidence, at will, and find its truth.

So, it is well-settled, that while humans became anatomically human as early as perhaps 200,000 years ago, which in geologic time is nothing, humans became more behavioral oriented about 50,000 years ago. Both archaeologic and supporting disciplines establish the "Great Leap Forward" evolving about that time as symbolic and syntactic language was acquired and developed. This was also the time when humans made that "Out Of Africa" Exodus following through the Levant, East across the Red Sea at the Gate of Grief and began to colonize the world.

As I read books on evolution and even delved into a few scientific treatises, I became increasingly disturbed with attempts in the religious/political arena to stifle proven facts about evolution and application of its principles in biology, microbiology, genetic code sequencing, biochemistry, anthropology, ethnology, sociology, human history, and anthropology. These scientific categories were not just sympathetic magic. Even a layman such as I could see the critical analysis supporting many streams of evidence.

I was sad because of the loss of Texas in intelligent education, but I was somewhat accustomed to it because of other venues. Then, the "Second Scopes Trial" came into being. It occurred in Pennsylvania and once again history repeated itself, as from the first such trial, The State of Tennessee v. John Thomas Scopes (1925), as the famous defense attorney, Clarence Darrow, destroyed the prejudicial oratory of William Jennings Bryan on the issue of the evolutionary process.

The frightening thing about the Pennsylvania case wasn't so much the ignorance of the members of the Dover School Board; you see that in a lot of conservative fundamentalist Christian and Islamic areas. It was the underhanded design used through a Machiavellian approach to mandate ignorance and prejudice in the community. It is all laid out in the easily accessible transcript and Memorandum Opinion of the judge in the case of Kitzmiller v. The Dover Area School District, dated December 20, 2005, in the United States District Court for the Middle District of Pennsylvania. The judge expressed his intellectual feeling of contempt on page 137 of his memorandum decision when he stated:

"It is ironic that several of these individuals, who so staunchly and proudly touted their religious convictions in public, would time and again lie to cover their tracks and disguise the real purpose behind ID Policy."[70]

Sadly, Texas secondary education and many junior colleges and lesser four-year colleges have been permeated with such tactics and even teachers using such tactics for over a decade now. This, of course, creates a nation-wide cooperative groundswell for the federal level to enforce ID teaching as a science. The movement is not hidden, although its tactics are. Any citizen in Texas can easily encounter it simply by going to a school board meeting or a book selection committee in a state school. The situation hampering the teaching of the scientific method has turned for the worse, and there is little successful intervention. Unsatisfied with controlling the populace through evangelism, Christian literalists have controlled the state government for some 30 years in Texas, and now impose religious faith as part of education.

The judge in the Dover (Pennsylvania) case concluded his decision, after receiving treatises from both sides, in what came to be called "The Scopes II Trial," as follows:

"To conclude and reiterate, we express no opinion on the ultimate veracity of ID as a supernatural explanation. However, we commend to the attention of those who are inclined to superficially consider ID to be a true 'scientific' alternative to evolution without a true understanding of the concept the foregoing detailed analysis. It is our view that a reasonable, objective observer would, after reviewing both the voluminous record in this case, and our narrative, reach the inescapable conclusion that ID is an interesting theological argument, but that it is not science."[71]

My consternation, as I had come to live comfortably in my "Period of Disbelief," was that school boards, vis-à-vis government intervention and control of books, teachers and teaching would now raise a barricade against logical questioning. Had that happened to me, I could never have initiated or pursued my quest to find truth in religion or end-of-life answers. The presumption of truth and a religious answer would have been predetermined for me. Clearly, this was the ultimate goal that the religious right had in mind for the nation.

I decided to revisit history and just refresh myself on the First Amendment and the background leading up to it at the Constitutional Convention. My view had been that the history was clear, or so I thought. In listening to some of the ID arguments, however, issues were jumping around a bit, from one issue to another without completing any, and creating a haze. Since government and religion have now come together in America, I find it essential to delve into the meaning of the First Amendment and so-called separation of church and state.

PART IV

THE FIRST AMENDMENT AND SEPARATION OF CHURCH AND STATE

Chapter 26

Some History of the First Amendment

[NOTE: Traditional publishing would never approve of a book moving from a comparative study of Abrahamic religions to a dissertation of religious non-freedom in America. Of course, being a non-traditionalist, the advent of self-publishing gives me this opportunity. In my opinion, the sequence is both relevant and important.]

FOR MOST OF my life, the reading of American history has been a hobby. I dare say that it is a hobby of most lawyers, as someone in education had planted the seed in them when they were very young at just how admirable the structure of this democratic government is and how it came to be.

I have observed that both media and authors of currently popular books portray the government of today as more polarized than ever, and it only gets worse when considering the issue of "separation of church and state" under the First Amendment to the Constitution of the United States. "More polarized than ever" is a reach and comparison is probably counter-productive to understanding. To look at the problem, and the antics of the combating sides, it helps to look at the words of the amendment, itself, though this is truly not a starting point. It is perhaps more of a conclusion:

"Congress shall make no law respecting an establishment of religion, or prohibiting the free exercise thereof..."[72]

This was a seminal point in history and political enlightenment upon being enacted. It came from a dual motivation that most of the delegates developed from reaction to their European government-controlled religious heritages and the abuses they experienced to cherishing their freedom while at the same time protecting their faith. It took at least a decade of debate, wrangling, prejudicial oratory, experimenting and uniting in a war effort and a lot of maturing to reach this point. At every stage, there were ulterior motives and goals by diverse proponents of different aspects of the Christian religion and the religiosity stemming from various state sources.

One cannot look solely at the Constitutional Convention to understand what was going on that ultimately resulted in the mental shift to produce the prohibition against governmental establishment of religion. One cannot look solely at an individual "founding father" to say he was entirely responsible. These were complicated times just as they are today, and collateral issues, such as taxes for one example, helped push the paradigm towards religious freedom. The political leaders were for the most part highly educated, worldly experienced individuals that even today should not be stereotyped, but they were also adept politicians and knew how to maneuver in first opposition, then compromise, to get things done.

To understand the debate as well as the evolution of the mindset of those involved in the ultimate passage of the First Amendment, one has to at least go back to the paradigm change within the "Age of Enlightenment." From there, follow the writings of the nineteenth century British freethinkers, who tried to build their opinions on facts, scientific inquiry and logical principles, avoiding in their attempt any fallacies in logic that many people fall into, as much today as ever. They avoided the intellectually limiting effects of authority (church or government), confirmation bias, cognitive bias, so-called conventional wisdom, popular culture, prejudice, sectarianism, tradition, urban legend or supernatural dogma. Freethinkers, collectively, had identified each category as a mental trap to logic and truth and pursued logic and reason.

Many of these English freethinkers were Christians who separated from the Church of England from the sixteenth to the eighteenth century, often known as "Nonconformists" or "Rational Dissenters," and they were opposed to state interference in religious matters and funding religion, as England did with its official church. They founded their own churches, schools, colleges, and communities. Many of these men were scientists and philosophers and filled the coffeehouses for discussion and debate, and many of them were both friends and correspondents of Benjamin Franklin and Thomas Jefferson.

All were heavily influenced by the thought evolution of the 18th-century cultural movement, "The Age of Enlightenment," that had even followed to the colonies in America. Its main goal was to reform society using reason rather than tradition or faith and advance knowledge through science. Hundreds of leading philosophers, such as Voltaire (1694 – 1778), Rousseau (1712 – 1778) and Montesquieu (1689 – 1778) contributed and influenced men like Benjamin Franklin and Thomas Jefferson, as well as others who played a role in the American Revolution. It makes no difference what these men's personal beliefs were regarding a deity when looking at the First Amendment. What they were reacting to was government control of religion and one particular sect influence rising above all others. The only way to do this was to have a level playing field, essentially defined as having a separation between religion and governmental duty on the one side, and on the flipside, no religious interference with government. Each had separate responsibilities – – religion was for the soul; government was for the administration of the civil order.

As the drums of war began to pound in 1774, leaders of the colonies coalescing to fight the British regarded God's grace as universal. No one was denouncing God or saying there was not one, but by placing the drafting of the Declaration of Independence in the hands of Thomas Jefferson, he took care not to call upon evangelical rhetoric or the stayed Episcopalian dogma of the church-state of Virginia but to return to the verbiage of natural thought. In his first draft of the Declaration of Independence, Jefferson linked fundamental ideas – – that freedom is a gift of "Nature's God," that "all men are created equal," and that all "are endowed by their Creator with inherent and inalienable rights." This was a spiritual vision of the world with roots both in classical philosophy and in Holy Scripture. He drew from Aristotle and Cicero, as much as John Locke. He drew from freethinkers such as Joseph Priestley, the scientist and founder of the English Unitarian Church, Algernon Sydney, Lord Bolingbroke and others; the principle was that the "Creator" had invested the individual with rights no human power should, or in reality could take away.

One cannot read Jefferson, as complex as he is, without knowing that he saw civil society when successful as being neither wholly religious nor wholly secular but that strength lay in the balancing of freedom for both. As representatives came from the colonies, then states, to form a Constitution under which all could agree and live, they followed different paths to reach a balance between the secular, the no religious preference requirement, and religion.

The men who came together in the Continental Congress from the colonies to conduct a Revolutionary War, as well as those who later participated in the Constitutional Convention to draft a unifying document were of mixed orientation as politicians and philosophers. Indeed, some were truly sages; others committed warriors, churchmen, as well as doubters. Many were knowledgeable in history and literature, the arts of politics and negotiation, business, statecraft and soldiering. As one reads of their individual accounts and then their assembly arguments, it is fascinating how these divergent personalities could be vain yet selfless in the same man, or shortsighted but suddenly farseeing in another. They could be and often were temperamental; then they would suddenly be forbearing; or, some representatives may be bigoted at times; then turn around and be magnanimous at other times. There were broad complexities of personalities and egos.

The man who came to lead was not easy to anticipate or understand, either. Jefferson at a later time edited the Gospels by cutting out text relating to superstition. Men like Benjamin Franklin rephrased and rearranged the Book of Common Prayer used by the Anglican churches and recalled as a young man falling into sound boredom sleep in a Quaker meeting house. While some of the founders were deists, Jefferson and Franklin believed that God worked through Providence. For them, Jesus of Nazareth was a great moral teacher but not the Son of God. According to Jon Meacham, they saw the creation of the idea of the Holy Trinity as an invention of a corrupt church more interested in temporal power than in true religion.[73] For these men, the mind of man and the natural laws of the universe, not the self-made mysteries of the church, were the center of faith. This, along with the diversified history of Christian worship throughout the colonies from highly oppressive to individually freeing, from centralized by the colonial government to open without colonial government intervention, created a basis for a negotiated First Amendment.

At the same time, there had to be a thought that a centralized government religion could be a source of the downfall of the people. Throughout history, government, religion, and war were first cousins, each dependent upon the other for curtailing freedom of the common person. The timely and famous 1776 masterwork of Edward Gibbon, The Decline and Fall of the Roman Empire, was widely read. It argued that an overconfident and intolerant Christianity caused the Imperial decline of Rome. The English historian's basic thesis was that after the late fourth century, the Roman Empire made a state religion of Christianity, which until then had been just a minor sect, and that combination of church and state became crippling and divisive. The pendulum had swung from Christians being persecuted to being the persecutors, which helped bring down an already weakening Empire.[74]

Whether or not Gibbon's thesis was historically provable became the source of much debate, even as it is today. But the production of that masterwork at that particular time raised serious questions about the validity of centralized religion under government mandate, and there was much debate and consideration among the learned and intellectual in both England and the colonies.

While traditional church religion was influential in the colonies, just as it is in America today, there was also a dominant paradigm that there should not be a unification of religion. It was a time of independent thought and a desire to protect individual thought and faith. Grounded in this was the fact that each colony was different and had different religious heritages. But while Jefferson proceeded with "Age of Enlightenment" verbiage with the Declaration of Independence, an anonymous English writer produced a pamphlet entitled "Common Sense."

That anonymous writer, who later became an American and attacked religion in his "The Age of Reason," nevertheless wrote "Common Sense," in the style of the common people, forgoing philosophical and Latin references. It was like a Protestant sermon, which relied on biblical references to make the case to the common people that reason and cause for independence from England exist. Never let it be said that media cannot scheme against people. In that day, the media was the printed press and "Common Sense" did its job. It was published January 10, 1776, and became the bestseller throughout the colonies. Its author was Thomas Paine. The people were ready for war. It was not a religious war, but the idea of religious freedom was involved.

Paradoxically, this drive for non-government intervention rose out of a long colonial history of escaping governmental religious intolerance in England, while at the same time mandating religious intolerance within each local founded colony. But there was always, even in these early times, the marriage of capitalism with religion. It's quite fascinating to read the early charters of exploration and settlement of America. The deeply religious Pilgrims, early settlers of present-day Plymouth, Massachusetts, arranged with English investors to establish their colony in 1620. The investors sought to profit from trade and hoped of gold in the New World. Of course, if the pilgrims found gold, they would be worldly wealthy, as well.

Pilgrims were soon followed by even greater religious strictness, the Puritans, who established the Massachusetts Bay Colony at present-day Boston in 1630. It was a capitalistic venture strongly disciplined by religion. The colonial leadership exhibited complete intolerance for other religious views, including Anglican, Quaker, and Baptist theologies, but the monopolistic trade was the avenue to wealth.

In 1641, the colony formally adopted its first code of laws, the Massachusetts Body of Liberties. This document consisted of 100 criminal and civil laws, "specifying required behavior and punishments by appeal to the Judeo-Christian social sanctions recorded in the Bible."[75] Draconic and absurd as they work, they nevertheless set forth the early ideas of equal protection and protection against double jeopardy; of course these principle thoughts were later enshrined in the United States Constitution.

Religious conformity and mandate within Massachusetts was the basis for everything. However, smoking of tobacco, abusing your mother-in-law, profane dancing, kissing, pulling hair, sleeping during church services, a woman riding behind a man, playing cards, or being too active on the Sabbath could all lead to criminal prosecution. Disobedience from conformity or disagreement was not allowed. Margaret Jones, a female physician, was hanged for being a witch. A Quaker named Mary Dyer was hanged in Boston for repeatedly defying the law banning Quakers from the colony.[76] Ann Hutchinson stood trial for her dissenting religious views, was forced into exile in the wilderness and killed by the Indians. You just did not question nor contest, but the Massachusetts Bay Colony was a financial success, while simultaneously restrictive of thought.

Down the coast, however, the Jamestown and subsequent settlers to Virginia were capitalists first. Nearly all of the Virginia immigrants in the 1600s came for economic reasons – – to get rich, or richer if possible. They were not driven primarily by a desire for religious freedom. They did not have the paradigm of limitation to one form of worship; though it was evident that religion was vital to them. The first permanent settlers to come to Tidewater, Virginia, were motivated by wealthy desires, not the urge to proselytize the heathen or establish a one religion refuge.

The Virginians considered religion to be a fundamental part of both life and government. They assumed the Anglican Church would be the "established" church, supported by the taxes imposed by government authority, while in contrast in Massachusetts all colonists were mandated by the church to tithe out of their income to support the religion. But in Virginia, the King of England was the head of the Anglican Church, and King James, for whom Jamestown was named, had imposed a new translation of the Bible, The King James Version.

There was no expectation of separation of church and state in Virginia, but it was often hostile to its neighbors in Maryland, who had a Catholic religious base. However, to attract settlers, Virginian Anglicans consciously recruited Presbyterians and other Protestants belonging to various German/Swiss denominations to move from Pennsylvania to Virginia, west of the Blue Ridge. Even dissenters such as the "Pennsylvania Dutch" were invited to immigrate to the Shenandoah Valley. Religion didn't matter; settlement and profit did.

So, the founding of America varied from colony to colony and with varied European ethnicities and former nationalities. Religion, Christian religion with a very small silent influx of Jews, was always there, sometimes at the forefront, sometimes following the motivation for capitalist gain, and always in an environment of frontierism and settlement. This backdrop, this history, both divergent and unifying, had a century of vintage ripening as Jefferson put pen to paper to announce a Declaration of Independence from England for all colonies. One might wonder, had Jefferson cited Scripture as a basis for independence instead of natural law, would the Continental Congressional delegates have fallen into the abyss of theological debate; thus, undermining the very goal of independence and freedom of thought.

Nevertheless, having produced the Declaration and successfully severed the English ties by Revolutionary War, representatives from each colony then set about a substantial ten-year debate on the drafting of a document that would be the organizational source of authority for a central government bringing all colonies together as the United States of America. In viewing the First Amendment's response to established religion during this ten-year period, post-1776, it is important to remember the religious heritage of each state coming into that formative period. They each had a different influence, but it was Virginia that emerged as a leader from debates about religion within its own Assembly. What happened there had a seminal impact on the Constitutional Convention ultimately producing the creative First Amendment.

In Virginia, the Anglican Church was intimately connected to the government until disestablishment in 1786. At that time, the Virginia Assembly adopted the Virginia Statute for Religious Freedom. Political leaders of Virginia established a new tradition of maintaining a wall of separation between church affairs and government affairs. James Madison and Thomas Jefferson led the way first in Virginia, and then to the new United States. Integral to the debates of prohibiting government from delving into religious affairs involved two issues. The first one was the issue of taxation to support religion, which had become abhorrent. The second issue was that the invited immigrants had been prohibited from citizenship, because of their religious preference, while some of them had become successful and influential in the state.

In 1779, Jefferson proposed a bill that would guarantee complete legal equality for citizens of all religions, and of no religion, in his home state Assembly of Virginia. Jefferson's was the first plan in any of the 13 states to call for complete separation of civil and religious authority. It was monumental but not an easy plan to get through the Assembly. Different groups had different mindsets that had not reached that level of independence, and after seven years of fierce debate and political bargaining, a law was adopted, just in time for similar consideration and debate in the Constitutional Congress for the greater United States.

Virginia initially stood alone in marshaling a legislative majority that, as Jefferson observed, "meant to comprehend, within the mantle of its protection, the Jew and the Gentile, the Christian and the Mahometan, the Hindoo, and the infidel of every denomination."[77]

Within that seven-year debate and to counter Jefferson, Patrick Henry had introduced in 1784 a bill that would have assessed taxes on all Virginia citizens for the support of "teachers of the Christian religion." Its effect was to continue Virginia state support of religion, Christian religion, but also to replace the established

Episcopal Church with "multiple establishments." For many Virginians, this seemed reasonable as long as one was in continued favor of state taxation to support religion.

James Madison disagreed and went to the electorate with a petition signed by some 2000 Virginians and then conveyed his views to the Virginia General Assembly with his eloquent "Memorial and Remonstrance Against Religious Assessments." He delineated his concern:

"Who does not see that the same authority which can establish Christianity, in exclusion of all other Religions, may establish with the same ease any particular sect of Christians, in exclusion of all other Sects? That the same authority which can force a citizen to contribute three pence only of his property for the support of any one establishment, may force him to conform to any other establishment in all cases whatsoever?"[78]

Madison saw the battle as against government establishing religion, any religion. Jefferson viewed the battle of Virginia electorate as being between sects of the Christian religion. Virginia had been under the Anglican or Episcopalian thumb since its founding, and its citizens had always been taxed to support the church. Now, however, there was growing strength within sects in the Christian faith. Baptists, Quakers, Presbyterians, and Methodists were universal in their desire to thwart any attempt by the Episcopal Church to retain its privileged prerevolutionary position. Today, these sects are considered mainstream religions, and some, such as evangelical Baptists and Methodists, have changed their position about how government should impose religion, or how religion should be critically involved in government. But in the 1780s and 150 years later, evangelical faith would rest on a personal, independent, unmediated relationship between God and man, and any governmental influence upon the populace between state and church, church and state, was seen not only as encroachment but as an insult to the Creator, whose authority preceded and was outside of any civil government.

There was a petition from 400 Quakers, which called Henry's proposed bill "an infringement of religious and civil liberty established by the [Virginia] Bill of Rights." The debate on taxation for religion lasted two years and produced petitions with more than 13,000 signatures. This, in a state, with fewer than 100,000 white men over 21, which was the only segment of the population allowed at the time to vote. Ultimately, as Jefferson had politically designed with the early introduction of his bill for complete separation of civil and religious authority, the Jefferson plan was passed. Not only that, the lawmakers overwhelmingly defeated a move to acknowledge Jesus Christ rather than a nonsectarian deity. The guarantee of freedom of thought, as opposed to the mandate of religious dogma, was at the heart of the statute:

"Be it enacted by the General Assembly, that no man shall be compelled to frequent or support any religious worship, place, or ministry whatsoever, nor shall be enforced, restrained, molested, or burthened in his body or goods, nor shall otherwise suffer on account of his religious opinions or belief; but that all men shall be free to profess, and by argument to maintain, their opinion in matters of religion, and that the same shall in no wise diminish, enlarge, or affect their civil capacities."[79]

How wonderful a paradigm! Any consideration of what later became The First Amendment to the United States Constitution that does not incorporate this broad historical backdrop is incomplete and will lead to misinterpretation. The debate over the federal Constitution was just beginning, and secularists hailed Virginia's law as a model for the issue of religion within a new federal government. On the other side, those who favored the semi-theocratic systems that were still prevailing in most states denounced it. The Constitutional Convention opened in the summer of 1787. It could have followed the Massachusetts model in which the right to hold office extended only to Christians, but with limitations on Catholics that if they were to hold office, they had to renounce papal authority. The Convention could have followed the New York State model, which extended political equality to Jews but not to Catholics; or Maryland which guaranteed full civil rights to Protestants and Catholics but not to Jews, freethinkers or deists; or the Delaware model, where officeholders were required to take an oath affirming belief in the Trinity.

Instead, following debate and compromise, the Congress spoke to religion with the brevity that was consistent with the founding document when it came to service of federal elected and appointed officials. It required that they:

"shall be bound by Oath of Affirmation, to support this Constitution; but no religious test shall ever be required as a

Qualification to any Office or public Trust under the United States." Art. 6, sec. 3.[80]

"Congress shall make no law respecting an establishment of religion or prohibiting the free exercise thereof, or abridging the freedom of speech, or of the press; or the right of the people peaceably to assemble, and to petition the government for a redress of grievances." First Amendment to the United States Constitution.[81]

Chapter 27

The Fight for a Religious Oath

IT IS A MIRACLE that nonsectarian or secularist (terms which were probably not even used at the time) rights were protected, and the United States Constitution got on with the business of conducting and managing the civil government.

My observation is that it happened not because the majority of delegates were interested in religious freedom for all, but because without nonsectarian protection each was afraid that a Christian sect from some other state would be the central Christian religious sect to the exclusion of theirs. True, each feared Jews, Mahometans, as they called Islamists, and Catholics if they were not from Maryland, but their greater fear was that of a more significant or different Christian sect. Each state had a different Christian religious history, beginning from its earliest founding as a colony. And, while they all agreed that there was one Supreme God, a Christian God, the majority sect in each state was a different sect or denomination with differing interpretations and fear of the power of other sects, similar to the very beginning of Christianity.

This fear and distrust of the other in a central federal government, coupled with the ongoing brutal battle waged by Thomas Jefferson and James Madison in Virginia, not only against a government tax for establishment of a central denomination, but for religious freedom to all citizens in the context of natural law, weighed heavily on the minds of delegates to the Constitutional Convention.

No state, before the Constitutional Convention, had been racked by more bitter religious disputes than Virginia. Its 1776 Constitution said nothing about religious qualifications for voting and holding office, although it taxed its citizens for the support of the state-authorized Anglican Church. But in June 1779, Thomas Jefferson proposed a statute on religious freedom and introduced its unequivocal words to the State Assembly:

"... but that all men shall be free to profess, and by argument to maintain, their opinion in matters of religion, and that the same shall in no wise diminish, enlarge, or affect their civil capacities."[82]

This statute broke new ground. Every colony, now state, had been behooved to create and pass its governing document, a Constitution, now that a joint Declaration of Independence from England had been issued. In most states, there was a hot debate on whether a Christian oath must be taken, or more appropriately what it will contain, to ensure that only Christians can serve in public offices, thereby ensuring control by the Christian religious sect of the majority of that particular state. In the minds of state assemblypersons, freedom of religion meant freedom of religion within Christian sects, and everyone else was excluded from participating in the political process. The typical state assembly battle was what must say the oath of the Christian religion.

No majority in a state assembly thought beyond that. So, when Jefferson proposed a statute on related religious liberty in Virginia in 1779, it was a whole new thought. He wasn't just talking about how Virginia should word a mandatory political Christian oath. He addressed the thought that the concept of religion in a civil, democratic society should be personal to the individual and that no religious oath for government service should be required. Of course, many Virginians regarded this as an attack on Christianity.

A vortex of petitions for and against the bill flooded the legislature. Jefferson had dropped the gauntlet of natural thought on religion as he had done in drafting the Declaration of Independence. Christian fear peaked in letters to newspapers arguing the wisdom of exalting individual freedom at the expense of majority religious faith. A contributor to the "Virginia Gazette" admitted that "Jews, Mahometans, atheists or deists" should be tolerated, but they had no right to hold public office or to promote their "singular opinions." I would classify this as a liberal view of the time, that of even recognizing non-Christians.

A petition from Culpeper County, Virginia, asked the legislature to reject Jefferson's bill and to adopt the one that would institute a form of Christian religious establishment, since a majority of Virginians were Christians. Amherst County started a petition requesting that any toleration accorded to Catholics be "guarded and limited," and that no Catholic, "Jews, Turk, or infidel," be permitted to hold any civil or military position in the state.

The battle raged for several years and then settled a bit, but James Madison took up the fight. While he secretly authored "a Memorial and Remonstrance" and his friend, George Mason, widely distributed it, he argued against taxation to support religion:

"Who does not see that the same authority which can establish Christianity, in exclusion of all other Religions, may establish with the same ease any particular sect of Christians, in exclusion of all other Sects? That the same authority which can force a citizen to contribute three pence only of his property for the support of any one establishment, may force him to conform to any other establishment in all cases whatsoever?"[83]

In 1786, Madison reintroduced Jefferson's bill on religious freedom, which passed, but not before last-minute attempts to alter the wording to insert the words "Jesus Christ" after the words "our Lord" in the preamble which would have implied a restriction on the liberty defined in the bill.

We know that in Philadelphia in 1787, the combinations of principle and necessity proved irresistible in the face of fear between Christian sects. Article 6, section 3, was the result. It said:

"No religious test shall ever be required as a qualification to any office or public trust under the United States."[84]

But for the leadership of Jefferson, Madison, John Adams, and Benjamin Franklin and to some extent, George Washington, this early history could have easily been instead of religious liberty for all, an America governed by Protestants only, who tolerated others but rejected their quest for equality. The delegates who voted for Article 6, section 3, were often from states in which they supported mandated religious oaths that barred either non-Christians or non-Protestants from holding office. They saw little contradiction by granting equality on the federal level for fear that some sect other than their own would control.

I have assumed that the fight for religious freedom centered around the First Amendment, but not so much. By the time it was submitted to the states for ratification in 1789, the discussion in the Virginia Assembly over religious freedom and the bitter battles over oaths in various states had pretty much run their course. So, Article 6, section 3, would guarantee that no one sect or a combination of sects would ever become so powerful – as in England – so as to design a religious test oath that would exclude others from office on the national level.

Realistically, history shows that many Federalists, without whom neither Article 6, section 3, nor the First Amendment would have been instituted, envisioned the American future as a federation of Christian states. In such a federation, the majority churches would be supported by local compulsory taxation, or at the very least, real power would reside in state governments controlled by Protestants only. It would appear that they were not too far off the mark. Tax law in its present form provides no federal taxation of churches and under the 2018 tax code, churches cannot only support a candidate for federal or state office, they can provide financial backing for that candidate without losing their tax exemption. While fundamentalist Catholics and Protestants have now buried the hatchet, Christianity does indeed control state governments.

In the end, Article 6, section 3, and the First Amendment had distinctively different purposes. The former was written to protect government from religion; the latter to protect religion from the government. Of course, in today's America and after 250 years, we have seen numerous slips in application by our highest court, not to mention the circumvention by fundamentalist Christian groups requiring state legislators to sign privately a religious test oath.

We often hear the statement made that "America was founded on Christian principles." Indeed it was, but which ones would you like to select; the Puritan restiveness of Massachusetts, the xenophobia of New Hampshire, the restriction of speech of New York or the advice of Samuel Adams to inaugurate a "reign of political Protestantism." When you think about it, "founded on Christian principles" is meaningless. First, which Christian principle? Most are contradictory. I doubt that the one making the statement is referring to "love thy neighbor as thyself" or "do unto others as you would have them do unto you," but if the speaker is, it must be noted that every major religion of the world professes such a principle. It is true that the colonies were founded by a rival of Christian sects, all disagreeing with each other, each seeking control, and each having differing principles. That is hardly a foundation for a historical argument that we should have a government dominated by religion.

To give you a feel for the early state constitutions, look at the following in the different approaches for excluding non-Christians from the government:

Pennsylvania. 1776: "That no person, who acknowledges the being of a God and a future state of rewards and punishments, shall, on account of his religious sentiments, be disqualified to hold any office or place of trust or profit under this Commonwealth."[85] (Obviously, if you don't believe there is a God, or a heaven, or ostensibly a hell if that can be included as a reward, you could not hold office, serve as a trustee of a trust, executor of an estate, etc., etc. in the state of Pennsylvania.)

Delaware. 1776: "Every person who shall be chosen a member of either house, or appointed to any office or place of trust, before taking his seat, or entering upon the execution of his office, shall take the following oath, or affirmation if conscientiously scrupulous of taking an oath, to wit: 'I, ____, will bear true allegiance to the Delaware State, submit to its Constitution and laws, and do no act wittingly whereby the freedom thereof may be prejudiced.

"And also make and subscribe the following declaration, to wit: I, ____, do profess faith in Almighty God the Father, and Jesus Christ His only Son, and the Holy Ghost, One God, Blessed for Ever More; and I Do Acknowledge the Holy Scriptures of the Old and New Testament to Be Given by Divine Inspiration."[86]

Morton Borden in his books "Jews, Turks, and Infidels" covered several states and their early state constitutions.

New Hampshire -- the demand for political restrictions against non-Protestants was nearly universal.

Connecticut remained without a constitution for more than 40 years. It afforded a larger measure of religious liberty as did Rhode Island, though none of Connecticut's various "acts of toleration" provided political equality to Jews, and it was not until the Constitution of 1842 that the Rhode Island Jews got their political emancipation.

New York Constitution (1777) was the only state without restrictions on holding office by Jews. However, it discriminated against Catholics.

The Maryland Constitution (1776) had a different take on Christian prejudice. There, one had to declare a belief "in the Christian religion" to hold "any office of trust or profit." So, Catholics and professing Protestants, other than Unitarians and Congregationalists, possessed full and equal civil rights, except for Jews and freethinkers

South Carolina. 1778: the Constitution made "the Christian Protestant religion… the established religion of this state."

North Carolina. In 1776, Presbyterian Rev. David Caldwell, insisted upon the inclusion of a provision in the state constitution whereby "no person, who shall deny the being of God or the truth of the Protestant religion, or the divine authority of the Old or New Testaments, or who shall hold religious principles incompatible with the freedom and safety of the State, shall be capable of holding any office or place of trust or profit in the civil department within this State."

Georgia. 1777: the Constitution required that representatives be "of the Protestant religion."

New Jersey. 1776: the Constitution disqualified non-Protestants implicitly rather than explicitly by stating that "all persons, professing a belief in the faith of any Protestant sect...shall be capable of being elected into any office."

Massachusetts. 1778: the Constitution limited religious freedom to Protestants only, and non-Protestants could not hold office.

Massachusetts. 1780 (second Constitution): all "Christians… shall be equally under the protection of the law." (It also specified that holding office was open to Christians. However, Catholics can qualify by taking a test oath renouncing the superiority of papal authority "in any matter, civil, ecclesiastical, or spiritual.")[87]

At the time when it became necessary for then-colonies, in 1776, to create their governing documents, their constitutions, religious test oaths were a prevailing paradigm. As they completed their work on their Constitution and sent delegates to Philadelphia to create a national Constitution under which all states and their constituents would come together to form a union, many Protestants favored religious provisions in the federal Constitution. Nevertheless, religious self-protection produced what we have today.

The Constitution did set an example for four states, which between 1789 and 1792, altered their constitutions to correspond to that of Virginia and the federal government. Delaware abandoned its requirement of a Trinitarian oath. Pennsylvania removed its references to the New Testament, permitting Jews to hold office for continuing to bar atheists. South Carolina and Georgia struck all religious restrictions. Nevertheless, eight other states did not, with several refusing to make any changes for many decades, or ever, depending upon the state.

The following potpourri of statements and events hopefully provide a feel for what was going on in the debate on religion and religious dedication. Between the Declaration of Independence and the ratification of the United States Constitution, political leaders not only wrestled with their state constitutions, but the federal, as well. Morton Borden described it well in his book Jews, Turks and Infidels:

The artist John Trumbull recalled being invited to a dinner party at the home of Thomas Jefferson in 1793, at which "a discussion of the Christian religion ensued." Christianity, he reported, was "powerfully ridiculed on the one side, and weakly defended on the other." It was "a rather freethinking dinner party." One guest, William Branch Giles, "proceeded so far at last, as to ridicule the character, conduct, and doctrines of the divine founder of our religion." Jefferson listened, "smiling and nodding approbation on Mr. Giles." A Jewish guest, David Franks – – at the time first cashier of the Bank of the United States – – disturbed by the vehemence of Giles' remarks, argued in favor of Trumbull, who was a devout Congregationalist. Trumbull was so struck by this that he remarked to Jefferson, "Sir, this is a strange situation in which I find myself; and a country professing Christianity, and at a table with Christians, as I supposed, I find my religion and myself attacked with severe and almost irresistible wit and raillery, and not a person to aid me in my defense, but my friend Mr. Franks, who is himself a Jew.

Famous Baptist leader in Massachusetts, Isaac Bacchus, who usually argued in favor of separation of church and state, wrote differently in one of his last pamphlets entitled "a Door Opened for Equal Christian Liberty" (1783): "no man," he commented, "can take a seat in our (state) legislature till he solemnly declares, 'I believe the Christian religion and have a firm persuasion of its truth.'"

The Roman Catholic Bishop John Carroll of Maryland wrote an essay for "The Colombian Magazine" in 1787 in which he thanked "the genuine spirit of Christianity" by which several states "have done... justice to every domination of Christians, which ought to be done to them all, of placing them on the same footing of citizenship, and conferring an equal right of participation in national privileges. Freedom and independence, acquired by the united efforts, and cemented with the mingled blood of Protestant and Catholic fellow – citizens, should be equally enjoyed by all."

The anonymous author of "The People the Best Governors; Ora Plan of Government Founded on the Just Principles of Natural Freedom" (1776) recommended: "that no person shall be capable of holding any public office except he possesses a belief of one only indivisible God, that governs all things; and that the Bible is his revealed word; and that he be also an honest, moral man."

In 1776, Samuel Adams advised Americans to inaugurate a "reign of political Protestantism."

Jefferson wrote to John Adams that Christianity must be cleansed of its superstitions: "the day will come when the mystical generation of Jesus, by the supreme being as his father in the womb of a virgin will be classed with the fable of the generation of Minerva in the brain of Jupiter."

George Washington: "I am not amongst the number of those who are so much alarmed at the thought of making people pay towards the support of that which they profess, if of the denomination of Christians, or declare themselves Jews, Mahometans or otherwise, and thereby obtain proper relief."

At the Constitutional Convention and subsequent Ratification, participants in the debate made various statements:

Delegate Luther Martin of Maryland: "to think… That in a Christian country, it would be at least decent to hold out some distinction between the professors of Christianity and downright infidelity or paganism."

At the Massachusetts Ratifying Convention, delegate Major Thomas Lusk from West Stockbridge: "shuddered at the idea that Roman Catholics, Papists, and pagans might be introduced into office."

At the New Hampshire Ratifying Convention, Deacon Mathis: [the absence of a religious test] "would leave the Bible, the precious jewel, the pearl of great price, without support... The blood of all martyrs would rise up against us."

Another New Hampshire delegate stated that if the president were not compelled to take a proper religious oath: "a Turk, a Jew, a Roman Catholic, and what is worse than all, a Universalist, may be President of the United States."

At the North Carolina Ratifying Convention, Rev. David Caldwell warned that the lack of a religious test would be: "an invitation for Jews and pagans of every kind to come among us. At some future, this might endanger the character of the United States."[88]

Leverett Saltonstall, a Massachusetts lawyer, predicted the ruin of Massachusetts if the religious test was removed: "as to Jews, Mahometans, deists, and atheists, they are all opposed to the common religion of the Commonwealth and believe it an imposition, a mere fable, and that his professors are under a wretched delusion. Are such persons suitable rulers of the Christian state?"[89]

A Massachusetts Unitarian minister on removing the Massachusetts religious test: "Either the religion of Jesus Christ is from God or it is not. Either we are accountable to God for all our means and opportunities of advancing the interests of this religion, or we are not. (...) If men should be elevated to high and responsible stations, who are enemies of Christianity, may we not look with some apprehension to the consequences?"[90]

Sometime before the New York Constitutional Convention in 1821 a man named Ruggles had been arrested, tried, and convicted for blasphemy. He said in public that "Jesus Christ was a bastard, and his mother must be a whore." He was sentenced to three months in jail and fined $500. The problem was that there was no written law in New York against blasphemy or defining it. The state Supreme Court upheld his conviction. Chancellor James Kent ruled that it was legal to blaspheme any non-Christian religion, "and for this plain reason, that the case assumes we are a Christian people and the morality of the country is deeply grafted upon Christianity, and not upon the doctrines or worship of those impostors."[91] He followed a judicial principle that Christianity was a part of the common law and to blaspheme Christianity was to violate it.

Gen. Erastus Root, at the New York Convention, who was a freethinking Republican, moved to add a section to the state constitution depriving the judiciary of the power to "declare any particular religion to be the law of the land" or to "exclude any witness on account of his religious faith."[92] Root argued that Jews held state office. In fact, a Jew was currently serving as Sheriff of a large city. The Ruggles decision would mean "is guilty of blasphemy every time he enters a synagogue."[93] That could be considered an anti-Christian act.

Kent, another member of the Convention, responded that the authors of the 1777 New York Constitution "meant to preserve…

the morals of the country, which rested on Christianity as the foundation. They meant to apply the principles of common law against blasphemy, which they did not believe the Constitution ever meant to abolish. Are we not a Christian people? Do not ninety-nine hundredths of our fellow citizens hold the general truths of the Bible to be dear and sacred?"[94]

The clarification on the Jew Sheriff in New York as found in James Fenimore Cooper's Notions of the Americans: "the Sheriff of the city of New York, an officer elected by the people, was, a few years ago, a Jew! Now all the Jews in New York united, would not probably make three hundred voters (...) Notwithstanding all this, the country is as much, or more, a Protestant and Christian country than any other nation on earth."[95] In reality, Noah, the sheriff, was appointed to the office of Sheriff; when it later became an elected position, Noah campaigned for it but was defeated.

New Hampshire was notoriously xenophobic of Catholics and Jews. Isaac Hill, who served as governor and publisher of "the New Hampshire Patriot," however, defended the delivery of mail on Sunday, because to do otherwise was to violate the separation of church and state. Abner Kneeland, who was tried and convicted of blasphemy in Massachusetts, and frequently argued in behalf of Catholics, Jews, shakers, Universalists, and other minority groups, editorialized: "our [state] Constitution, to our discredit, does contain a religious test... Does anyone pretend, in this enlightened day, that a pious and conscientious Catholic is less worthy to be a governor than many persons who call themselves Protestants?"

In Maryland, new Jew could serve in any office of the state, or be commissioned in the state militia, or follow the profession of the law. A bitter political battle for equality had occurred in 1801, but the "Jew Bill" was defeated. But in 1818 a freshman delegate, Thomas Kennedy, resurrected the issue with a new bill, stating: "there is only one opponent that I fear at this time, and that is Prejudice – – our prejudices Mr. Speaker, are dear to us, we all know and feel the force of our political prejudices, but our religious prejudices are still more strong, still more dear; they cling to us through life, and scarcely leave us on the bed of death, and it is not the prejudice of a generation, of an age or a century, that we have now to encounter. No, it is the prejudice which has passed from father to son, for almost eighteen hundred years..."[96]

As frontier expansion continued in states were added, the fight for religious control state-by-state under the auspices of "States Rights" never ceased. The constitutional development of each state was different, as one would expect. Some instituted religious oaths, some did not, some did but later changed the wording or omitted the oath altogether.

Early states' rights allowed individual states complete discretion regarding the inclusion of religious test in their state constitutions. Today, there are only nine states left that legally establish religious superiority to the exclusion of other citizens[97]:

Arkansas State Constitution, article 19, section 1:

"No person who denies the being of a God shall hold any office in the civil departments of this State, nor be competent to testify as a witness in any court."

Maryland's Declaration of Rights: article 36:

"that as it is the duty of every man to worship God in such manner as he thinks most acceptable to Him, all persons are equally entitled to protection in their religious liberty; wherefore, no person ought by any law to be molested in his person or estate, on account of his religious persuasion, or profession, or for his religious practice, unless, under the color of religion, he shall disturb the good order, peace or safety of the State, or shall infringe the laws of morality, or injure others in their natural, civil or religious rights; nor ought any person to be compelled to frequent, or maintain, or contribute, unless on contract to maintain, any place of worship, or any ministry; nor shall any person, otherwise competent, be deemed incompetent as a witness, or a juror or, on account of his religious beliefs; provided, he believes in the existence of God, and that under His dispensation such person will be held morally accountable for his acts, and be rewarded or punished therefore either in this world are in the world to come."

Article 37: "that no religious test ought ever to be required as a qualification for any office of profit or trust in this State, other than a declaration of the belief in the existence of God."

Massachusetts State Constitution, article 3:

"Any denomination of Christians, demeaning themselves peaceably, and is good subjects of the Commonwealth, shall be equally under the protection of the law: and no subordination of any one sect or denomination to another shall ever be established by law." (Note: inferential he, one would have to say non-Christians are not "equally under the protection of the law.")

Article 3 of the Massachusetts State Constitution was later changed or amended to become Article XI, reading as follows:

"Instead of the third article of the Bill of Rights, the following modification and amendment thereof is substituted. As the public worship of God and instructions and piety, religion and morality, promote the happiness and prosperity of the people and the security of a republican government; – – therefore, the several religious societies of this Commonwealth, whether corporate or unincorporate, at any meeting legally warned and Holden for that purpose, shall ever have the right to elect their pastors or religious teachers, to contract with them for their support, to raise money for erecting and repairing houses for public worship, for the maintenance of religious instruction, and for the payment of necessary expenses; and all persons belonging to any religious society shall be taken and held to be members, until they shall file with the clerk of such society, a written notice, declaring the dissolution of their membership, and thenceforth shall not be liable for any grant or contract which may be thereafter made, or entered into by such society: – – – and all religious sects and denominations, demeaning themselves peaceably, and is good citizens of the Commonwealth, shall be equally under the protection of the law; and no subordination of any one sect or denomination to another shall ever be established by law."

Mississippi State Constitution. Article 14, section 265:

"No person who denies the existence of a Supreme Being shall hold any office in this state."

North Carolina State Constitution. Article 6, section 8:

"Disqualifications of office. The following persons shall be disqualified for office: first, any person who shall deny the being of Almighty God."

South Carolina State Constitution. Article VI, section 2:

"No person who denies the existence of the Supreme Being shall hold any office under this Constitution."

Section 5: [the oath of office ends in:] "so help me God."

Pennsylvania State Constitution. Article 1, section 4:

"No person who acknowledges the being of a God and a future state of rewards and punishments shall on account of his religious sentiments, be disqualified to hold any office or place of trust or profit under this Commonwealth." [Again, inferentially disqualifying others.]

Tennessee State Constitution. Article 9, section 2: "No person who denies the being of God, or a future state of rewards and punishment, shall hold any office in the civil department of this state."

The Texas Constitution. Article 1, section 4: "No religious test shall ever be required as a qualification to any office, or public trust, in this State; nor shall any one be excluded from holding office on account of his religious sentiments, provided he acknowledge the existence of a Supreme Being."

Chapter 28

The Evolution of the Religious Right and Republicanism

𝔉OR AS LONG as I can remember, men have sat around in coffee shops and bars and talked politics, but seldom religion. I can remember as early as five years old, my favorite uncle allowing me to tag along with him to his favorite watering hole in Dallas, not far from where he lived, as the locals would gather for a beer, discuss and debate the politics of the mid-40s. I loved it. I didn't so much have a concept of the issues, but I had a scoring system as to whom I thought was winning.

Such traditions, I now know, go back centuries and were not unique to my uncle's time, but as I followed my quest for religious truth and end-of-life answers, I observed that people didn't sit around coffee shops and watering holes and discuss the New or Old Testament, or end-of-life questions. They just accepted whatever their faith was supposed to be, and if questioned, became seriously defensive. At least, this is what I observed up until the fundamentalist and the Pentecostal resurgence of the late 70s, early 80s. But even then, it became more of a bumper sticker, quick statement sort of thing, rather than an open coffee shop sort of discussion, and there always seemed an underlying fear of contradiction, anger and threatened counterattack with the bumper sticker phrasing.

Nevertheless, by retirement, I determined that there was not one piece of credible evidence that religion could present to me that would lead to an end-of-life answer of immortality. Science is the search for truth. Religion is the defense of myth. But because American politics became religion, and faith became political with fervent aggression in the last quarter of the twentieth century and continuing to present, I have come to fear that we are losing the freedom of religion. The First Amendment is under attack by the religious right who want to ensure a theocratic state, and some of whom, such as the Baptists, were the very allies of Jefferson in establishing the First Amendment, but now, oh how they have changed their color.

As I progressed through each of my periods ("Acceptance," "Gandhi," "Doubting," "Re-Search," "Disbelief"), I viewed each Abrahamic religion with respect, but with a critical eye. As I read the scientific deductions from various disciplines (anthropology, archaeology, evolutionary psychology, genetics, and physics), I believe I maintained a consistent critical view. My quest lasted 60 years, and within that period, societal patterns developed seeking power within American culture and government, conservative, regressive religious forces that to me were anti-Democratic and contrary to Jefferson/Madison principles on the issue of religion, or no religion at all. For me, I wanted to be free of being controlled on religious matters. I don't want my children or grandchildren to be prescribed on religious beliefs, but to be allowed to have an open questioning mind, and to have a choice in their beliefs. I am of the opinion that this would be healthy for all Americans.

This sort of freedom has always come with great difficulty and strife in America, and today, the contingent elements of control are different from before. By this time in our two-and-a-half-century history, we are well entrenched in American theocracy, and it is now pretty easy to see how we got here and how a pattern of control developed. It is now clear that while we have a First Amendment prohibiting the government from establishing a religion, nevertheless we have a government in which the Christian God is recognized as the supreme civil ruler. While the church may still be separated from the state, religion is not. There were always shades of this in our political history, even without a well-orchestrated Machiavellian drive to solidify it. Even the Constitutional Convention opened with prayer.

I don't think 50s America was shocked in 1956 when Congress adopted as the official motto, "in God we trust," and printed it on paper money. After all, we were afraid of communists and felt like we needed supernatural protection. That move, of course, replaced the more erudite and less understood "E Pluribus Unum" (out of one, many), adopted in 1782. Nevertheless, the motto "In God We Trust" began appearing on metal currency in 1864, ostensibly surrounding the turmoil and heightened religious sentiment during the Civil War.

While the United States has a long history of going back to a Christian deity through government in times of uncertainty and fear, it also has that rather mystical, iconic history of symbols. One of them is the "Eye of God" (some called it Providence) looking down upon us (I guess from Egypt), in the creation of the Great Seal of the United States back in 1782. Government deification has been around in one form or another since the beginning, in spite of Jefferson, Madison, and the First Amendment. Pop culture has taken its shot at these slogans, as in Jean Shepherd's 1966 book title, In God We Trust, All Others Pay Cash, or the movie Oh, God!, where George Burns plays God and says to his reluctant disciple, "trust me. Like it says on the money."

Our presidents have mostly closed their speeches with "God bless the United States, God bless America," and all of this can be understood because the vast majority of Americans are Christians. Within that vast majority is a large fundamentalist segment who thinks that this is the way it is supposed to be, it's "the American Way," and there is an even larger segment of moderate Christians who are not repulsed by fundamentalist verbal infringements, codified or otherwise, on the First Amendment. Basically, they say, "let it pass."

At this new period of my life, what I now call "the old man's political observation period," I have become concerned with one question. How did we end up with Congresspersons, Senators, judges, and presidents who were dedicated to doing "God's will" from their official position, by a deified view of civil authority domestically and a drive for Empire globally, and within that purview a vision for passing statutes of religious founding that restrict personal freedoms and impose religious law? It is almost as if our representatives became jealous of Islamic countries ruled by Sharia law and decided to implement Old Testament Temple law for us. We have, indeed, come to a theocratic, not secular, government, but it has come not through a grassroots movement, but through a backdoor instigated by a masterful organization.

I came to realize that my personal life paralleled two quests, running side by side. There was the quest for religious truth and end-of-life answers, but there was simultaneously the search for understanding of what was going on in American politics and government and how political events were interfacing with religion, itself. I began to think about it seriously during President Reagan's second term. I'm not sure what the stimulus was, but I could see evidence of that interfacing between politics and religion, especially where I lived and worked in West Texas, as most people were Protestant or Catholic fundamentalists, as well as conservative Republicans. My hometown was the hometown of the future president, George W Bush.

To access some understanding, I followed my usual approach, the same that I used in the practice of law. I asked myself a question. Was Christian fundamental belief amalgamating with the Republican Party? If so, why? If the answers were affirmative, my next question was – – how?

To have asked myself these questions in the mid-80s, which I originally did, was even then a bit of "Johnny-come-lately," since political scientists already knew what was going on and the move had been in process for some time. I reflected back to the time of my "Gandhi Period," 1962. My future mother-in-law, a wife of a Midland oil man, was concerned that I might have been infected with the thought after having represented Baylor at the United Nations in meeting Prime Minister Nehru of India. Predominant West Texas thought at the time was not only that we did not need the rest of the world, but also that the most of the world was our enemy. As to oil, we had plenty, and we could certainly produce all that we needed by ourselves. As to the United Nations, it was a communist organization designed by some dangerous people called "liberals."

My future mother-in-law invited me to attend a meeting on "history" with her on a night that I was home from college. It was the first Midland meeting of the John Birch society, and purportedly, we would be listening to a lecture on the United States history and current concerns. Of course, I went to the lecture, found it interesting and personally disturbing, and found that it certainly raised some questions in my mind, especially when it came to the history of Jews, banking, and geopolitics. The speaker at times boarded on vitriolic, but being a Southern Baptist boy, I was used to that demeanor of public speaking from evangelists.

I never went to another John Birch Society meeting, but I did learn some years later that it had been founded by candy magnate, Robert Welch Jr., of Massachusetts in 1958 to reestablish Christian principles in America, limited government, get us out of the UN, rollback government regulation and oppose redistribution of wealth.

That background, my John Birch Society meeting of 1962 and later learning of its founder, just sat there in my memory for decades. It was in the 2010 and 2012 political season in my retirement that I decided to take a look at just how the Republican Party became so powerfully connected to religiosity. I had noticed how the Koch brothers' father, Fred Koch, and his financial support had put it on the map. Koch's sons had followed the extremism of their father and now owned perhaps the largest private corporation in America enveloping such companies as Invita, Georgia – Pacific, Koch Fertilizer, Koch Minerals, just to name a few. Wealthy industrialists like Koch brothers were the financial backbone of the Republican Party, but I wanted to know where the religiosity came in. When did it become such a force in the Republican Party, and when did the Republicans become so dependent on fundamentalist religiosity?

I decided to look at history and cultural change as I had observed, as I had approached such research in the Abrahamic religions. Whether studying comparatively Abrahamic religions or trying to get a grasp on concepts such as culture, religion, and politics, I don't think one has to be inhibited for not being an academic historian, theologian, sociologist or scientist. Part of the joy of life is each person's own intellectual search for knowledge and understanding. To be sure, it is important to refer to and rely upon trained experts in each field, who are independent, and without motivated thinking, and to attempt to use self-discipline in critical thinking, without placing one's trust blindly in an expert, ideologue or guru.

As I saw it, the best I could do for the long historical period from reconstruction (1865 – 1877) to the civil rights movement of the 1960s was to call it the time of white, "conservative" control of the government. Of course, the Wilson years and the FDR years could be called an exception, but that was even debatable. My purpose for what I was looking for was what had happened in my life, and that seemed to begin really with the 60s.

The decade of the 60s had to be quite a shock for mainstream white adults in America. The Great Generation that had grown up through World War II in the 40s and then settled into a postwar decade of economic growth and prosperity of the 50s, must have thought that life would always be just the way it seemed at the time, as long as we could find communist infiltrators and root them out, and as long as Russia didn't attack us with a nuclear bomb. For me, the 50s was high school, pep rallies, football games and playing baseball. Everyone was white, believed in God and Jesus, abided by the law and interacted in mannerly fashion with others. If you heard of poverty, you didn't know where it was, and you doubted that it existed. You pretty much assumed everyone was just like you, but you didn't think about it much.

The cultural turbulence of the 1960s had to do with the question of national identity and persistent questioning. History has shown the same to be true in the revolutionary 1790s, the anti-revolutionary 1860s, the revolutionary 1930s, and what I call the "take back America" cultural religious movement of the 80s, 90s, and early twenty-first century.

In the 1960s movement, the youth rebellion questioned just about everything, debunked national myths, mocked in satirical television programs, and as with all youth rebellions, sex played a significant part. The movement wasn't just an American movement, although our egocentricity often makes it seem so. Similar cultural protests were occurring in Europe and Great Britain. In Britain in 1960, Lady Chatterley's Lover, first published in Italy in 1928 was published in Britain as the full unexpurgated edition by Penguin Books in 1960, and Penguin stood trial under the Obscene Publications Act of 1959. It was a major test of the new obscenity law. However, defense was allowed if Penguin could show that the book had literary merit. The prosecution objected to the frequent use of the word "fuck" and its derivations, as well as the word "cunt."

Penguin prevailed and readers on both sides of the Atlantic rushed for a copy of Lady Chatterley's Lover, the story of the physical relationship between a working-class man and an upper-class woman with explicit descriptions of sex, and the use of then-unprintable words. Cultural taboos of both words and actions were breaking down in the nation. In the fall of 1962, the Communists sent missiles to the communist island, Cuba, testing the new Catholic president Kennedy. White Protestants had not yet embraced their conservative Catholic counterparts and still had a general distrust of Catholics, conservative or liberal. It just seemed like stability was evaporating and "American values" were being undermined. It certainly must have something to do with the Communists.

Then came the period from 1962 to 1972, a decade of student demonstrations against the Vietnam War. The war somehow emboldened young college students to question settled principles of society and culture, far beyond objections to the draft and the war itself. Marijuana, which had been around legally forever and used by jazz musicians and the poor became almost as popular as alcohol, and then along with it came, or about the same time, the sexual revolution and the perception of sexual honesty and freedom. It was all happening so fast, and it was both distasteful and fearful to suburban-house America. American values were being lost. Even the way language was used was no longer cloistered in niceness.

1970 brought a massive effort to retake control. Many average people and certainly all religious bases viewed the previous decade like the actions of the children of Israel while Moses was on the mountaintop. They had wandered away from God. The American youth had lost their way, and there was the fear that America could be lost. The conservatives felt that the populace must be brought back into a disciplined, semi-free moderation of control. Industry was best served when there was no public unrest and no riots. Religious centers of sects and denominations recognized that church and mass attendance was down, and they needed new directions to bring the fold back, as well as to convert the heathen. There must be a silent Moral Majority, and they must take back America.

It seems to me that the first thrust came from the political vanguard in 1970. The new president, Richard Nixon, viewed the problem as a power struggle between young Americans who had lost their way, primarily as a result of "communist infiltration and influence," and the power of government. In campaigning, he had urged two strong traditional Republican themes: first, individual freedom; second, strong law enforcement in order to defeat crime and the criminal growth we had seen over the last decade. Of course, what history has proven relative to that dual Republican mantra is that what is meant by "individual freedom" is deregulation and corporate and industrial laissez-faire, and by "strong law enforcement and criminal justice" is meant to curtail the individual and instill a peaceful populace.

Nevertheless, Nixon acted quickly and characteristically with strength and authority. Three months after taking office he brought Congress to pass The Controlled Substances Act (CSA). This act listed prohibited drugs by class and assign punishments for possession on a graduated scale. Marijuana was given the most restrictive designation – – Schedule I – – along with heroin. The motivation, we now know from presidential archives, before Nixon had that propensity for erasure, was that if you took the drug away from college students and threw their leaders in jail for its use you could demoralize counter-movements and demonstrations. To back this up and implement incarceration, he formed the new Drug Enforcement Agency (DEA) and along with J. Edgar Hoover placed FBI spies into any youth organization that had organizational ability or networks. The strategy, though hardly democratic, worked. Authoritarianism usually does work when it comes to subduing the opponent.

However, Nixon's triumph of stabilizing the masses was short-lived, as his ego undermined his strength in 1972. Fearing his Democratic opponent in the presidential election, he approved the break-in (felonious burglary) of the Democratic National Committee office headquarters at the Watergate office complex in Washington DC. Ultimately, he was forced to resign as president on August 9, 1974. One might have thought that while Nixon had made great governmental inroads into subverting cultural changes of the 60s he had defeated himself by his own actions. This was true to an extent, but it didn't spill over to the ebb and flow of evolutionary American cultural change.

On the national domestic level, it seemed to slow liberal cultural change such as general acceptance of drug use or sexual equality, but it didn't seem to do anything towards restoring Christian fundamentalist values in people or governmental representatives or employees. The Nixon and Hoover authoritarianism was more of a political power move. On the horizon, however, there were geopolitical events that the American public had no way of anticipating and yet would create a wondering by many, such as "was our morals affecting our destiny?" Events would again shake the feeling of consistency and evenness of American life and drive a fearful public uneasiness that could be used to say "God was not happy with the American people. We had better straighten up."

1973 brought the first oil embargo, shortages of gasoline, and higher gasoline prices. Americans first began to learn that, "no we

IN GOD WE TRUST

did not produce all the oil that we needed." We imported a lot of oil from the Middle East, particularly from places called Saudi Arabia and Iran, and what was worse, we were importing more and more. We were energy hungry, and these countries knew we couldn't keep up with demand in our own production. We had become their hostage, and we resented the fact that suddenly we could not jump into our car and drive anywhere we wanted, anytime we wanted. It was un-American not to be easily mobile. With great diplomatic effort, however, America negotiated a settlement, albeit for more money to the Middle East, and the crisis passed. It almost seemed that things were returning to normal on the front of the oil importation, but there was still a domestic irritant that wasn't subsiding. It was a strange resistance to cultural change that was coalescing as the Moral Majority.

The CSA and efforts of the DEA seemed to be working. At least far more people were being arrested for using prohibited drugs, being tried by the courts and imprisoned. One concern was that the budgets and resulting costs for law enforcement and the building of additional prisons were going up. The other concern was "how long is this War on Drugs supposed to last?" There was one school of thought that argued that prolonging the prohibition effort was the popularization of a new drug, at least newly popular in the mass – – cocaine. It also was growing by leaps and bounds. It too had been around forever like marijuana but was now illegal because it became popular among the young people who were getting "hooked" on it; there was even evidence that many young, white, educated executives were beginning to use it extensively.

289

Government and religion were frustrated by this drug revolution that had begun back in the 60s and seemed to be growing, not lessening. The new and growing anti-drug army should have taken care of it by now. President Nixon had announced the War on Drugs back in 1971 to take back the country from the influence of drugs. Surely, the War should have been won by now.

In 1979, a Democratic president and moderate Southern Baptist had hardly begun his presidency when both he and the American populace were quickly hammered with a series of unsettling events, all of which shocked both the confidence of the American people and their feeling of stability. The fear level of the populace began to rise, and there was a prevailing feeling of loss of confidence and perhaps loss of prosperity.

First, on January 16 Islamist fundamentalists overthrew the Shah of Iran, a puppet ruler the United States and Great Britain had put in place to ensure the flow of oil. Then, the militants took 60 American hostages from the American Embassy in Tehran and held them for 444 days. During that time, American forces failed in an attempt to rescue them and lost all their men's lives and helicopters. It was a national embarrassment. The flow of oil to the US dropped to a trickle, and a perfect cataclysmic economic storm was produced – – high gasoline prices, shortages, and then Iraq invaded Iran and commenced a major Middle East war, again more oil shortage in the US.

From 1979 to 1981, the American people blamed the Carter presidency for everything except sin – – the hostage-taking, the Iraq/Iran war, recession, hyper-inflation that stagnated the economy (called "stagflation"), the nuclear crisis of the three-mile island, the Soviet invasion of Afghanistan and the boycott of the 1980 Summer Olympics, not to mention the return of the Panama Canal to Panama. American hubris had been that we were the best in the world at everything and that we were the most powerful. We were great at denial when we failed at the image of most powerful, such as our defeat in Vietnam. With this rapid course of negative events and still feeling the hangover of cultural changes from the 60s and early 70s, there was a rising consensus in the populace that we must do something to become strong again. We needed it, and we wanted to feel it. Someone had to lead us back.

Along came Ronald Reagan. History has proved that you don't have to be particularly smart to be president – – not that Reagan wasn't. He was of average American intelligence. You have to be able to be an administrator, make decisions and communicate with the public. Reagan could do all of that, and his background as an actor didn't hurt. The smart people needed to run a nation could all be hired and brought into the inner circle, while Reagan captained the ship. For a variety of reasons, the period of Reagan's two-term presidency (1981 – 1989), saw the country rise from the doldrums of the 70s with a felonious egocentric president followed by one who was buried by negative geopolitical and economic forces. Enough time had passed from the earlier cultural changes and the disillusionment of losing the Vietnam War so that a new political and religious alliance could develop, but another element was needed to make strong alliances of this sort work, and that was the American industry. The Republican brain trust was waking up to what had been in front of their face all along. If you combine religious fundamental and evangelical fervor with political conservatism, financed and strengthened by a powerful industrial base, you can mold a powerful coalition that can not only pass the laws it wants, but can also permeate every branch of federal and state government with its own ideology. The man who came to the forefront, the new President Reagan, had already tested the idea of such a coalition and could now assist it to evolve into a new paradigm of power.

A triple force amalgamation (political party, fundamentalist Protestants, and Catholics and strong corporate backing on social issues) could deliver what had been segregated elements into a unified central force that would deliver what each had wanted. The time came. The time was now, and intelligent, committed Republican strategists could see the opportunity and the way of design to bring each element into that perceived unified central force.

The genius of the strategic leaders from each segment (Republican politicians, religious fundamentalists, industrialists) was the recognition that they did not have to agree on every issue. As long as each had support on their favorite issue, it could overlook other issues where it might not agree. For the religious segment, the most pressing issue might be the recall or diminishment of Roe v. Wade, for the industrialist it might be less regulation and lower taxes, and for the Republican, it would be control of Congress, the presidency, and reelection. An industrialist might not be against abortion, or a religious group might be in favor of protecting the environment, but they could each overlook such issues if they could amalgamate agreement and power on their favorite issue. They developed a sense of compromise between their diverse elements, while at the same time establishing a covenant to never compromise with those who opposed them on their favorite issues.

Chapter 29

The Heritage Foundation, the Council for National Policy and the Moral Majority

$\mathbb{D}$ISPARATE PARTS OF society in the 70s (the churches, Wall Street industrials and the Republican Party) felt that they were the minority and that the moral, cultural and political changes of the 60s (including Johnson's "War on Poverty" and the Civil Rights Act) had disenfranchised them, but they were the real America. You could see the seeds of establishing a counter-front, a counter-blow, with the early establishment of The Heritage Foundation in 1973 by Joseph Coors, Paul Weyrich, and Edwin Feulner.

One of the most influential conservative research organizations, today, is The Heritage Foundation. Its mandate in 1973 and continuing was to lead in government policy change. It was well-funded, and increasingly so, by wealthy industrialists such as Richard Mellon Scaife and Edward Noble. In the nine years leading up to Ronald Reagan's Republican nomination for president, it formulated conservative public policies based upon the principle of free enterprise, limited government, individual freedom, traditional American values, and strong national defense. While each of those tenants could be described and believed in from a liberal viewpoint, that was not the place of the Heritage Foundation. Its charge was to solidify conservative definitions and propose them in formulated governmental policy.

In the history of any movement, there is a prehistory where ideas, forming paradigms and courses of actions to be followed are not completely clear, but are developing. In the 60s, Protestant fundamentalists did not recognize the strength of joining with their Catholic counterparts in the political arena, having competed against each other for so long in proselytizing. But as the "Christian Right" grew increasingly vocal and organized in reaction to a series of United States Supreme Court decisions, a synergy began to counter the feminist movement and engage in battles over pornography, obscenity, abortion, state-sanctioned prayer in public schools, textbook contents concerning portrayal of American history and creationism, homosexuality and sexual education. New fundamentalist organizations began to see their conservative Catholic counterparts as a source of strength rather than competition. From every pulpit and homily, a Christian attack on the First Amendment and the Fourteenth Amendment was urged, without naming them but expressing what they stood for as anti-Christian and anti-American.

While all of this was melding in the 70s, the birth of the New Christian Right is usually traced to 1979 and the creation of a "Moral Majority" organization by televangelist Jerry Falwell. He followed through with the early thought that had been evolving through the decade of bringing together religion, industry and political organization. Through that decade, televangelism had provided a medium of growing popularity among Pentecostals and evangelicals and Falwell, himself, had a massive following. He reached out to activists and strategists like Richard Viguerie, a direct-mail political writer, co-founder of the Heritage Foundation and Wisconsin newspaper journalist and Goldwater Republican Paul Weyrich, and Howard Phillips, the Republican National Committee leader who had served on Nixon's cabinet.

With this leadership, it was clear that strength lay in inclusiveness. While any group gains strength early on by believing that they are on the outside, the ones who are abused, which has a unifying effect, there comes a time to convince the populace that they are the majority thought and should be joined. This time came for the disparate elements of political conservatism and the Religious Right. While the new Moral Majority appealed mainly to Christians, it invited all "morally conservative" Americans who believed in its tenets, including Orthodox Jews, Mormons, evangelical Protestants and conservative Catholics to join them. They needed to become a unified voting block with a mantra of taking America back, through opposing abortion, equal rights for homosexuals, sex education in schools, pornography as they defined it, through fighting communism and supporting Israel against Arab and Islamic states. It created religious tests for political candidates to take lest the candidate would lose such a block vote, as the John Birch society had done in the 60s, to determine candidate morality and to ensure that they would "defend the free enterprise system, the family, and Bible morality." Often, a candidate was required to sign an oath, if they wanted to be considered for support.

All of this coalesced just in time for Ronald Reagan's nomination, and he embraced it all. In the 1980 election, the Moral Majority claimed a constituency of 50 million. The message was not only that it is time to take back the morals of America and family values, but also that this is the majority thought and if you are not with us, you are against us to your own exclusion in society. There were numerous organizations such as the Christian Voice, the National Conservative Political Action Committee, and others, but they cooperated and served under one umbrella. Through a groundswell of conservative sentiment, they defeated Sen. George McGovern (D – SD), Frank Church (D – ID), John Culver (D – IA), Birch Bayh (D – IN) and many state legislators. Unlike moderates or liberals, they were energized and showed up to vote, and they organized at the precinct level from out of the churches. The Moral Majority packed the Republican caucus in Alaska, for insurance, and won all 19 delegates to the national convention for Ronald Reagan, while they achieved similar victories in Iowa and Alabama.

This was the beginning, as the country moved out of the 60s and 70s to a new conservatism that would last well into the next century. In 1981, Tim LaHaye founded the Council for National Policy (CNP). It operated in secrecy with a few hundred of the most powerful conservatives in the country networking industrial and right-wing donors together with top conservative operatives to plan long-term movement strategy. Its strong supporters were the new developing amalgamation of religion represented by the Moral Majority organizations and committed industry leaders such as Nelson Bunker Hunt of Hunt foods, T. Cullen Davis from the oil industry and others from political strategy orientation. Over decades to come, such notables as General John Singlaub, shipping magnate J. Peter Grace, Edwin J. Faulner, Jr. of the Heritage Foundation, Reverend Pat Robertson of the Christian Broadcasting Network, Jerry Falwell, Senator Trent Lott, retired Texas Court of Appeals Judge Paul Pressler, former United States Attorneys Generals Ed Nice and John Ashcroft, gun-rights activist Larry Pratt, Colonel Oliver North, mother of Eric Prince, founder of the Blackwater private security firm, and over time, quite a number of legislators and appellate judges, all belonged to the Council for National Policy.

Even though the Council for National Policy is more of a directive organization for various independent religious, commercial and political organizations, it is respected and followed and it provides centralized communication and leadership. Its membership list is "strictly confidential," the locations of its meetings secret, as well as its communications to its affiliates. Its founder, fundamental Baptist pastor Tim LaHaye is the author of The Battle for the Mind (1980) and the Left Behind series of books. The Council is known to have links with the World Anti-Communist League and is typically a speaking forum by invitation only for major political candidates, as represented in the past by VP Dick Cheney (Halliburton) and former Massachusetts governor Mitt Romney in the 2007 campaign; however, Rudy Giuliani, though invited did not appear. Before that election season, in 1999 George W. Bush gave a speech in the CNP, and it is thought that his appearance helped him gain the support of conservatives in his successful bid for the United States presidency in 2000. It was a secret speech, and neither CNP nor Bush has ever released its contents. There is speculation that it laid out pretty well what eventually occurred under the Bush paradigm.

The Republican Party and the Religious Right had mastered two principles; one, amalgamation; two, bringing multiple organizations under a common cause organization. Interestingly, although never an official member, leaders of the US military became ideological compatriots of the movement, as they saw it strengthening the military industrial complex. Part of that strength of what was now a well-organized movement was the clarity of its agenda which was preached from every pulpit, altar, and precinct political stump. There was no modulation of words or presentation. It was, indeed, evangelical, whether promoting Christianism, Old Testament morals or restrictive government. It produced voter guides, campaign, raised industrial contributions to tax-exempt political organizations wherein businesses could get tax deductions for making political contributions and interviewed candidates one-on-one to ensure they would vote on and initiate legislation that would undergird theocracy in America, often requiring the signing of an economic and or moral pledge.

By the turn of the century, America changed from what it had ever been before. While it had separated church and state, it was theocratic in legislation and judicial administration. The strong core of federal Congressmen, Senators and judges belonged to the moral conservative base, even if they had a separate caucus from which they came.

Astute Democratic candidates sometimes worked their way into governance, but they did so by never attacking the religious right but by "triangulating" towards that mass, which was just a nice way of being more in tune with what the religious right wanted. They certainly triangulated to the right when it came to the industrial complex because small contributions from the general public don't amount to much, while business contributions to political campaigns do. Now, under the new tax law, churches will have that massive contributory power. They can be huge, and while the religious right action committees might get larger amounts from the industrial complex and the churches, the more moderate candidates or party won't be able to compete. Industry under the Citizens United ruling has proven more than willing to buy off political candidate which affects both parties, while at the same time ensuring what had developed into Theocratic Corporate America by riding the successful founding of the Moral Majority back at the time of the great communicator, President Ronald Reagan. Now, churches will be able to have directly that same power.

So there you have it, as seen through the eyes of a singular observer for 50 years who is now in his "old man's political observation period." Of course, just like a river, many tributaries flowed into the making of this theocratic government, and I haven't covered nearly all, but I do believe this was the crux of the matter, at least from what I was able to observe.

Chapter 30

Revival and Osama bin Laden

IF YOU HAVE fought for the control of the mind of the masses for two decades and finally succeeded; if you have fought for control of government in order to pass religious laws without establishing a government religion and accomplished your mission; if you have established a judiciary to enforce those laws, how do you maintain the position of control and superiority of power? This is always the test for those who come to power with a fervent ideological view. To maintain that fervor and control is hard work, which tends to wane.

While the new Amalgamated force of industry, religion, and Republican politics had lurched under President Reagan, it modulated under Bush I and went through a malaise of frustration through the Clinton years. The strength and organization were there and ultimately enough fervor to sneak it back for George W. Bush, but there was clearly a need for revival. After two recounts for the 2000 election and candidate Gore filing suit for a third recount, the Supreme Court in a highly controversial decision, Bush v. Gore, held in favor of Bush.

The revival for the Religious Right came that same year, as Osama bin Laden and his Islamic fundamentalists struck the heart of New York City and the Pentagon of Washington, killing more than 3000 people and injuring and sickening many thousands more. It was a prayerful, sickening shock for all Americans, and the persistent, repeated scenes on television and in print were making an end-of-the-world nightmarish scene. For at least a couple of years after the attack, the publics' initial panic, anomie, and fear hung on. While psychologists documented sleeplessness and stress, even a year later 50% of US adults surveyed by CBS News felt "somewhat uneasy" or "under danger from terrorist attacks."

If you are a person who has grown up in a religious revivalist tradition and has ever stepped back to analyze it, you know that there are some key elements in which you must come to believe. First, there is a standard of conduct for both the individual and society that is accepted by God. Second, breach of that code of conduct must be punished. Third, by asking for forgiveness after punishment and reestablishing the conduct of the will of God, all will be forgiven, the spirit and the protection of the spirit revived.

Islam, even though Abrahamic, was portrayed as the antichrist and War was the will of the Christian God to render retribution. The 9/11 travesty upon American soil was a perfect vortex for revival, and the new conservative President was the evangelist that could bring about the ultimate religious government. He, himself, was a fundamentalist and believed in the literal word of the Bible.

Interestingly, as the drums of war pounded and the Republican Administration consolidated its legislative power, it was a Baptist minister, later a professor in the Department of Religion at Wake Forest, Charles Kimball, who published the book, When Religion Becomes Evil, in 2002. He set forth five warning signs for when religion, which is good when following its true purpose, is about to cause devastation:

Absolute Truth Claims

Blind Obedience

Establishing the "Ideal" Time

The End Justifies Any Means

Declaring Holy War.[98]

While the signs applied to bin Laden, they were the absolute paradigm of George W. Bush and supported by the industrial and military complex, as well as the Christian fundamentalist religion, Pentecostal, Protestant, and Catholic. Without a doubt, the United States was going to counterattack someone, but whom? History speaks for itself, today, without repetition here. Bush declared a global War on Terrorism and in a classical nation-to-nation war invaded Iraq following a congressional mandate in March 2003. To hell with the international law. The UN Charter applied to everyone else. Not us!

In his first term, Bush passed education legislation which opened the door for religious control of textbooks and religious teachings in schools on a state-by-state basis, by overshadowing the purpose of the standardized testing and the requisite legislative title of "No Child Left Behind." He pushed legislation of Partial Birth Abortion prohibition, faith-based welfare initiatives, withdrew funding from the United Nations Population Fund, withdrew funding from any nongovernmental organization that would provide an abortion service, restricted stem cell and genetic research, tried to privatize Social Security, and stacked the Supreme Court with social conservatives and laissez-faire justices, along with the same throughout the national federal judiciary.

A theocracy without establishing a state-authorized religion is created by emphasizing issues with Christian theological importance and then passing statutes with influence in that direction. Public schools and textbooks are pressured toward prayer and theological correctness on matters ranging from science and evolution to sex education. Family life is perceived in the patriarchal sense, and foreign policy established to both proselytize and control. The federal government is urged to restrain public morality at odds with interpretations of the Bible, shifting its regulatory preoccupation away from business and the economy, except for purposes of electioneering rhetoric and placing governmental focus on issues of life and death, including immortality, sex control, and family.

This is the religion of government, and it is the legacy of George W. Bush, the Religious Right and the first decade of the twenty-first century in America. What to me personally seems so strange, as I look back to some periods of my life, particularly the "Re-Search" period, was that my national government was now prepared to answer my initial questions concerning truth, religion and end-of-life questions, but it should not have come to this. If my own study brought me to a conclusion of invalidity in the promises of the Abrahamic religions, nevertheless, my government was here to reassure me by legislative authority.

Chapter 31

Theocratic Government

JANUARY 20, 2013, President Obama began his second term in office. The amalgamated Republican Party lost the presidential race for Obama's second term, but retained control of the House of Representatives. There was a lot of finger-pointing going on within the Party about why the Party did not retake the White House, but any thought that the amalgamation was cracking would have been foolish. It was then and is today here to stay, and its religious segment will always be working to pass legislation to maintain a Christian theocratic government. The Party will always be attacking the First Amendment, and that attack will take many different forms, as it has in the past.

This is not to suggest that the Democratic Party is the protector of separation of church and state. There may be times when it drives to support minority freedoms such as same-sex marriage, or the right of a woman to make a choice, but its history shows that many times it turned a blind eye to legislation that encroaches on the First Amendment protection. It's all about politics and not doing anything that would upset the Christian constituents. The Democratic Party may not be as aggressive in establishing and maintaining a Christian theocratic government as the Republican Party, and as an ideology, the Democratic Party may not even want a Christian theocracy, but that doesn't mean that as a group it will go out of its way to fight against theocracy.

The point is this. The only entities which are really going to fight against legislation that undermines the First Amendment right against theocracy are independent, private groups. Groups like the Freedom from Religion Foundation or the Secular Coalition for America or the Atheist Alliance of America are the "David" in the David/Goliath story. The religious right organizations that I've identified ("Goliath") are wealthy beyond imagination, well-organized and intend to continue having the theocratic government we know today on both the state and federal level. They're not going away nor are they going to let up. They are the Goliath of misinformation when it comes to the First Amendment.

In Congress, the religious right has its own caucus. I don't think you will find Congresspersons in a First Amendment caucus. I don't think you will find a Freethinkers caucus in Congress. But there is a clear joinder of religion and legislation when you see a Christian fundamentalist caucus of Senators and Representatives.

Alan Abramowitz of Emory University points out in his book, The Disappearing Center: Endangered Citizens, Polarization, and American Democracy, that the Founders saw political parties as "dangerous fomenters of conflict." That was at a time when a so-called "party" was just a small group who may agree on one issue, but disagree on others.

James Madison in the "Federalist No. 10," cited complaints "everywhere heard" that "the public good is disregarded in the conflicts of rival parties, and that measures are too often decided, not according to the rules of justice and the rights of the minor party, but by the superior force of an interested and overbearing majority." He saw "a zeal for different opinions [and] an attachment to different leaders ambitiously contending for pre-eminence and power." Madison lamented that it had "divided mankind into parties, inflamed them with mutual animosity, and rendered them much more disposed to vex and oppress each other than to cooperate for their common good."[99]

Our very first President, George Washington, in his 1796 farewell address, stepping down from the presidency, warned of hyper-partisans. "They serve to organize faction, to give it an artificial and extraordinary force; to put, in the place of delegated will of the nation the will of a party, often a small but artful and enterprising minority of the community."[100]

I am neither an academic nor a historian, but it is clear to me that these and other similar statements at that time prove that the Founding Fathers, the writers of the Constitution, wrestled with the intuitive knowledge that parties, as organized and factitious groups, could undermine the direct representation of the people by their representatives and the government, and in essence can cause a nullification of democracy in favor of special interests. Of course, that has come to pass, and as admirable as the creators of the constitutional document were in separating and protecting the three branches of government with checks and balances, they failed and could not do the same in protecting the citizenry with insurance of direct, democratic representation. They did their best, by ensuring certain minority rights within the document, but those protections went more towards protecting the individual from the powerful government, through the Bill of Rights, than the structure and dynamic of how an individual Congressman must be directly responsible to his constituency, both majority and minority.

The ultimate effect, as we know it today, is a two-party system in which the Party controls individual Congresspersons, and if they break off from the party's caucus, they can count not only on not being appointed to a meaningful congressional committee, but also on a likely defeat in the next election. Beyond that, a renegade party member will not receive money from the Party to run in the next election. It is a top-down governing system in which the voter now votes for the Party, while the Congressperson is less than important, but often pre-committed to a special interest group.

It is clear to me that the framers of the Constitution perceived an electorate who could choose their representatives on the basis of what they wanted or didn't want from the government, based upon clear and complete information easily acquired through a free press. Propaganda was alive and well not only then but for centuries before, but it did not have the mediums of today or the organized financial power to control thought that exists in the current technological environment. Each party, today, spends billions making sure their geographical strongholds (gerrymandered as they may be) are told how to think, rather than the other way around, individual thinkers with a full deck of information telling their individual Congressperson how they want their representation.

As Mickey Edwards states in his book, The Parties versus The People:

"In a sane world, in which the men and women we elect to Congress supply their own research and intelligence to the important decisions that confront them, we would expect some number of Republicans to vote with Democrats and some Democrats to line up with Republicans. But on the big issues, the ones that matter most, solid blocs face solid bloc of the other, unmovable, and unflinching in their loyalty to the Party 'team.' And that is because of the framework within which our politics unfolds… Party leaders control important committee assignments, provide or withhold money for reelection campaigns, and advance or block team members' legislative priorities; in our political system, one often pays a significant price for exercising independent judgment."[101]

"We have engendered a political system in which the necessary and inevitable 'interest-based factions' the Founders anticipated, understood, and worried about have been supplanted by permanent factions whose primary focus is on gaining and retaining political power."[102]

While historians point out the concerns of parties as they infused themselves into our democratic system, the modern day concern for First Amendment advocates is how a religious political Caucus had married itself to one of those political parties, sometimes in control, sometimes in partial control. The concern is that there exists no counter-balance.

So, where does that leave those of us who do not want to be controlled by such a structure, those of us who may have a different thought, or who would want freedom from religious codification in the laws that Congress enacts? We must understand that we are one of America's multitudes of minorities, and we always will be. Ours is a minority of thought, a view of what freedom and democracy should be, which makes us less identifiable as say an ethnic minority. Whether we and our thoughts of freedom shall survive depends on the effectiveness of organization and funding and the persistence and tenacity to fight for our vision of freedom. In structure, paradoxically, the Religious Right set the formula, but whether it is the organizing ability of a Cesar Chavez type on a financial shoestring or the Religious Right with substantial corporate funding and backing, the key is to organize and intelligently select the battlegrounds to battle a tougher, stronger opponent. This is the key to success.

I have never been an organizer and I don't know how I would do that, but I have served my time in courtrooms against overwhelming odds of opposing rows of litigators backed by a wealthy Corporation or an aggressive government. What I learned was that the "David" must select his engagement with the stronger force on a limited but strategic basis. You must do so with an intelligent identification of the opponent's most likely weakness and know the perfect timing of when and how to strike to gain maximum effectiveness. If, on the other hand, the "David" tries to contest the more powerful "Goliaths" on each issue, all of the time, he becomes fatigued and overwhelmed.

I would think that trial strategy would also apply to the broader context of organizing to protect a minority right. Obviously, the very beginning of the First Amendment battle is to understand where we are today and how we got here. Much of that battle centers on religion interfacing with government public education, though in reality, it goes far beyond that, in many different and subtle codifications outside public or private education.

Before the landmark 1947 Supreme Court decision of Everson v. Board of Education, only two Establishment Clause disputes about government funding of religion had reached the court, and the court in those cases refrained from defining the clause "respecting the establishment of religion" or what that clause means. In Bradfield v. Roberts (1899), where the court had upheld the federal government's funding of a hospital because even though the hospital was owned and staffed by a religious order, its primary function was to provide secular healthcare services. But it was in 1947 when the Court discussion started on what should or should not be funded, only to begin down a slippery slope after that, as the following shows:

Everson v. Board of Education (1947):

Applied the Establishment Clause to state and local governments and announced that the clause erected a "wall of separation" between religion and government; upheld a New Jersey statute that allowed local school boards to reimburse parents for the cost of busing their children to religious schools.

Board of Education v. Allen (1968):

Upheld a New York State program that required local school boards to loan textbooks at no cost to students in both public and private schools, including religious schools.

Lemon v. Kurtzman (1971):

Announced an important Establishment Clause standard now known as the "Lemon Test"; invalidated Rhode Island and Pennsylvania programs that in various ways subsidized instruction in secular subjects in private schools, most of which were religious.

Tilton v. Richardson (1971):

Upheld the 1963 Higher Education Facilities Act, a federal statute that awarded construction grants to colleges and universities, including those affiliated with religious institutions; declared that government-funded buildings must not officially be used for school-sponsored religious activities.

Committee for Public Education v. Nyquist (1973):

Invalidated a New York State program that granted tuition tax credits to parents of children in private schools, many of which were religious; invalidated grants for maintenance and repair of the schools because the facilities were used for worship and religious instruction.

Mueller v. Allen (1983):

Upheld a Minnesota statute that allowed parents to deduct from their state income taxes any money they spent on "tuition, textbooks, and transportation" for their children attending elementary and secondary schools, including religious schools.

Aguilar v. Felton (1985):

Invalidated a federal program that paid New York City public school teachers to provide remedial secular instruction to students living in low-income areas. This instruction was provided to students in both public and private schools, a substantial number of which were religious.

Grand Rapids School District v. Ball (1985):

Invalidated two school programs in Grand Rapids, Michigan that provide public funds for supplemental secular instruction in private schools, many of which were religious.

Witters v. Washington Department of Services for the Blind (1986):

Upheld the use of tuition grant at a religious college in accordance with a Washington State program that paid tuition for blind people at institutions of higher education or vocational training.

Bowen v. Kendrick (1988):

Upheld the eligibility of religious groups to receive funding under the 1981 Adolescent Family Life Act, a federal program that awarded grants to private groups that provided teen sex education.

Zobrest v. Catalina Foothills School District (1993):

Ruled that the Establishment Clause allowed the government to provide a sign-language interpreter for a hearing-impaired student during instruction at his religious high school.

Agostini v. Felton (1997):

Overruled Aguilar v. Felton, thus upholding a federal program that offered secular remedial services inside New York City religious schools; more generally held that the government may directly provide aid to religious institutions when the aid is secular and the government provides safeguards to ensure that recipients use the aid for secular purposes.

Mitchell v. Helms (2000):

Upheld a federal program that provided instructional materials and equipment to public and private schools, including religious schools, which educated children who lived in low-income neighborhoods.

Zelman v. Simmons – Harris (2002):

Upheld a Cleveland, Ohio, program that gave vouchers to low-income parents who chose to send their children to eligible private schools, most of which were religious.

Locke v. Davey (2004):

Upheld a Washington state program that denied scholarships to students pursuing theology degrees at religious schools.

Hein v. Freedom From Religion Foundation (2007):

Denied taxpayers the right to challenge the Executive Branch's use of discretionary funds for programs that support religious groups.[103]

With the Supreme Court having given a free Executive pass to the unification of government with religion, we can only anticipate that the movement will grow and become even more intertwined with society, societal acceptance, and thinking. From a purely political position, it is now well established that a President can give governmental support to any religious organizational authority, which clearly inures to the political benefit of his party and can provide not only massive boots on the ground at election time, but a resolving voice for religion in government, laws and election of representatives. The Executive Branch's ability to use discretionary funds for this purpose completely undermines the First Amendment.

This set of cases does not speak to the multitude of layered First Amendment issues such as the school prayer, the death penalty (itself Abrahamic-based), religious education in textbooks and classrooms, gay marriage and homosexuality (Abrahamic prohibition, but not in secular legalization), signing of religious covenants by candidates for public office, teaching creationism, executive privileges to establish religion to come, prayer and government facilities, religious displays in courts and governmental institutions, and all manner of issues relating to the Free Exercise Clause.

A fighter for religious freedom, while carrying the battle for the moral freethinking minority, should maintain in every argument that the logically and semantically placed statement, "Congress shall make no law respecting an establishment of religion…" conversely means there should be no religion in the laws passed by Congress, nor funding for laws that allow religious establishment. The mandate "shall" does not allow for government will, and the term "shall", being defined as a mandatory statement, has judicial foundation existing for centuries. Unfortunately, as interpreted by the Supremes, this does not apply to the Executive Branch. Beyond that, any foundation or other entity, or a Congressperson, who fights for religious freedom, should be aware of practical political caveats if and when they win a legal or legislative battle. You can see it in the 1971 Tilton case upholding the 1963 Higher Education Facilities Act that allowed Congress to award construction funds to religious institutions, as long as the buildings were not officially used for school-sponsored religious activities. A number of later cases expanded to other areas in this line of thinking. The problem is that the high court makes a judicial determination, but it has no oversight or enforcement power. Congress does. When Congress grants money to build buildings on behalf of and for religious universities, it does nothing more than follow the prohibition about not using the buildings for religious purposes in a bland statement in the financial award, to maintain the wall of separation, or at least its appearance.

Congress has never passed such an oversight or enforcement statute to ensure such prohibition. Then, the final caveat about judicial opinions, when they are brought in someone's favor, is that they are handicapped by Congress, who passes an enforcement statute, but without funding, so it can't be used. Thus, we have so-called separation laws with no oversight or oversight with no funding. It undermines the whole idea of separation of religion from government.

If we look back to the high court's 1971 "Lemon Test," we find that later courts wrestled with this legal doctrine because they did not like the strictness of separation of church and state. The Lemon Test had set out a three-part test for determining when a law violated the Establishment Clause, or on the flipside when a law was in compliance. The law must:

1. Have a secular purpose
2. Have a predominantly secular effect
3. Not foster "excessive entanglement" between government and religion.[104]

As can be seen, however, while the wall of church-state separation reached its apex in 1985, in the Ball and Aguilar cases, and other Supreme Court cases around the same time started to put some cracks in that wall. Basically, in spite of the Lemon Test, Supreme Court decisions undermined that test through inconsistency. For example, the standard laid out in "Mitchell" dramatically increased the government's options for partnering with religious groups. It was a monumental change when, prompted by the Mitchell case, Pres. George W. Bush announced his faith-based initiative, which sought to eliminate all federal policies that disqualified religious groups from participating in government-funded social welfare programs. The effects, of course, was government subsidy of Christian proselytizing.

In an admirable attempt to counter the President's destruction of the wall that separates government from religion, the Freedom from Religion Foundation (FFRF) brought to the High Court in 2007 the "Hein" case. It's argument focused on the question of whether taxpayers have legal standing (the right to sue) to challenge the government's funding of religion solely because the plaintiff, the one bringing the suit, the one desiring to contest the Bush program, is a taxpayer. Not just anyone can bring a suit to contest the government action or law. They must have "standing" to do, and the judicial doctrines of "standing," are quite erudite and complicated.

In the "Hein" case, the FFRF alleged that various federal executive agencies had violated the Establishment Clause by using tax dollars to promote faith-based initiatives. It argued that it had the standing to bring the "Hein" suit because its members pay taxes. But the court dismissed the suit by a five – four vote, reasoning that taxpayer standing applies only when the "legislative" branch specifically authorizes the use of tax dollars for religious institutions or purposes, not when the Executive Branch uses discretionary dollars funded by Congress without that legislative authority. In 2009, Pres. Barack Obama announced his faith-based initiative as "Executive." It is called the "White House Office of Faith-Based and Neighborhood Partnerships" which purports to broaden the scope of church – state partnerships.[105]

However, with the tenacity of a true First Amendment advocate, in 2012, the Freedom from Religion Foundation returned to court. This time they sued the Internal Revenue Service over its failure to enforce electioneering restrictions against churches and religious organizations.

Their argument before the US District Court for the Western District of Wisconsin was that the restrictions placed upon a Sec. 501(c) (3) (nonprofit) organization against political electioneering is intentionally not being enforced by the IRS, which violates the Establishment Clause of the First Amendment and FFRF's equal protection rights. It is well documented that in the 2012 national election, thousands of churches were electioneering from the pulpit and church facilities. The point is simply this. To be a nonprofit and be exempt from federal taxes, which saves churches and religious organizations an estimated $100 billion per year, such organizations do not have the right to a political purpose. Their purpose is for the private welfare, education and religious teaching of the citizenry, not the purpose of political control.

Freedom comes only to those who fight for it, and it is the same for freedom from theocracy. Organizations like the Freedom from Religion Foundation may be the "David," but they must keep slinging the shot if there is to be equal protection under our laws. These First Amendment litigation fights will now become more difficult to win, as the Religious Right continues to stack all courts with theocratic preferences.

Chapter 32

What to Do

IN SPITE OF Executive Privilege to establish a theocracy, proponents of religious freedom must develop a template to fight back. I have a few suggestions for any individual or group who desires to advocate for First Amendment enforcement:

1. Take (steal) from the Religious Right the public relations paradigm that they are the ones under attack and show that in fact we, First Amendment protection proponents, are the ones under attack.

2. Recognize that we are a minority and always will be. Why? Because blind faith is easy; critical thinking is difficult. It's work.

3. Speak out that to be a nonbeliever, a freethinker, is not odd but admirable. It is indicia of intelligence.

4. Create our own memes, short, specific verbal responses to use in conversation that can conjure truth and reason. This

may be the bumper sticker fallacy, but it works for those who can only think that far.

5. As distasteful as it may be, accept that money is a power that pushes thought, at least mass thought, and is needed to protect rights. The Religious Right tapped industrialists. Where can the funding source for the First Amendment protection be found?

6. To counter religious prejudice and influence, organize local community groups of freethinkers throughout the land, perhaps along the 18th-century coffeehouse model.

7. To counter the blind faith of the Religious Right, get the word out on the inconsistencies of the Gospels.

8. At Christmas, organize a parade of mourners for the Jewish children murdered, effectively protecting Jesus, in the Herod story.

9. To counter the blind faith of the Religious Right, prepare a simple presentation showing myth is not evidence.

10. The demographics of the 2012 election showed the changing ethnicity of America. Don't leave them out in teaching about the First Amendment. Include the Asian and Hispanic population on their own terms, communicating in their way.

11. Create and launch a social media campaign educating about the separation of church and state and utilize cartoons in the message.

12. Call into question the purpose behind preachers and priests lying about the veracity of the Bible. Expose their true motivation.

13. The religious Right has well organized and well-funded think tanks (Heritage Foundation, Cato Institute, etc.). Work to establish a Freethinkers First Amendment policy think tank.

14. Retail merchants fear loss of business if they don't placate the Religious Right. Freethinkers should also vote with their dollars and let it be known.

15. While the Executive Branch has provided government funds for religious social welfare programs, a campaign should commence for government funds for a Freethinker social welfare program.

16. Media sources have been cowed from reporting on free thought or critical thinking. Every local newspaper has a religion section. Organize and force a free thought section.

17. Do not accept the thought that critical thinking is too difficult for a large contingent of the populace to learn.

In support of this last suggestion, Wayne R Bartz, the retired clinical psychologist, sets forth the paradigm of critical thinking so simply in his book, Critical Thinking: the Antidote for Faith. He uses the acronym CRITIC for easy learning:

C – Claim? Exactly what is being proposed?

R – Role of the claimant? Who is making the claim?

I – Information backing the claim? What is the evidence to support the claim?

T – Test? How might we design an adequate test of this claim?

I – Independent testing? What was the test that others used? Was it unbiased? Was it adequate?

C – Cause proposed? Does the explanation fit within known laws of the physical universe?[106]

We can teach this in the same way public television children shows teach phonetics or arithmetic, and we need to get the word out. Simplicity is the key.

Of course, setting out what needs to be done is the easy part. The difficult part is the implementation, effort, workforce, and money it takes to do these things. To succeed, it takes organization at the grassroots level. The Religious Right had the necessary ingredients for success before the great political organizers showed up. They were already wealthy, and the churches had armies of middle-aged women who were and are willing to commit for this cause. The amalgamation, as I call it, the three separate segments (industry, government, Christian religious base), each already had a base. It was just a matter of identifying a common goal in coming together. They had what I call a pre-organization. When leaders recognized this, it was just a matter of bringing the three segments together to form unbeatable power.

For those of us who want freedom from religion and preference for free thinking, we are a truly disorganized minority. The thought of what it takes to compete against our amalgamated adversary is overwhelming. Where will we find the boots on the ground to carry the battle? Where will we find the money to match the financing? How will we convince legislators, Presidents, judges and governors that freedom from religion is what the First Amendment means and that should not be undermined? These are the same questions and the same fears every minority group asked themselves at the beginning of their campaign to organize. The Freedom from Religion Foundation has taken intelligent steps in recognizing the courtroom as a viable battleground. When you don't have that massive volunteer organization the churches have, you can nevertheless gain momentum through litigation. Even if you don't win the case, you create a consciousness that wasn't there before. If you do win, all the better.

Finally, study the techniques of such organizers as Fred Ross, Cesar Chavez and Saul Alinsky. Read Alinsky's 1946 book, Reveille for Radicals, where he described the nuts and bolts of effective organizing. Read his 1971 book Rules for Radicals, which provides a toolkit of principles and tactics for organizing the cause. Interestingly, after Obama took office in 2009, conservatives like Glenn Beck and the Tea Party attacked Obama for being an "Alinsky-ite" and a "socialist," and they began recommending Alinsky's book as a training tool for building a right-wing movement. First Amendment advocates can follow the same path, because the basics for organizing are the same for everyone. The only difference is an added tool that we have today, the Internet and social media.

As I am coming to the end of this long journey with numerous segregated periods of thought in my quest, I ask myself why it was so important to me to make my own comparison of Abrahamic religions. Why from the early seminal questioning of death at the killing of my dog was it so important to know the answers to end-of-life questions? I finally know the answer. It became clear that either through unintentional ignorance or intentional lying I was being given answers that lacked evidence. It became clear that there was no one I could trust for the truth. I had to dig it out for myself.

Mid-stream in my quest, I came to realize that fundamentalist religion had packaged answers and controlled thought. I never had a chance to think differently, to think critically, because I never heard anything but fundamentalist dogma as I was growing up. There was nothing in my West Texas world that would allow even a whisper of questioning, but somehow I broke loose and found intellectuals, those brave critical thinking individuals, who paved the way for investigation and critical thinking and real historical evidence beyond myth.

I became angry at the religion that had lied to me, but that anger was mild compared to what I felt as I learned how the First Amendment had been undermined and a theocratic government had evolved. It didn't seem fair that a myth-based religion should be forced by the government when the Bill of Rights plainly protected against that. These epiphanies brought frustration in my mindset, and I came to realize that most Americans don't even think about such things because the voice which is telling them that they should is so small. I am thankful that there is a voice at all, but I now know that freedom comes only to those willing to fight for it; and knowledge and freedom from religion is a natural and fundamental right. The Religious Right has sold the mass of citizenry the idea that the governments are out to stop their religious worship and therefore their religious freedom is in danger, that they are the persecuted just as in the time of Jesus. Of course, the opposite is true, and this is disinformation, but it sells. The mass of voters believe it, but just like being raised fundamentalist, the mass has never asked the question, "Is that really correct? What is the data that proves it?"

Nevertheless, I see a day coming when Christian fundamentalism will lose its stranglehold on American thought. I see a time when the pendulum will begin to swing back towards free thought. I see a time when freethinkers will join in an organization saying that they have had enough. I see a time of resurgence for freedom from religion. Indeed, I see a time when the myth is called into question, and we can be free at last.

Chapter 33

The Case for Religion

WHILE MUCH OF this book could be characterized as an attack on religion, my view is that religion, or more particularly, churches, synagogues, and mosques of Abrahamic religions offer more good than harm, most of the time. This may not be so in the hierarchy of religion and politics, but at the ground base, in the community, much good has been done.

Forget the test of a preponderance of evidence showing there is no God, that Jesus is not coming back, and that someone manipulated the writings of the New Testament, the book that Jesus did not write. It makes not a scintilla of difference.

"Jesus Is Risen!" Indeed, He has risen through groupthink and association. In my community, we have billboards stating the existence of God and citing Scripture. At Easter, there are signs everywhere saying "He Is Risen." This brings the church community together throughout the countryside in song, sermon, and affirmation.

Churches give one a community of support, belonging and togetherness. When a loved one is lost, the thought that you will be with them again in heaven is comforting in the surging grief.

The out-giving of Christian churches, synagogues, and mosques to the poor is indeed a loving support. The moral code of the New Testament, even when used in motivated thinking and bumper sticker misrepresentation, nevertheless sets an identifiable standard, a moral gauge.

The local religious meeting place is a community, coming together at one centerfold of belief, a belief in a higher power and authority that has predestined our path or upon faith can change our path. By joining together in prayer, a cathartic practice that brings ease, peace and an acknowledgment that not one of us is in control of what is going on around us, let alone in our personal life. It gives credence to the belief that a supernatural power is in control and can help us in our time of need. It gives us a chance to plead our case and ask for help.

What is wrong with that? Absolutely nothing. Faith, relying on claims yet to be proved, has stood the test of time. Whether it is based on an original myth makes no difference and need not be considered. It brings us together, and together we feel assuredness and confidence. The songs, rituals, sermons or homily create unity. It strengthens every community.

How many times have we seen religion save a young life from addiction, or give a Marine strength to carry on? How many have reached their emotional end in a state of depression, yet pulled through with a faith in God and then kept on going? There is much to be said in favor of the psychological effect of a belief in something, someone higher and larger that can help us through pain, remorse, difficulty, guilt, and tragedy, even raising us to an accomplishment greater than we thought possible.

This might be a short and even incomplete proposition of the need for religion and community provided by Christian churches, synagogues, and mosques. However, that proposition is not the focus of this book. Critical thinking is. Nevertheless, without these religious foundations, it is difficult to perceive what might be in their place, or how we might come together in our local communities. An alternative structure does not exist at the moment.

Chapter 34

Final Reflection

I HAVE CONCLUDED that there is no preponderance of evidence that God exists, and the premise that Jesus will return to earth has no foundation. If myth is not evidence, then there is no evidence of a supernatural God. It is only wishful thinking.

However, there are two more stones that I must turn. The first has always been a conundrum to me, and it is that I have often watched trained critical thinkers lose their critical thinking, seemingly by choice. The second is that I must argue in favor of the benefits of myth.

Beginning with the first stone, I use medical doctors as an example. I am well aware that medical training lasts 7 to 14 years. It is intense, grueling, and centered upon the principles of critical thinking and reliance on the application of the scientific method. One would think that kind of training would cause doctors to think critically in every aspect of their life and their life's philosophy, but my observation of many doctors I have known is that they leave critical thinking in the course of everyday life. To be fair, my observation is not scientific and can only provide my personal impression. Of course, not only doctors lose their critical thinking. Such a loss in reason seems to occur in persons of every profession that teaches logic and critical thinking.

I'm reminded of my cardiologist, a highly intelligent man. Not only is he a medical doctor, but he holds a Ph.D. from Columbia in epidemiology. He wrote and published a practical guide for laypeople to help the average person navigate the medical maze. It was well-written and explained well the processes of testing medicines, as well as treatments, and how critical thinking and the scientific method are an integral part. Throughout the book, however, he placed boxed inserts which he called the "Christian Perspective." He correlated stories of Job with the scientific revolution and attributed the Bible as the cause of the scientific revolution, and he often quoted Jesus and made other biblical references, asserting their validity.

It was striking to read a book that set forth logic so well in its description of the medical and pharmacological field, and yet viewed the Bible as written as a credible unit, valid in all respects. The attempts at causal connection were clearly motivated thinking. Having observed such conundrums of intelligent people of different disciplines, I can only conclude that logical, critical thinking is innate to no one. It is a tool. A person may be intelligent and may learn to use a given tool. Whether they choose to use it by definition is a matter of choice. They may do so; they may not, but the mere fact that they have learned to use the tool is not self-imposing.

That brings me to the last stone, the benefits of common myth. The image of death is most likely the beginning of mythology. The earliest evidence of anything like mythological thinking is associated with graves. There is no evidence that humans thought about death in a significant way until the Neanderthal period when weapons and animal sacrifices occur with burials.

Death has always been fearful and mysterious to the human psyche, as the brain evolved. As a Neanderthal would see a fellow person alive, then later dead, it wasn't a great leap to the idea of a continued life beyond the visible one, a plane of being that is behind the visible plane, one that is somehow supportive of the visible one to which we relate.

The idea of invisible support is connected to the human psyche in that we each intuitively know that we do not dictate all that happens. We are not in control. The idea of invisible support also relates to our psyche, in that we know we are limited in our individual capacity, but someone or something behind that veil can help us do more.

The feeling of invisible support comes from the connection with one's society, as well. Society was there before you; it is there after you are gone; you are a member of it. It is clear that the same myths that link you to your social group, the tribal myths, affirm that you are an organ, a part of the larger organism. The myths of society are not to be questioned. They grow and adjust with time and event, and the rituals link the individual to a larger morphological structure than that of his/her own body.

It doesn't take long to conceive a supernatural power behind the veil of invisibility, but myth is easier to tell from generation to generation than explaining a God. God is beyond description, yet we feel compelled to try to describe it. Heroes help to bring a description of what that God must be like, so many religions begin with their own heroes and heroic stories – – teaching the good law brought back by Buddha, the blessed laws brought down from Mount Sinai by Moses, the healings of Jesus, or the liberation by Muhammad. From that place come the stories that will connect us to God.

Of course, from the stories of the heroes comes the reduction of mythology to theology. Most myths are self-contradictory, but fluid. Some cultures have four or five myths, all giving a different version to the same mystery, just to make sure all bases are covered. Then theology comes along and says it has to be just a certain way. Within divining that certain way, there are struggles for influence and power until one version is established to the exclusion of all the others. Codes are made, and as one myth survives the battle, flexibility is gone. God is likely up there, and this is literally what an individual comes to think. You have to reject certain others, or accept or reject certain others or different ideas. This is the way you've got to behave in your society to get into a proper relationship not only with your community but with that God up there.

What is the benefit of this picture that has existed for 30,000 years? Community. Being a part of something. Support.

Acceptance, a vehicle by which to suppress the fear of death. If you are a Catholic, your feeling of strength comes from that religious community, if a Protestant fundamentalist, the same. You have a place to be born, to wed, to have children, to educate those children and allow them to become part of the community, and to die. You have organizations that you can belong to and help people who are less fortunate, and in the time of crisis, you band together with like-minded others. But it all began with communal myth, the glue of the tribe that survives.

All of this touches the spirit, the feeling within and the comfort provided by numbers. What is it that exists but not within logic, critical thinking, or the confirmation by the scientific method? It is the spirit – – that internal part of us that is not definable. We may call it will or soul, or being, but it is what myth speaks to and theology deducts into a set of rules and a way of life.

For those of us who are freethinkers, we do not want such a tribal, ritualistic life, and we see not only the failure of truth but the manipulation of the goals with it. We know very well, and have seen many times, that the codified texts such as the Qur'an or Bible can be used for any proposition – – anger management or anger enhancement, the eradication of prejudice or the creation of it, the pursuit of peace or the demand for war. For a small segment of society, it is not for us.

For the vast majority, they are willing to suspend disbelief when immersed in the religion. It may last for only a few hours on Sunday, or for others with discipline and dedication an extended period, but ultimately, the doubt will return, even if periodically.

The believer wants to believe that, although they have entered through the portals of other people's imagination from a different time and age, the stories of that imagination actually exist, and they happened as told. The common knowledge about historical writings is that it is the nature of many people's recollections that entails some degree of embellishment, exaggeration, and the bias of opinion. In religion, such realistic defects are either dismissed or suspended for a perceived higher purpose.

It is important, however, that we never take the attitude that it is they versus us, we versus them. Of course, it is well to state our truths in public and in private. In this democracy, we have the First Amendment right, and truth should neither be intimidated nor hidden. But the clear statement of truth should not be an attack upon or confrontation with religious society. It should simply be stated for its own worth and be protected from coercive proselytizing.

In my world, human intelligence is not an imprisoned spirit from afar, but an aspect of the whole intricately balanced organism of the natural world. Universes and earth are alike members of this organism, and nature is as much our father as our mother. One who has stood still long enough sees that on this Goldilocks little planet of ours, all sentient beings and non-sentient elements are interconnected. That does not require a god. Recognizing the inherent worth and dignity of every being does not require a god, but religion can indeed and often does reinforce this earthly requirement, regardless of how it gets to that understanding. There must be nonreligious respect for the interdependent web of all existence of which we are part. This is where Spirit lives; this is where peace is.

There is an exception of course, as there always is. Political representatives, whether federal, state or local should be taken to task whenever an individual politician acts in his/her official capacity to undermine the separation of church and state, whether in speech or action. They must be named and called out. They, their action, and their organization must be named and called out and brought to the awareness of the general public. In like manner, those secret Christian fundamentalist organizations to which some congressmen and senators belong and whose signed and committed mission is to undermine the separation of church and state must be continually unmasked and brought to public awareness. Here, again, however, it is important to attack issues, not the individual; to fight the clandestine maneuvers of the secret political organizations by disclosure and debate, but not to personally attack its members. Theocrats are always eager to legislate morality, their version of it. It is irrelevant to them that their proposed laws violate the very freedom of constitutional government; therefore, we must fight each attempt towards theocratic government, issue by issue, court by court.

We should not allow a paradigm among us that seeks to destroy any religious community. People need their myths for their own comfort, and they need their religious community for being a part of their tribal group. Much good often comes from this, and while we disagree with their prejudices, we should equally recognize the good that they do on the community level.

What we, freethinkers, want is freedom in a free democratic society. We do not want a theocratic government, where we are forced to live with laws that imply or impress upon us a codification of religious thought. To this end, when a legislative enactment attacks our freedoms or when the First Amendment is undermined, we must, by our right as an American, contest such actions in a court of law. It is our duty. It is also our duty as freethinkers to attack and debate the issues. We gain nothing by attacking the religious proselytizers, lest we become as they are.

LETTER TO SCHATZIE

WELL SCHATZIE, TIME is about up. I missed you very much when you were gone. There were times when I was riding my bicycle, but I thought you were still there running along beside me. Exploring places we hadn't seen before just wasn't the same after you left. I was determined to find out how, when and where I would get to see you again.

You are my best friend, and somehow, in my childish way, I thought we would be together real soon, and things would get back to normal. Well, things didn't happen quickly, and it took a very long time to figure out the answers – – in fact, an entire lifetime. I was told a lot of different things by a lot of different people, some of whom claimed to have all the answers. The trouble was that they didn't have evidence for the answers they claimed, or on other occasions, what they called evidence like Bible verses, really wasn't evidence at all.

A religious man, a preacher, told me that I must have faith that I would see you in heaven. I tried very hard to do that, because it made me feel better, at least for a little while. Perhaps it would've worked, the feel better part, if I hadn't met intelligent people that taught me to ask questions. Once I started doing that, things got a little complicated. Questions require answers. You can have answers that you like or just want to hear, or you can search for answers that are true and correct and based on fact. There is a complete testing process for the latter, but it takes away the thought, or the feeling, or the intuition of what you want the answer to be. Most of the time, you either end up with the probability of the hard, cold truth or the actual true answer, itself. Many times, the answer is not what you wanted to hear.

And Schatzie, I'm afraid that's where we are. I searched, and I studied, and I know you cannot hear what I'm saying because when that car hit you, that was it. It (life) was over. We won't be seeing each other again Schatzie, and I really hate that. There is neither dog heaven nor human heaven. But what I do have as long as I am alive is my wonderful memories of you.

You were such a hoot! You were interested in anything that moved. Life totally intrigued you. As I sit here thinking about it, I can feel that same feeling of peace I had riding my bike through the drifting yellow fall tree leaves, with you running and barking happily along by my side. We had some great times together and that, in itself, is its own beauty.

Goodbye, Schatzie, my love.

REFERENCES, SOURCE NOTES, AND EXPLANATIONS

WHILE THIS BOOK was written in the final form in my retirement, it was not until retirement that I anticipated writing it. The epic search for answers and research seeking those answers lasted a lifetime. Through that lifetime many notes were taken, outlines designed, sources documented, but seldom in preparatory fashion for writing a book. Much research and note taking was done before the advent of computer usage or search engines.

Through the first eight chapters, I seldom cite a source for the reason that much of the text is experiential; while at the same time some of the note-taking and early note-sourcing in research was lost over the years. However, periodically, in these first chapters, I insert current thinking scholars even though I did not have the benefit of their analysis at the time. For example, in Chapter Three, I reference Stephen Prothero. 2010. God Is Not One. Harper One. N.Y.

Otherwise, in these early chapters, I did refresh the memory of earlier research by visiting a few scholars or going to the Qur'an and Old Testament texts, individually. These chapters are not meant to be an academic examination but more the story of my search at the time.

I am totally inconsistent in use of BC, BCE, and CE. I used whatever designation was in my mind at the time. The terms BCE (Before Common Era and CE Era, which was first invented in the Sixth Century A.D.) are now the rule of order to express politically correct sensitivity to non-Christians. To me, it's much ado about nothing. The Gregorian calendar is used as the starting point for each designation.

Finally, as to internet citations in Source Notes, I incorporate each source citation used by the author, because I have utilized them all, in addition to hard print study. On occasion, the internet citation seen as a source is duplicitous of the same text in another but different source in hard print.

SOURCE NOTES

Source Notes for Chapter 3

Prothero, Stephen. *God Is Not One: The Eight Rival Religions that Run the World – and Why Their Differences Matter.* New York: HarperOne, 2010.

Source Notes for Chapter 4

Brandewie, Ernest. *Wilhelm Schmidt and the Origin of the Idea of God.* Lanham: University Press of America, 1983.

Source Notes for Chapter 5

"Zoroastrianism at a glance". BBC. Accessed February 23, 2018. http:// www.bbc.co.uk/religion/religions/zoroastrian/ataglance/glance. shtml

Source Notes for Chapters 9, 10 and 11

That period of several months in my first sabbatical, where I could visit libraries in New York City, occurred in 1972. I outlined and took copious notes of text and subject matter separately; I documented sources. Unfortunately, in later years and before the writing of this book my source list was lost, though not my text notes.

In writing the referred to chapters, I have relied heavily on my text notes from that earlier time in the works of Bart D. Ehrman, a scholar on the history of the New Testament and John Shelby Spong, an Episcopal Bishop and scholar on the subject of understanding the culture in which the Bible was written.

While numerous other books and treatises on the same subject influenced my research, writing ability of Ehrman and Song to reduce vast quantities of research to succinct understanding is most admirable and causes me to rely on them in these chapters.

Books by Bart D. Ehrman:

Misquoting Jesus, the Story Behind Who Changed the Bible and Why. San Francisco: Harper, 2005.

Lost Christianities: The Battles for Scripture and the Faiths We Never Knew. New York: Oxford University Press, 2003.

Jesus, Interrupted: Revealing the Hidden Contradictions in the Bible. New York: Harper Collins Publishers, 2009.

Forged: Writing in the Name of God--Why the Bible's Authors Are Not Who We Think They Are. New York: HarperOne, 2011.

(Bart D. Ehrman has written numerous other books and treatises and is a James A. Gray Distinguished Professor of Religious Studies at the University of North Carolina at Chapel Hill.).

Books by John Shelby Spong:

Rescuing the Bible from Fundamentalism: A Bishop Rethinks the Meaning of Scripture. New York: HarperCollins, 1991.

Eternal Life: A New Vision: Beyond Religion, Beyond Theism, Beyond Heaven and Hell. New York: HarperCollins, 2009.

Re-*Claiming the Bible for a Non-Religious World.* New York: HarperCollins, 2011.

(John Shelby Spong is a retired American Bishop of the Episcopal Church who dedicated his life to scholarly research, authoring many books and treatises.)

These scholars and scholars like them refresh the knowledge that the evolution of language complicates the documentation of human experience, as gaps in documentation exacerbate the attempt. As one looks back over centuries of Biblical interpretation the words of German philosopher Theodore Lessing come to mind – – how writers in each century "give meaning to the meaningless" through acts of creativity.

Cox, Steven L. Easley, Kendell H. *Holman Christian Standard Bible Harmony of the Gospels*. Nashville: B&H Publishing Group, 2007.

"Inconsistencies of the New Testament". The Nazarene Way of Essenic Studies. Accessed February 26, 2018.

http://www.thenazareneway.com/new_testament_biblical_inconsistencies.htm

Pastor Kyeyune, Stephen. *A Miracle at Prairie Avenue: The Quest for Faith*. Bloomington: Authorhouse, 2011.

Stinson, Vance A. "The Resurrection - Real Event or Historical Hoax?" Accessed February 26, 2018.

https://static1.squarespace.com/static /50438d1dc4aa994481346f77/t/54f757c0e4b08d5963bbd850/1425496000855/The+Resurrection.pdf

"Who was Theophilus at the beginning of Luke and Acts?". Got Questions. Accessed 27 February 2018. https://www.gotquestions.org/Theophilus-Luke-Acts.html

Source Notes for Chapter 12

"Historicity of Jesus". Wikipedia – The Free Encyclopedia. Accessed 27 February 2018. https://en.wikipedia.org/wiki/Historicity_of_Jesus

Feldman, Louis H, Hata, Gōhei. *Josephus, the Bible, and History*. Detroit: Wayne State University Press, 1989.

Mason, Steve. *Josephus and the New Testament*. Peabody: Hendrickson Publishers, 2003.

Paget, James Carleton. "Some Observations on Josephus and Christianity." Journal of Theological Studies, 2001, 52 (2): 539-624.

Wells, George Albert, *The Jesus Legend*, Chicago: Open Court Publishing Company, 1996.

Whealey, Alice. *Josephus on Jesus: The Testimonium Flavianum Controversy from Late Antiquity to Modern Times*. New York: Peter Lang, 2003.

Source Notes for Chapter 13

What an interesting tale. If only it were true, it would be a more sensible story than the mythical one we now have.

As to The Essenes and The Purported Letter from Jerusalem, scholars have exposed it as a fraud, first published in German, in Leipzig in 1849. The later discovery of the Dead Sea Scrolls, which were unavailable to the writer of this document, established its lack of factual authenticity.

Armstrong, Karen. A *History of God, the 4000-year Quest of Judaism, Christianity and Islam*. New York: Ballantine Books, 1993.

Crucifixion by an Eye-Witness. Chicago: Indo-American Book Company, 1907.

Ehrman, Bart D. *Forged: Writing in the Name of God--Why the Bible's Authors Are Not Who We Think They Are.* New York: HarperOne, 2011.

Ehrman, Bart D. *Lost Christianities: The Battles for Scripture and the Faiths We Never Knew.* New York: Oxford University Press, 2003.

Ehrman, Bart D. *Forged: Writing in the Name of God--Why the Bible's Authors Are Not Who We Think They Are.* New York: HarperOne, 2011.

Haywood, John. *The New Atlas of World History: Global Events at a Glance.* Princeton: Princeton University Press, 2011.

Kiraz, George A. (Ed.), *Anton Kiraz's archive on the Dead Sea Scrolls,* Piscataway: Gorgias Press, 2005.

Richards, Chris. *The Illustrated Encyclopedia of World Religions.* New York: Barnes & Noble, 1997.

Schuler, Eileen M. *The Dead Sea Scrolls: What Have We Learned?* Louisville, KY: Westminster John Knox Press, 2006.

Tov, Emanuel, Davis, Kipp, Duke, Robert (Eds.). *Dead Sea Scrolls Fragments in the Museum Collection,* Leiden: Brill Academic Pub, 2016.

Zimmer, Carl. *Smithsonian Intimate Guide to Human Origins.* New York: Harper Perennial, 2005.

For the study of the evolution of Hebrew and Abrahamic Judaism, see the Jewish Virtual Library, A Division of the American – Israeli Cooperative Enterprise (www.jewishvirtuallibrary.org):

The Torah

The Holy Scriptures - Tanakh

The Babylonian Talmud

The Zohar, for mystical interpretations of the above.

Source Notes for Chapter 14

Albertz, Rainer. A *History of Israelite Religion in the Old Testament Period: Volume I: From the Beginnings to the End of the Monarchy.* Louisville, KY: Westminster John Knox Press, 1994.

Armstrong, Karen. A *History of God, the 4000-year Quest of Judaism, Christianity and Islam.* New York: Ballantine Books, 1993.

Barton, John, Stavrakopoulou, Francesca (Eds.). *Religious Diversity in Ancient Israel and Judah.* London: T&T Clark, 2010.

Cohen, Jennie. "6 Things You May Not Know About the Dead Sea Scrolls". History. Accessed 4 March 2018. http://www.history.com/news/history-lists/6-things-you-may-not-know-about-the-dead-sea-scrolls

Crucifixion by an Eye-Witness. Chicago: Indo-American Book Company, 1907.

"Daughter of Jairus". Religion Wiki. Accessed 4 March 2018.

http://religion.wikia.com/wiki/Daughter_of_Jairus

Source Notes for Chapter 15

Armstrong, Karen. A *History of God, the 4000-year Quest of Judaism, Christianity and Islam.* New York: Ballantine Books, 1993.

"History of ancient Israel and Judah". Wikipedia – The Free Encyclopedia. Accessed 4 March 2018. https://en.wikipedia.org/wiki/History_of_ancient_Israel_and_Judah

While I had lost many of my source notes from my early sabbatical, I still had some, and I reviewed the following in my later life to support my early text notes.

For general history, see:

"Mesopotamia time". Accessed 9 March 2018.

http://www.mesopotamia.co.uk/time/home_set.html

Zimmer, Carl. *Smithsonian Intimate Guide to Human Origins*. New York: Harper Perennial, 2005.

For the polytheism of Israel and the true personality of Muhammad, see:

Wright, Robert. *The Evolution of God: The origins of our beliefs*. London: Little, Brown. 2009.

For the early myths, see:

Armstrong, Karen. *A Short History of Myth*. Edinburgh: Canongate Books, 2005.

For the divergence, Israel/Judah:

Ahlstrom, Gosta W. *The History of Ancient Palestine*. Minneapolis: Fortress Press, 1993.

Barton, John, Stavrakopoulou, Francesca (Eds.). *Religious Diversity in Ancient Israel and Judah*. London: T&T Clark, 2010.

For revealing epigraphy of the period, see:

"Inscriptions of Israel/ Palestine". Brown Library. Accessed 12 March 2018. http://cds.library.brown.edu/projects/Inscriptions/

For the significance of archaeology and anthropology of the periods, see:

Amihai Mazar. *Archaeology of the Land of the Bible: 10,000 – 586 B.C.E.* New York: Doubleday, 1990.

Scarre, Chris. *Smithsonian Timelines of the Ancient World*. New York: DK Adult, 1993.

For continued discussion, see:

"Frontiers of Anthropology". Accessed 12 March 2018. http://www.frontiers-of-anthropology.blogspot.com

Source Notes for Chapter 16

World and Its Peoples: Greece and the Eastern Balkans. New York: Marshall Cavendish Reference. 2010.

"The Epic of Gilgamesh / Nimrod: Second Oldest Writing – From the Lost Book Of Enki". True Democracy Party. Accessed 6 March 2018.

http://truedemocracyparty.net/2012/07/the-epic-of-gilgamesh-nimrod-second-oldest-writing-from-the-lost-book-of-enki/

Source Notes for Chapters 18 and 19

For general background and references on Judea and Israel, BCE, see:

Armstrong, Karen. A *History of God, the 4000-year Quest of Judaism, Christianity and Islam.* New York: Ballantine Books, 1993.

Armstrong, Karen. *The Bible: A Biography (Books That Changed the World).* New York: Atlantic Monthly Press, 2007.

For general background and references on the prehistory of Hebrews, Israelites and Judaism, see:

Albertz, Robert. *A History of Israelite Religion in the Old Testament Period, Volume I: From the Beginnings to the End of the Monarchy.* Louisville, KY: Westminster John Knox Press, 1994.

Hetzron, Robert (Ed.). *The Semitic Languages.* New York: Routledge, 1997.

Paas, Stefan. *Creation and Judgment: Creation Texts in Some Eighth Century Prophets.* Boston Brill Academic Publishing, 2003.

Van der Toorn, Karel, Becking, Bob, Van der Horst, Pieter W. (Eds.) *Dictionary of Deities and Demons in the Bible.* Grand Rapids, MI: Wm. B. Eerdmans Publishing Company, 1999.

Vikander Edelman, Diana (Ed.). *The Triumph of Elohim: From Yahwisms to Judaisms*. Grand Rapids, MI: Wm. B. Eerdmans Publishing Company, 1995.

Grabbe, Lester L. *The History of the Jews and Judaism in the Second Temple Period*. London: T&T Clark, 2004.

Nodet, Etienne. *A Search for the Origins of Judaism: From Joshua to the Mishnah*. London: T&T Clark, 1997.

For general background and references on the evolution of Judaism, see:

Cohn-Sherbok, Dan. *The Hebrew Bible*. London: Continuum International, 1996.

Coogan, Michael David. *The Oxford History of the Biblical World*. London: Oxford University Press, 1999.

Lipschitz, Oded. *The Fall and Rise of Jerusalem: Judah Under Babylonian Rule*. Winona Lake, IN: Eisenbrauns, 2005.

"The Destruction of the Second Holy Temple", Chabad.org. Accessed 12 March 2018. https://www.chabad.org/library/article_cdo/aid/913023/jewish/The-Second-Temple.htm

For archaeological data and references, see:

Akkermans, Peter M. M. G., Schwartz Glenn M. *The Archaeology of Syria: From Complex Hunter-Gatherers to Early Urban Societies (c.16,000 – 300 BC)*. New York: Cambridge University Press, 2003.

Finkelstein, Israel, Silberman Neil Asher. *The Bible Unearthed: Archaeology's New Vision of Ancient Israel and the Origin of Its Sacred Texts*. New York: Free Press, 2001.

Grabbe, Lester L. (Ed.). *Israel in Transition: From Late Bronze II to Iron IIa (c. 1250 – 850 B.C.E.) Volume 1. The Archaeology*. New York: T&T Clark, 2008.

Killebrew, Ann E. *Biblical Peoples and Ethnicity: An Archaeological Study of Egyptians, Canaanites, Philistines, and Early Israel, 1300–1100 B.C.E.* Atlanta: Society of Biblical Literature, 2005

Levy, Thomas E. *Archaeology of Society in the Holy Land*. New York: Continuum Publishing, 1998.

Simmons, Alan H. *The Neolithic Revolution in the Near East: Transforming the Human Landscape*. Tucson: University of Arizona Press, 2007.

For understanding the Natufians:

Bar-Yosef, Ofer, Belfer-Cohen, Anna. "Encoding information: Unique Natufian objects from Hayonim Cave, Western Galilee, Israel". *Antiquity*, 1999, 73(280), 402-410. doi:10.1017/S0003598X00088347

Bar-Yosef Ofer, Valla Francois R. (Eds.). *The Natufian Culture in the Levant*. Ann Arbor, MI: International Monographs in Prehistory, 1991.

Source Notes for Chapter 20

"The Levant". Accessed 6 March 2016. http://www.crystalinks.com/Levant.html

Wright, Robert. *The Evolution of God: The origins of our beliefs*. London: Little, Brown. 2009.

Source Notes for Chapter 21

"Joseph Campbell". Pantheism. Accessed 6 March 2018. https://pantheism.com/about/luminaries/joseph-campbell/

"Joseph Campbell". Psychology Wiki. Accessed 6 March 2016. http://psychology.wikia.com/wiki/Joseph_Campbell

Armstrong, Karen. *A Short History of Myth*. Edinburgh: Canongate Books, 2005.

Campbell, Joseph, Moyers, Bill. *The Power of Myth*. New York: Anchor Books, 1991.

Klein, Richard G. "Archaeology and the Evolution of Human Behavior." *Evolutionary Anthropology* 9: 17 – 36, 2000.

Smith, Fred H., Spencer, Frank. *The Origins of Modern Humans: A World Survey of the Fossil Evidence*. New York: A.R. Liss, 1984.

For general understanding of Out of Africa:

Arsuaga, Juan Luis. *The Neanderthal's Necklace: In Search of the First Thinkers*. New York: Four Walls Eight Windows, 2002.

Klein, Richard G., Edgar, Blake. Dawn of Human Culture: A Bold New Theory on What Sparked the 'Big Bang' of Human Consciousness. New York: John Wiley & Sons/Peter N. Nevraumont, 2002.

Wade, Nicholas. *Before The Dawn: Recovering the Lost History Of Our Ancestors*. New York: The Penguin Press, 2006.

Source Notes for Chapter 22

Armstrong, Karen. *A Short History of Myth*. Edinburgh: Canongate Books, 2005.

Campbell, Joseph, Moyers, Bill. *The Power of Myth*. New York: Anchor Books, 1991.

Haywood, John. *The New Atlas of World History: Global Events at a Glance*. Princeton: Princeton University Press, 2011

"Joseph Campbell". Pantheism. Accessed 6 March 2018. https://pantheism.com/about/luminaries/joseph-campbell

"Joseph Campbell". Psychology Wiki. Accessed 6 March 2016. http://psychology.wikia.com/wiki/Joseph_Campbell

For an understanding of current Free Thought Atheism, see:

Dawkins, Richard. *The God Delusion*. Boston: Houghton Mifflin Company, 2006.

Dennett, Daniel C. *Breaking the Spell: Religion as a Natural Phenomenon*. London: Penguin Books, 2006.

Harris, Sam. *The End of Faith: Religion, Terror, and the Future of Reason*. New York: W. W. Norton & Company, 2004.

Hitchens, Christopher. *Mortality*. Boston: Twelve, 2012.

Stenger, Victor J. *The New Atheism: Taking a Stand for Science and Reason*. New York: Prometheus Books, 2009.

For an understanding of the scientific discovery of the Higgs Boson, see:

Baggott, Jim. *Higgs: The Invention and Discovery of the 'God Particle'*. London: Oxford University Press, 2012.

Source Notes for Chapter 23

Cohen, Morris F. *An Introduction to Logic and Scientific Method*. New York: Harcourt, Brace & World, 1934.

"Elements of Critical Thinking". The Sourcebook for Teaching Science. Accessed 13 March 2018. https://www.csun.edu/science/ref/ reasoning/critical_thinking/elements.html

Garner, Bryan A. *Black's Law Dictionary*. St. Paul, MN: West Publishing Co, 1999

Goldstein Rebecca. *36 Arguments for the Existence of God: A Work of Fiction*. New York: Vintage, 2011.

Hawking, Stephen, Mlodinow, Leonard. *The Grand Design*. New York: Bantam Books, 2010.

Hoover, Kenneth, Donovan, Todd. *The Elements of Social Scientific Thinking*. Boston: Wadsworth, 2011.

Lilly, Graham, Capra, David, Saltzburg, Stephen. *Principles of Evidence*. St. Paul, MN: Thomson Reuters, 2009.

Littrell, Dennis. *Understanding Evolution and Ourselves*. CreateSpace Independent Publishing Platform, 2011.

Martin, Michael, Monnier, Ricki. *The Impossibility of God*. Amherst: Prometheus Books, 2003.

Ruggiero, Vincent Ryan. *Thinking Critically About Ethical Issues*. Mountain View, CA: Mayfield Publishing Company, 1982.

"New Atheism", Wikipedia – The Free Encyclopedia. Accessed 6 March 2018, https://en.wikipedia.org/wiki/New_Atheism

"The rise of the 'New Atheists'". CNN. Accessed 6 March 2018. http://edition.cnn.com/2006/WORLD/europe/11/08/atheism.feature/index.html

Weinberg, Steven. "Why the Higgs Boson Matters". The New York Times. Accessed 7 March 2018. http://www.nytimes.com/2012/07/14/opinion/weinberg-why-the-higgs-boson-matters.html?pagewanted=all

Source Notes for Chapter 24

Brockman, John (Ed.) *Intelligent Thought: Science Versus the Intelligent Design Movement*. New York: Random House, 2006.

Deckman, Melissa M. *School Board Battles: The Christian Right in Local Politics*. Washington DC: Georgetown University Press, 2004.

Frazer, Sir James. *The Golden Bough*. New York: Dover Publications, 2002.

Forrest, Barbara. Gross, Paul R. *Creationism's Trojan Horse, the Wedge of Intelligent Design*. New York: Oxford University Press, 2004.

Garner, Bryan A. *Black's Law Dictionary*. St. Paul, MN: West Publishing Co, 1999.

Klein, Richard G., Blake, Edgar. *The Dawn of Human Culture: a Bold New Theory on What Sparked the "Big Bang" of Human Consciousness.* Hoboken, NJ: John Wiley & Sons, 2002.

„Philosophy 101". Evolutionary Philosophy. Accessed 7 March 2018. http://www.evphil.com/philosophy-101.html

Tammy Kitzmiller, et al, v. Dover Area School District, et al. "Memorandum Opinion. In The United States District Court for The Middle District of Pennsylvania." 2005. Accessed 7 March 2018. https://ncse.com/files/pub/legal/kitzmiller/highlights/2005-12-20_Kitzmiller_decision.pdf

Tuckwell, William. *Reminiscences of Oxford.* New York: E.P. Dutton and Company, 1908.

Source Notes for Chapter 25

Buckley, Thomas E. *Church and State in Revolutionary Virginia, 1776 – 1787.* Charlottesville, VA: University of Virginia Press, 1977.

Conkin, Paul K. "The Religious Pilgrimage of Thomas Jefferson." *Jeffersonian Legacies.* Peter S. Onuf (Ed.), 19–49. Charlottesville, VA: University of Virginia Press, 1993.

Ragosta, John. *Wellspring of Liberty: How Virginia's Religious Dissenters Helped Win the American Revolution and Secured Religious Liberty.* New York: Oxford University Press, 2010.

Source Notes for Chapter 26

"Massachusetts Bay Colony". En Academic. Accessed 6 March 2018. http://enacademic.com/dic.nsf/enwiki/130064

Meacham, Jon. *American Gospel: God, the Founding Fathers, and the Making of a Nation.* New York: Random House Publishing Group, 2007.

"Memorial and Remonstrance against Religious Assessments, (ca. 20 June) 1785". Accessed 7 March 2018. https://founders.archives. gov/documents/Madison/01-08-02-0163

Phillips, Kevin. *American Theocracy: The Peril and Politics of Radical Religion, Oil, and Borrowed Money in the 21ˢᵗ Century.* New York: The Penguin Group, 2006.

"The Constitution of the United States". Accessed 7 March 2018. https://constitutioncenter.org/media/files/constitution.pdf

"Thomas Jefferson and the Virginia Statute for Religious Freedom". Virginia Museum of History and Culture. Accessed 7 March 2018. https://www.virginiahistory.org/collections-and-resources/virginia-history-explorer/thomas-jefferson

"Thomas Jefferson, July 27, 1821, Autobiography Draft Fragment, January 6 through July 27, from the Thomas Jefferson and William Short Correspondence, Transcribed and Edited by Gerard W. Gawalt, Manuscript Division, Library of Congress". Accessed 7 March 2018. http://www.loc.gov/resource/mtj1.052_0517_0609

For Original Meanings underlying the language of First Amendment religion clauses, see:

Curry, Thomas J. *The First Freedoms: Church and State in America to the Passage of the First Amendment.* New York: Oxford University Press, 1986.

For the idea of Natural Rights and Natural Law, see:

Tuck, Richard. *Natural Rights Theories, Their Origin and Development.* London: Cambridge University Press, 1982.

For the Virginia debates, see:

"Memorial and Remonstrance against Religious Assessments, (ca. 20 June) 1785". Accessed 7 March 2018. https://founders.archives. gov/documents/Madison/01-08-02-0163

Madison excerpt: "The Religion then of every man must be left to the conviction and conscience of every man; and it is the right of every man to exercise it as these may dictate. This right is in its nature an unalienable right. It is unalienable, because the opinions of men, depending only on the evidence contemplated by their own minds cannot follow the dictates of other men: It is unalienable also, because what is here a right towards men, is a duty towards the Creator. It is the duty of every man to render to the Creator such homage and such only as he believes to be acceptable to him."

"Thomas Jefferson and the Virginia Statute for Religious Freedom". Virginia Museum of History and Culture. Accessed 7 March 2018. https://www.virginiahistory.org/collections-and-resources/virginia-history-explorer/thomas-jefferson

Excerpt from Virginia Statute (1786): "Be it enacted by the General Assembly, that no man shall be compelled to frequent or support any religious worship, place, or ministry whatsoever, nor shall be enforced, restrained, molested, or burthened in his body or goods, nor shall otherwise suffer on account of his religious opinions or belief; but that all men shall be free to profess, and by argument to maintain, their opinion in matters of religion, and that the same shall in no wise diminish, enlarge, or affect their civil capacities."

(Note: in 1789, James Madison introduced in Congress proposed amendments to the Constitution that would eventually become known as the Bill of Rights. The First Amendment's first 16 words, divided into two clauses, guaranteed unprecedented freedom of religion in the early United States.)

For understanding what Madison called "the great rights of mankind's quote and the American Court that interpreted them, see:

Buckley, Thomas E. *Church and State in Revolutionary Virginia, 1776 – 1787*. Charlottesville, VA: University of Virginia Press, 1977.

Ives, Joseph Moss. *The Arc and the Dove: The Beginning of Civil and Religious Liberties in America*. New York: Longmans, Green and Company, 1969.

James, Charles F. *Documentary History of the Struggle for Religious Liberty in Virginia*. Lynchburg: J. P. Bell Company, 1900.

Rutland Robert A., Rachal, William M. E. (Eds.) *The Papers of James Madison, vol. 8, 10 March 1784–28 March 1786*. Chicago: The University of Chicago Press, 1973.

Schwartz, Bernard. *The Great Rights of Mankind: A History of the American Bill of Rights*. New York: Rowman & Littlefield Publishing, 1992.

For strong feelings against non-Protestants in North Carolina, see the instructions of the county representatives at the Hillsborough Congress of August 1775:

Alexander, John B. *The History of Mecklenburg County [Nc]*. Baltimore: Genealogical Publishing Company, 2009.

Protestant Christianity was to be "the religion of the State to the utter exclusion forever of all and every other (falsely, so-called) religion, whether Pagan or Papal…"

Cappon, Lester, J. (Ed.) *The Adams-Jefferson Letters: The Complete Correspondence between Thomas Jefferson and Abigail and John Adams, 2 vols*. Chapel Hill: University of North Carolina Press, 1959.

Chase, Frederick, Lord John K. *A history of Dartmouth College. 2 vols*. Cambridge: Wilson, 1891.

Douglas, Elisha P. *Rebels and Democrats: The Struggle for Equal Political Rights and Majority Rule During the American Revolution*. Chapel Hill: University of North Carolina Press, 1955.

Elliott, Jonathan (Ed.). *The Debates in the Several State Conventions on the Adoption of the Federal Constitution, 5 vols.* Ithaca, NY: Cornell University Library, 2009.

Ferrand, Max (Ed.). *The Records of the Federal Convention of 1787, 4 vols.* New Haven, CT: Yale University Press, 1966.

Hanley, Thomas O'Brien (Ed.) *The John Carroll Papers, 3 vols.* Notre Dame, IN: University of Notre Dame Press, 1976.

Journal of Debates and Proceedings in the Convention of Delegates chosen to Revise the Constitution of Massachusetts. Ithaca, NY: Cornell University Library, 1853.

Kinney Jr, Charles B. *Church & State: The Struggle for Separation in New Hampshire, 1630 – 1900.* New York: Bureau of Publications, Teachers College, Columbia University, 1955.

McLoughlin, William G (Ed.) *Isaac Backus on Church, State, and Calvinism: Pamphlets, 1754 – 1789.* Cambridge: Belknap Press of Harvard University Press, 1968.

Reports of the Proceedings and Debates of the Convention of 1821, assembled for the purpose of amending the Constitution of the State of New York. Ann Arbor, MI: Scholarly Publishing Office, University of Michigan Library, 2005.

Rutland, Robert A (Ed.). *The Papers of George Mason, 1725–1792.* Chapel Hill: The University of North Carolina Press, 1970.

Silverman, Morris. *Hartford Jews 1659 – 1970.* Hartford, CT: The Connecticut Historical Society, 1970.

Sizer, Theodore (Ed.) *The Autobiography of Colonel John Trumbull, Patriot – Artist, 1756–1843.* New Haven: Yale University Press, 1953.

Source Notes for Chapter 27

Borden, Morton. *Jews, Turks, and Infidels*. Chapel Hill: The University of North Carolina, 1984. https://reader.paperc.com/books/Jews-Turks-and-Infidels/901178/f04_contents

Carter, Nathaniel Hazeltine, Stone, William Leete. *Reports of the Proceedings and Debates of the Convention of 1821 Assembled for the Purpose of Amending the Constitution of the State of New York.* Albany, NY: E. and E. Hosford, 1821.

"Constitution of Delaware; 1776". Yale Law School, Lillian Goldman Law Library. Accessed 7 March 2018. http://avalon.law.yale.edu/18th_century/de02.asp

"Constitution of the Commonwealth of Pennsylvania – 1790". Duquesne University. Accessed 7 March 2018. http://www.duq.edu/academics/gumberg-library/pa-constitution/texts-of-the-constitution/1790

Cooper, James Fenimore. *Notions of the Americans: Picked Up by a Travelling Bachelor*. Albany, NY: SUNY Press, 1991.

Journal of Debates and Proceedings in the Convention of Delegates Chosen to revise the Constitution of Massachusetts. Boston: Office of the Boston Daily Advertiser. 1821. https://ia800209.us.archive.org/16/items/journalofdebates00mass/journalofdebates00mass.pdf

"People v. Ruggles". Amendment I (Religion). Accessed 7 March 2018. http://press-pubs.uchicago.edu/founders/documents/amendI_religions62.html

"State Constitutions". U.S. Constitution. Accessed 7 March 2018. https://www.usconstitution.net/stateconst.html

"Thomas Jefferson and the Virginia Statute for Religious Freedom". Virginia Museum of History and Culture. Accessed 7 March 2018. https://www.virginiahistory.org/collections-and-resources/virginia-history-explorer/thomas-jefferson

Urofsky, Melvin I. *Religious Freedom: Rights and Liberties Under the Law*. Santa Barbara: ABC-CLIO, 2002.

For an understanding of the goals of the religious right, see:

Brown, Ruth Murray. *For a Christian America: A History of the Religious Right*. New York: Prometheus Books, 2002.

Martin, William. *With God on Our Side: The Rise of the Religious Right in America*. New York: Broadway Books, 1997.

Oldfield, Duane M. *The Right and the Righteous: The Christian Right Confronts the Republican Party*. Lanham, MD: Rowman and Littlefield, 1996.

For a review of the 60s, see:

Gitlin, Todd. *The Sixties: Years of Hope, Days of Rage*. New York: Bantam Books, 1987.

For an understanding of Biblical Law as the foundation for American codification, see:

Rushdoony, Rousas John. *The Institute of Biblical Law, Volume I*. Phillipsburg, NJ: P&R Publishing, 1973.

Rushdoony, Rousas John. *The Institute of Biblical Law, Volume II: Law and Society*. Phillipsburg, NJ: P&R Publishing, 1973.

Rushdoony, Rousas John. *The Institute of Biblical Law, Volume III: The Intent of the Law*. Phillipsburg, NJ: P&R Publishing, 1973.

For the goals and effects of Evangelicalism, see:

Balmer, Randall. *Encyclopedia of Evangelicalism: Revised and Expanded Edition*. Waco, TX: Baylor University Press, 2004.

Bebbington, David W. *Evangelicalism in Modern Britain: A History from the 1730s to the 1980s*. London: Unwin Hyman, 1989.

Marty, Martin E., Appleby, R. Scott. *Fundamentalisms Observed.* Chicago: The University of Chicago Press, 1991.

For President Reagan's statements on such subjects as prayer in schools, stem cell research, climate change, etc., see:

"Public Papers of the President". Ronal Reagan, Presidential Library & Museum. Accessed 15 March 2018. https://www.reaganlibrary.gov/sspeeches

"The Report of the President's Commission on Campus Unrest." Accessed 15 March 2018. https://files.eric.ed.gov/fulltext/ED083899.pdf

Source Notes for Chapters 28 – 31

Bartz, Wayne R. *Critical Thinking: The Antidote for Faith.* Stillwater: River's Bend Press, 2010

Edwards, Mickey. *The Parties Versus the People: How to Turn Republicans and Democrats Into Americans.* New Haven: Yale University Press, 2012

"Funding for Faith-Based Social Services". Pew Research Center. Accessed 7 March 2018. http://www.pewforum.org/2009/05/14/shifting-boundaries8/

Kimball, Charles. *When Religion Becomes Evil.* New York: HarperCollins, 2003.

"The Federalist Papers". Congress.gov. Accessed 7 March 2018. https://www.congress.gov/resources/display/content/The+Federalist+Papers#TheFederalistPapers-10

"Washington's Farewell Address 1796". Yale Law School, Lillian Goldman Law Library. Accessed 7 March 2018. http://avalon.law.yale.edu/18th_century/washing.asp

"Significant Supreme Court Rulings". Pew Research Center. Accessed 7 March 2018. http://www.pewforum.org/2009/05/14/shifting-boundaries10/

Mandate for Leadership Series:

Heatherly, Charles (Ed.). *Mandate for Leadership: Policy Management in a Conservative Administration.* Washington DC: The Heritage Foundation, 1981.

Butler, Stuart M., Sanera, Michael, Weinrod, W. Bruce. *Mandate for Leadership II: Continuing the Conservative Revolution.* Washington DC: The Heritage Foundation, 1984.

Heatherly, Charles (Ed.). *Mandate for Leadership III: Policy Strategies for the 1990s.* Washington DC: The Heritage Foundation, 1988.

Butler, Stuart M., Holmes, Kim R. *Mandate for Leadership IV: Turning Ideas into Action.* Washington DC: The Heritage Foundation, 1997.

The Heritage Foundation (Ed.) *Mandate for Leadership 2000 (Mandate V).* Washington DC: The Heritage Foundation, 2000.

The Heritage Foundation (Ed.) *Mandate for Leadership (Mandate VI).* Washington DC: The Heritage Foundation, 2005.

Aberbach Joel D., Peele, Gillian (Eds.). Crisis of Conservatism?: The Republican Party, the Conservative Movement and American Politics after Bush. New York: Oxford University Press, 2011.

Bartz, Wayne R. *Critical Thinking: The Antidote for Faith.* Stillwater: River's Bend Press, 2010

Blackmore, Susan. *The Meme Machine.* Oxford: Oxford University Press, 1999

Boston, Robert. *The Most Dangerous Man in America?: Pat Robertson and the Rise of the Christian Coalition.* New York: Prometheus Books, 1996.

Brown, Ruth Murray. *For a Christian America: A History of the Religious Right*. New York: Prometheus Books, 2002.

Brubaker, Jack. "Bush quietly meets with Amish here; they offer their prayers". Lancaster Online. 2004. Accessed 15 March 2018. http://lancasteronline.com/news/bush-quietly-meets-with-amish-here-they-offer-their-prayers/article_81ee51db-5772-5613-8e50-d5db1ae3e537.html

"Church-State Law". Pew Research Center. Accessed 15 March 2018. http://www.pewforum.org/topics/church-state-law/

Council for National Policy. Accessed 15 March 2018. https://www.cfnp.org/

Deckman, Melissa M. *School Board Battles: The Christian Right in Local Politics*. Washington DC: Georgetown University Press, 2004.

Diamond, Sara. *Roads to Dominion: Right-Wing Movements and Political Power in the United States*. New York: The Guilford Press, 1995.

Kimball, Charles. *When Religion Becomes Evil*. New York: HarperCollins, 2003.

Neuhaus, Richard John, Cromartie, Michael (Ed.). *Piety and Politics: Evangelicals and Fundamentalists Confront the World*. Lanham MD: University Press of America, 1988.

Phillips, Kevin. *American Theocracy: The Peril and Politics of Radical Religion, Oil, and Borrowed Money in the 21st Century*. New York: The Penguin Group, 2006.

"Policy Counsel". Council for National Policy. Accessed 15 March 2018. https://www.cfnp.org/page.aspx?pid=223

Posner, Sarah. *God's Profits: Faith, Fraud, and the Republican Crusade for Values Voters*. Sausalito, CA: PoliPoint Press, 2008.

Posner, Sarah. "Secret Society: Just who is the Council for National Policy, and why isn't it paying taxes?" Alternet. 2005. Accessed 15 March 2018. https://www.alternet.org/story/21372/secret_society

(Endnotes)

1   Stephen Prothero is Chair of the Department of Religion at Boston University and the author of numerous books, such as Why Liberals Win the Culture Wars (New York: HarperOne, 2016), God Is Not One: The Eight Rival Religions that Run the World – and Why Their Differences Matter (New York: HarperOne, 2010), and the New York Times bestseller Religious Literacy: What Every American Needs to Know – and Doesn't (New York: HarperOne, 2007). He received his BA from Yale in American Studies and his PhD in the Study of Religion from Harvard. More on Prothero can be found at: http://stephenprothero.com/about/

2   Stephen Prothero, God Is Not One: The Eight Rival Religions that Run the World – and Why Their Differences Matter (New York: HarperOne, 2010), 11.

3   Ibid, 3.

4   Ernest Brandewie, *Wilhelm Schmidt and the Origin of the Idea of God* (Lanham: University Press of America, 1983).

5   "Zoroastrianism at a glance", BBC, accessed 23 February 2018, http://www.bbc.co.uk/religion/religions/zoroastrian/ataglance/glance.shtml

6   Bart D. Ehrman, *Forged: Writing in the Name of God—Why the Bible's Authors Are Not Who We Think They Are* (New York: HarperOne, 2011), 14.

7   Ibid, 14-15.

8   Bart D. Ehrman, *Misquoting Jesus: The Story Behind Who Changed the Bible and Why* (San Francisco: HarperSanFrancisco, 2005), 65.

9   Ibid, 66.

10   Ibid, 66.

11   Vance A. Stinson, "The Resurrection – Real Event or Historical Hoax?", accessed February 26 2018. https://static1.squarespace.com/static/50438d1dc4aa994481346f77/t/54f757c0e4b08d5963bbd850/1425496000855/The+Resurrection.pdf

12   Ibid.

13   The whole list of inconsistencies can be found at: "Inconsistencies of the New Testament", The Nazarene Way of Essenic Studies, accessed February 26, 2018,

     http://www.thenazareneway.com/new_testament_biblical_inconsistencies.htm.

14   John Shelby Spong, *Rescuing the Bible From Fundamentalism: A Bishop Rethinks the Meaning of Scripture* (San Francisco: HarperCollins, 1991), 150.

15   Pastor Stephen Kyeyune, *A Miracle at Prairie Avenue: The Quest for Faith* (Bloomington: Authorhouse, 2011), 73 – 74.

16 Stewart Henry Perowne, "Herod: King of Judaea", Encyclopaedia Britannica, accessed 27 February 2018, https://www.britannica.com/biography/Herod-king-of-Judaea

17 Ibid.

18 Ibid.

19 Ibid.

20 "Who was Theophilus at the beginning of Luke and Acts?", Got Questions, accessed 27 February 2018, https://www.gotquestions.org/Theophilus-Luke-Acts.html

21 Ibid.

22 "Historicity of Jesus", Wikipedia – The Free Encyclopedia, accessed 27 February 2018, https://en.wikipedia.org/wiki/Historicity_of_Jesus

23 *Crucifixion by an Eye-Witness* (Chicago: Indo-American Book Company, 1907), 35.

24 Ibid, 37.

25 Ibid, 40.

26 Ibid, 61.

27 Ibid, 85-86.

28 Ibid, 91-92.

29 Ibid, 92.

30 Ibid, 103.

31 Ibid, 103.

32 Ibid, 127.

33 Ibid, 127.

34 Ibid, 128.

35   Ibid, 128.

36   Ibid, 125.

37   "Daughter of Jairus", Religion Wiki, accessed 4 March 2018, http://religion.wikia.com/wiki/Daughter_of_Jairus

38   Karen Armstrong, *A History of God, the 4000-year Quest of Judaism, Christianity and Islam* (New York: Ballantine Books, 1993), 89.

39   Jennie Cohen, "6 Things You May Not Know About the Dead Sea Scrolls", History, accessed 4 March 2018, http://www.history.com/news/history-lists/6-things-you-may-not-know-about-the-dead-sea-scrolls

40   "History of ancient Israel and Judah", Wikipedia – The Free Encyclopedia, accessed 4 March 2018, https://en.wikipedia.org/wiki/History_of_ancient_Israel_and_Judah

41   Ibid.

42   Ibid.

43   Ibid.

44   Ibid.

45   Karen Armstrong, *A History of God, the 4000-year Quest of Judaism, Christianity and Islam* (New York: Ballantine Books, 1993), 32.

46   Ibid, 32.

47   Ibid, 32.

48   *World and Its Peoples: Greece and the Eastern Balkans* (New York: Marshall Cavendish Reference, 2010), 1460.

49   "The Epic of Gilgamesh / Nimrod: Second Oldest Writing – From The Lost Book Of Enki", True Democracy Party, accessed 6

March 2018, http://truedemocracyparty.net/2012/07/the-epic-of-gilgamesh-nimrod-second-oldest-writing-from-the-lost-book-of-enki/

50 "The Levant", accessed 6 March 2016, http://www.crystalinks.com/Levant.html

51 Robert Wright, *The Evolution of God: The origins of our beliefs* (London: Little, Brown), 2009.

52 "The Levant", accessed 6 March 2016, http://www.crystalinks.com/Levant.html

53 Ibid.

54 "Joseph Campbell", Pantheism, accessed 6 March 2018, https://pantheism.com/about/luminaries/joseph-campbell/

55 "Joseph Campbell", Psychology Wiki, accessed 6 March 2016, http://psychology.wikia.com/wiki/Joseph_Campbell

56 Campbell, Joseph, Moyers, Bill. *The Power of Myth* (New York: Anchor Books, 1991).

57 Karen Armstrong, *A Short History of Myth* (Edinburgh: Canongate Books, 2005), 6.

58 John Haywood, *The New Atlas of World History: Global Events at a Glance* (Princeton: Princeton University Press, 2011)

59 Ibid.

60 "The rise of the 'New Atheists'", CNN, accessed 6 March 2018, http://edition.cnn.com/2006/WORLD/europe/11/08/atheism.feature/index.html

61 "New Atheism", Wikipedia – The Free Encyclopedia, accessed 6 March 2018, https://en.wikipedia.org/wiki/New_Atheism

62 Ibid.

63   Steven Weinberg, "Why the Higgs Boson Matters", The New York Times, accessed 7 March 2018, http://www.nytimes.com/2012/07/14/opinion/weinberg-why-the-higgs-boson-matters.html?pagewanted=all

64   Bryan A. Garner, *Black's Law Dictionary* (St. Paul, MN: West Publishing Co, 1999)

65   Ibid.

66   „Philosophy 101", Evolutionary Philosophy, accessed 7 March 2018, http://www.evphil.com/philosophy-101.html

67   Bryan A. Garner, *Black's Law Dictionary* (St. Paul, MN: West Publishing Co, 1999)

68   Ibid.

69   William Tuckwell, *Reminiscences of Oxford* (New York: E.P. Dutton and Company, 1908), 55.

70   Tammy Kitzmiller, et al, v. Dover Area School District, et al. "Memorandum Opinion. In The United States District Court For The Middle District of Pennsylvania.", 137. Accessed 7 March 2018. https://ncse.com/files/pub/legal/kitzmiller/highlights/2005-12-20_Kitzmiller_decision.pdf

71   Ibid, 89.

72   "The Constitution of the United States", Accessed 7 March 2018, https://constitutioncenter.org/media/files/constitution.pdf

73   Jon Meacham, *American Gospel: God, the Founding Fathers, and the Making of a Nation* (New York: Random House Publishing Group, 2007)

74   Kevin Phillips, *American Theocracy: The Peril and Politics of Radical Religion, Oil, and Borrowed Money in the 21st Century* (New York: The Penguin Group, 2006), 221.

75 "Massachusetts Bay Colony", En Academic, accessed 6 March 2018, http://enacademic.com/dic.nsf/enwiki/130064

76 Ibid.

77 "Thomas Jefferson, July 27, 1821, Autobiography Draft Fragment, January 6 through July 27, from the Thomas Jefferson and William Short Correspondence, Transcribed and Edited by Gerard W. Gawalt, Manuscript Division, Library of Congress", 57, accessed 7 March 2018, http://www.loc.gov/resource/mtj1.052_0517_0609

78 "Memorial and Remonstrance against Religious Assessments, (ca. 20 June) 1785", accessed 7 March 2018, https://founders.archives.gov/documents/Madison/01-08-02-0163

79 "Thomas Jefferson and the Virginia Statute for Religious Freedom", Virginia Museum of History and Culture, accessed 7 March 2018, https://www.virginiahistory.org/collections-and-resources/virginia-history-explorer/thomas-jefferson

80 "The Constitution of the United States", Accessed 7 March 2018, https://constitutioncenter.org/media/files/constitution.pdf

81 Ibid.

82 "Thomas Jefferson and the Virginia Statute for Religious Freedom", Virginia Museum of History and Culture, accessed 7 March 2018, https://www.virginiahistory.org/collections-and-resources/virginia-history-explorer/thomas-jefferson

83 "Memorial and Remonstrance against Religious Assessments, (ca. 20 June) 1785", accessed 7 March 2018, https://founders.archives.gov/documents/Madison/01-08-02-0163

84 "The Constitution of the United States", Accessed 7 March 2018, https://constitutioncenter.org/media/files/constitution.pdf

85   "Constitution of the Commonwealth of Pennsylvania – 1790", Duquesne University, accessed 7 March 2018, http://www.duq.edu/academics/gumberg-library/pa-constitution/texts-of-the-constitution/1790

86   "Constitution of Delaware; 1776", Yale Law School, Lillian Goldman Law Library, accessed 7 March 2018, http://avalon.law.yale.edu/18th_century/de02.asp

87   Morton Borden, *Jews, Turks, and Infidels* (Chapel Hill: The University of North Carolina, 1984), https://reader.paperc.com/books/Jews-Turks-and-Infidels/901178/f04_contents

88   Ibid.

89   *Journal of Debates and Proceedings in the Convention of Delegates Chosen to revise the Constitution of Massachusetts* (Boston: Office of the Boston Daily Advertiser, 1821), 104, https://ia800209.us.archive.org/16/items/journalofdebates00mass/journalofdebates00mass.pdf

90   Ibid, 87.

91   "People v. Ruggles", Amendment I (Religion), accessed 7 March 2018, http://press-pubs.uchicago.edu/founders/documents/amendI_religions62.html

92   Nathaniel Hazeltine Carter, William Leete Stone, *Reports of the Proceedings and Debates of the Convention of 1821 Assembled for the Purpose of Amending the Constitution of the State of New York* (Albany: E. and E. Hosford, 1821), 462.

93   Ibid, 463.

94   Ibid, 463.

95   James Fenimore Cooper, *Notions of the Americans: Picked Up by a Travelling Bachelor* (Albany: SUNY Press, 1991), 458.

96   Melvin I. Urofsky, *Religious Freedom: Rights and Liberties Under the Law* (Santa Barbara: ABC-CLIO, 2002), 229

97   "State Constitutions", U.S. Constitution, accessed 7 March 2018, https://www.usconstitution.net/stateconst.html

98   Charles Kimball, *When Religion Becomes Evil* (New York: HarperCollins, 2003).

99   "The Federalist Papers", Congress.gov, accessed 7 March 2018, https://www.congress.gov/resources/display/content/The+Federalist+Papers#TheFederalistPapers-10

100 "Washington's Farewell Address 1796", Yale Law School, Lillian Goldman Law Library, accessed 7 March 2018, http://avalon.law.yale.edu/18th_century/washing.asp

101 Mickey Edwards, The Parties Versus the People: How to Turn Republicans and Democrats Into Americans (New Haven: Yale University Press, 2012)

102 Ibid.

103 "Significant Supreme Court Rulings", Pew Research Center, accessed 7 March 2018, http://www.pewforum.org/2009/05/14/shifting-boundaries10/

104 "The Lemon Test", Pew Research Center, accessed 7 March 2018, http://www.pewforum.org/2009/05/14/shifting-boundaries6/

105 "Funding for Faith-Based Social Services", Pew Research Center, accessed 7 March 2018, http://www.pewforum.org/2009/05/14/shifting-boundaries8/

106 Wayne R. Bartz, *Critical Thinking: The Antidote for Faith* (Stillwater: River's Bend Press, 2010)

Index

A

Abraham, 49, 51, 162–164

Abrahamic history, 53

Abrahamic religions (generally). *See also specific religions*
in 700-600 BC, 167–168
suppression of independent thought, 20

Abramowitz, Alan, 310–311

Abu Bakr, 49, 52

"Acceptance Period," 11, 23

Adam, 51, 68

Adams, John, 260, 268

Adolescent Family Life Act, 317

afterlife
in Islam, 59
in Jewish tradition, 172–175
in Qur'an, 71

Age of Enlightenment, 27–28, 243–244

Agostini v. Felton, 318

agriculture, during Neolithic, 189, 191

Aguilar v. Felton, 317, 318, 321

Ain Mallaha archaeological site, 187

Akkad Empire, 195–196

Akkadian language, 196

Alexander the Great, 157

Alexandria, Egypt, 140, 141

Alexandrian Brethren, 143, 144

Alinsky, Saul, 329

Allah, 59, 69, 70

Allat, 40

alphabetic script, 166–167

American Revolution, 244–245

the Americas, Christianity in, 201

Amorites, 196

Anatolia, 193

Anglican Church
freethinkers and, 243
in Virginia, 250, 253, 258

Annunciation, 90

Ansari, 41

Antioch, 129

Antipater, 126–128

Antiquities of the Jews (Josephus), 136

antiwar movement, 286

www.ingramcontent.com/pod-product-compliance
Lightning Source LLC
Chambersburg PA
CBHW071312090426
42738CB00012B/2684